Intimate Strangers

In the series *Asian American History and Culture*, edited by CATHY SCHLUND-VIALS, SHELLEY SANG-HEE LEE, and RICK BONUS. Founding editor, SUCHENG CHAN; editors emeriti, DAVID PALUMBO-LIU, MICHAEL OMI, K. SCOTT WONG, and LINDA TRINH VÕ.

ALSO IN THIS SERIES

Ruth Maxey, ed., *The Collected Short Stories of Bharati Mukherjee*
Y-Dang Troeung, *Refugee Lifeworlds: The Afterlife of the Cold War in Cambodia*
George Uba, *Water Thicker Than Blood: A Memoir of a Post-Internment Childhood*
Long T. Bui, *Model Machines: A History of the Asian as Automaton*
erin Khuê Ninh, *Passing for Perfect: College Impostors and Other Model Minorities*
Martin F. Manalansan IV, Alice Y. Hom, and Kale Bantigue Fajardo, eds., *Q & A: Voices from Queer Asian North America*
Heidi Kim, *Illegal Immigrants/Model Minorities: The Cold War of Chinese American Narrative*
Chia Youyee Vang with Pao Yang, Retired Captain, U.S. Secret War in Laos, *Prisoner of Wars: A Hmong Fighter Pilot's Story of Escaping Death and Confronting Life*
Kavita Daiya, *Graphic Migrations: Precarity and Gender in India and the Diaspora*
Timothy K. August, *The Refugee Aesthetic: Reimagining Southeast Asian America*
L. Joyce Zapanta Mariano, *Giving Back: Filipino America and the Politics of Diaspora Giving*
Manan Desai, *The United States of India: Anticolonial Literature and Transnational Refraction*
Cathy J. Schlund-Vials, Guy Beauregard, and Hsiu-chuan Lee, eds., *The Subject(s) of Human Rights: Crises, Violations, and Asian/American Critique*
Malini Johar Schueller, *Campaigns of Knowledge: U.S. Pedagogies of Colonialism and Occupation in the Philippines and Japan*
Crystal Mun-hye Baik, *Reencounters: On the Korean War and Diasporic Memory Critique*
Michael Omi, Dana Y. Nakano, and Jeffrey T. Yamashita, eds., *Japanese American Millennials: Rethinking Generation, Community, and Diversity*
Masumi Izumi, *The Rise and Fall of America's Concentration Camp Law: Civil Liberties Debates from the Internment to McCarthyism and the Radical 1960s*
Shirley Jennifer Lim, *Anna May Wong: Performing the Modern*

A list of additional titles in this series appears at the back of this book.

Tritia Toyota

Intimate Strangers

Shin Issei Women and Contemporary Japanese American Community, 1980–2020

TEMPLE UNIVERSITY PRESS
Philadelphia • Rome • Tokyo

TEMPLE UNIVERSITY PRESS
Philadelphia, Pennsylvania 19122
tupress.temple.edu

Copyright © 2023 by Temple University—Of The Commonwealth System
 of Higher Education
All rights reserved
Published 2023

Library of Congress Cataloging-in-Publication Data

Names: Toyota, Tritia, author.
Title: Intimate strangers : shin Issei women and contemporary Japanese
 American community, 1980-2020 / Tritia Toyota.
Other titles: Asian American history and culture.
Description: Philadelphia : Temple University Press, 2023. | Series: Asian
 American history and culture | Includes bibliographical references and
 index. | Summary: "This book offers a story of new migration and
 community transformation. Via an ethnographic study of young Japanese
 women migrants (shin Issei), Tritia Toyota details how they make
 place/space for themselves among generations of Japanese Americans with
 shifting alterations of membership and belonging that are neither
 seamless nor easily acknowledged"— Provided by publisher.
Identifiers: LCCN 2023003797 (print) | LCCN 2023003798 (ebook) | ISBN
 9781439923511 (cloth) | ISBN 9781439923528 (paperback) | ISBN
 9781439923535 (pdf)
Subjects: LCSH: Women immigrants—California—Social conditions. | Japanese
 American young women—California—Social conditions.
Classification: LCC E184.J3 T69 2023 (print) | LCC E184.J3 (ebook) | DDC
 305.48/8956073—dc23/eng/20230607
LC record available at https://lccn.loc.gov/2023003797
LC ebook record available at https://lccn.loc.gov/2023003798

♾ The paper used in this publication meets the requirements of the
American National Standard for Information Sciences—Permanence
of Paper for Printed Library Materials, ANSI Z39.48-1992.

Printed in the United States of America

9 8 7 6 5 4 3 2 1

Contents

	Acknowledgments	vii
	Introduction	1
1	Wilting Office Flowers	25
2	Leaving Home	45
3	Precarious Life under the Radar	64
4	Surviving around the Neighborhoods	87
5	Racial Talk: Shin Issei Palefaces and Dark Nikkei	114
6	Shin Issei and Nikkei Searching for Community	145
	Epilogue	176
	Notes	185
	References	191
	Index	223

Acknowledgments

Epiphanies sometimes derive from small events—unrecorded, unseen, and unremarked upon except perhaps by the person for whom the experience bears significance. Such is one of the motivations for this ethnography: in the early 1990s, the subject of contemporary Japanese migration was brought home with stunning clarity. I was waiting in a long line at a small bakery shop in West Los Angeles. When my turn came, I quickly rattled off my doughnut order to the young *Yonsei* woman (fourth-generation American of Japanese ancestry) behind the counter: "TwoChocolateAndOneVanilla-Please."[1] She kept looking at me, so I repeated myself. No reaction. I pointed at the glass case using my fingers to indicate amount. "*Hai!*" (OK!) she said loudly. It was my turn to stare. The young woman, whom I had assumed to be a Yonsei, was, in fact, a recent arrival from Japan. I hadn't really thought about Japanese migration except in the context of early nineteenth-century Japanese like my great-grandfather and grandparents. In subsequently doing some research, I soon found there was virtually nothing written about the appearance of contemporary Japanese migrants in the United States, the challenges they faced in their new lives, or the effects their inclusion might have on a Japanese American community.

Japanese American community—flash back to twenty years earlier. While in graduate school, I spent several years living in a one-bedroom apartment not too far from that bakery. The apartment was adjacent to a community park where *Sansei* (third-generation Americans of Japanese ancestry) played tennis at night on the lighted courts. The park was in the heart of one of the oldest Japanese American neighborhoods in Southern California. Throughout this quiet community were small bungalows with carefully trimmed bonsai (trees and shrubs) in the front yards. There were *bon* festivals (honoring ancestors) every summer at the nearby Buddhist church, tiny restaurants serving chicken and beef teriyaki, nurseries offering meticulously grown plants, and mom-and-pop grocery stores where you could buy *gohan* (rice) or *manju* (sweet confections) or small packets of brightly colored origami (folding) paper. In short, this area I came to know as Sawtelle was local community—Japanese American style. I had not known this when I moved in; my apartment was simply the most affordable and nearest to the local bus route. I grew up in the Pacific Northwest—an English-only speaking Sansei who had limited contact with other Japanese Americans. Yet, here in Sawtelle, I felt a keen sense of immediate familiarity, of belonging to an amorphous and imagined family in these everyday happenings—comfort food for the soul with life experiences common to all *Nikkei*—Japanese Americans. My sense of Nikkei family and community that continues to endure was nourished by my maternal grandmother even though we were unable to fully converse with each other in Japanese or English. I cannot now imagine what courage it took for her to leave Japan. She never learned (or refused) to speak English after she was freed from incarceration, although I knew she understood what was being said. She was a lifelong, devout Christian who emigrated from the Shinshu area (renamed Nagano prefecture after 1868) and insisted on speaking to me only in Japanese—nineteenth-century *Meiji* Japanese.[2] Among the highly urbanized, recently arrived Japanese women with whom I now have friendships, listening to vestiges of my old, rural dialect and vocabulary always elicited much humor and raised eyebrows.

In 1980s Sawtelle, imperceptibly, the story of this unique American identity began to shift, its transformation effected by the swirling tides of new migration, the result of economic restructuring both at home and across the Pacific. Quite suddenly, or so it seemed to Americans of Japanese ancestry, there were new faces from Japan everywhere around the neighborhood—overwhelmingly the faces of young women. I will always call it Sawtelle, though perhaps it's wishful thinking (I am not alone in this, as the following pages will reveal). New migrants from Japan began calling it Little Osaka, and it seemed the moniker was here to stay after local press picked up the name (Gold 2013; Parsons 2012). Little Osaka lends itself to a more global conversation; migrants say it's because many of them are from the Kansai region of Japan, where the country's second-largest city is located. Others say it's to differentiate it from the more venerable Little Tokyo enclave in downtown Los Angeles. The name change was not well received by older residents of Sawtelle, and it became emblematic of social tensions between them and newcomers.

I still frequent Sawtelle to shop; meet friends for ramen (noodles in broth), *tonkatsu* (deep-fried pork cutlet), or curry rice; and attend community events and meetings. The biggest challenge these days is jockeying for a parking spot amid the dozens of new multiethnic restaurants and shops that crowd Sawtelle Boulevard. The blocks west of Sawtelle are still mostly residential, though now dotted with upscale condominiums and rebuilt single-family homes with seven-figure price tags. There are fewer bonsai gardens in front yards. The bakery is still there, and there are still lines. It's now part of an international chain with headquarters in Tokyo. The counter staff is not fluent in English, but they understand enough to fulfill the chocolate requests I utter in fragmented Japanese.

My investigation and positionality in this book have been achieved *in community* and constructed through ways in which researchers and the persons researched interact in constantly transforming social and political environments where imbalances and inequalities of power exist (Naples 2003). I can now see that what my grandmother and other *Issei*—first-generation Japanese migrants—experienced helped kindle my own involvement in Nikkei community over the past thirty-plus years. To all of them who risked life in a new home, thank you. To the many activist Nikkei with whom I have long-standing relationships, who generously offered their time and shared in my goals for this fieldwork project, I am grateful for your support. Indeed, the role between participant and observer in this ongoing assignment remains, for me, often indistinguishable—what one of my academic mentors, Lane Hirabayashi, called *mutuality* in inquiry, "an integral tool in ethically and politically informed social research leading to engagement and empowerment" (L. Hirabayashi 2015: 129).

Lane was more than a sounding board. He was fair but fiercely critical in deconstructing the nub of the argument. As an engaged anthropologist, he was about academic commitment but also about how research could benefit community change. He was keenly aware of contextualizing the historic moment, and his always politely framed questions about the subject of this book meant lively discussion, which usually finished over bowls of ramen. Without his guidance and approval, my teaching at University of California, Los Angeles (UCLA), would have been an abbreviated experience. I will always hear his caveats and admonitions about contextualizing community. His wise counsel and support are deeply missed.

Valerie Matsumoto deserves much gratitude for repeatedly volunteering to read manuscript drafts. Despite her heavy academic responsibilities, not to mention her efforts in completing her own book, *City Girls: The Nisei Social World in Los Angeles, 1920–1950*, she was amazingly generous in offering both her time and valuable suggestions about how to better craft my work—telling me in her gentle way to get to the point!

At Temple University Press, without Acquisitions Editor Shaun Vigil's unstinting support through a period of family crisis, this book would not have been finished. As well, thanks to the reviewers who quickly saw the point of my argument, obscured though it was. Their critiques about ambiguities that drove them "crazy" were well heeded.

Most of all, to the Japanese women I've met throughout the course of this ethnographic research, I am humbled by your trust in sharing with me your experiences in a new country. Thank you for your candid answers, friendship, and willingness to be part of this story. Without your life narratives, there would be no book.

I realize that researching Japanese women's lives as a singular experiential is presumptuous (similarly so for Nikkei). Always top of mind is the extraordinary diversity that continues to exist among *all* Japanese migrants and their descendants, a diversity built on a myriad of life experiences that make each individual's personal history unique.

Intimate Strangers

Introduction

I was the first one of my friends to come to the U.S. Thinking about it now, yes it was courageous, but I was young.

Rieko arrived in Los Angeles from Tokyo in 1983, armed with two suitcases, a student visa, and enough money saved to see her through most of one year. Almost immediately, she got a waitressing job at a small bar and restaurant in the downtown Los Angeles area of Little Tokyo. She was twenty-one, alone, with neither friends nor family and virtually no ability to speak or read English. Her agentive ability to seek a new life speaks to a boldness born of inexperience and daring. She lived in the interstices of American society, seeking out other new Japanese migrants like herself, watching televised broadcasts from Japan, and hoping to evade the gaze of U.S. immigration officers who could and would most likely deport her if they found she was a sometime student who was working full-time without the legal documentation required for employment.

Rieko was born in Osaka, the daughter of a middle-class bureaucrat. When she was five years old, her parents moved the family to Tokyo to take advantage of her father's job promotion. Growing up in Tokyo with its many international influences was exciting for her, in particular were images from America. Although she personally knew no Americans, she says she remembers visuals from television and magazines. "I thought people here looked good, everything looked different. They looked free." Those early imaginings helped formulate her future plans. She is a slightly built woman with small facial features and fluttering hands. When she is thinking hard about a subject, she will bring both her hands to her face, covering her cheeks. The subject is her initial decision to leave Japan, motivated by the fact that months of searching after she finished junior college did not yield a job paying a livable wage. She decided to move to the United States. Like other migrants from around the world, Rieko had long envisioned America as a place where she could survive economically and carve out a meaningful life. Her parents were less than impressed with her plans and wanted her home. She acquiesced and briefly returned to Japan. "The economy [in Japan] was really good then, before the collapse." Jobs were plentiful though not ideal. With limited education and few marketable job skills, the best Rieko could do was hire on as a temporary worker, which meant she had to live at home with her parents. She says it was good to be with family, and she might have stayed if she had been able to find full-time employment. Searching again for a better job yielded no results. After nearly a year, with a still-valid U.S. student visa, she returned to Los Angeles, and this time, her plans did not include a future in Japan.

Rieko has many similarly situated Japanese sisters around the world who are crafting new lives for themselves beyond Japan's borders, and they form the nucleus of this book. Here, their life experiences unfold primarily in Southern California, and as a result, they reveal transforming social relations in an American community—changes brought about largely by their late twentieth-century migration during the 1980s and 1990s. I label these contemporary flows of Japanese migrants shin Issei.[1] To more fully explore this, I utilize several Southern California social spaces historically inhabited by Nikkei whose families were Issei migrants in these social spaces at the end of the nineteenth century.[2] Sawtelle in western Los Angeles, Little Tokyo in downtown Los Angeles, and the area in southern Los Angeles County known as the South Bay are indicative of alterations in Nikkei community place and space. These areas appear here as emblematic of the idea of connecting geographic locations as encounters where differences in membership and belonging are constructed through shared spaces and will be further expanded upon (Simonsen and Koefoed 2020).

While shin Issei transformations expand our knowledge about the effects of migration on long-standing racial and ethnic communities of Nikkei in Southern California, it does not mean there were no significant changes occurring in other Nikkei communities in the United States because of contemporary Japanese migration. I am, however, reluctant to draw parallels, as each community has its own history, its own dynamics, and its own way of dealing with social change where competition and tension for space or place are involved. The reader may draw any further inferences.

Nikkei wanting to preserve a long-standing identity in specific Japanese American space are finding that contemporary migration has restructured and shifted meanings of membership. Fundamental in the constructions of identity are actors and their practices that result in the creation of new social spaces (de Certeau 1984). Inherent in the concepts of *contemporary* and *change* are tacit conversations about what was before and how the motivations and actions of individuals and groups precipitated alterations in the social landscape. So how have shin Issei recreated social spaces; what are their narratives of migration; how have they positioned themselves as new actors?

To be clear, this book is not about *all* contemporary Japanese migrants but about its gendered majority—young women. Specifically, I define shin Issei women by what they are not. They are not World War II brides of American servicemen who brought their Japanese wives to the United States after 1947, nor employees of Japanese multinational corporations, nor economic tycoons from Japan who bought up signature properties in the United States in the 1980s. Rather, they were young twenty-something women when they migrated beginning in the 1980s and were primarily members of Japan's middle and lower-middle classes. In Japan, these class positions were produced in the successful rebuilding and prosperity of Japan. They were the first postwar generation—baby boomers—who did not have an "inferiority complex toward America" but, rather, a curiosity and emulation of the former occupier (Sakurai 2004: 17). In this stage of beginning adult lives, they should have been entering the Japanese workforce, establishing families, and becoming participatory members of their communities. Instead, they opted to leave their homes and lives behind to begin anew elsewhere in the world. The primary reason was the disintegration of the once-vaunted Japanese economy in the 1980s. Burgeoning jobs and consumer demand and lifetime employment disappeared, replaced by low-wage temporary and part-time work as businesses attempted to compete in global markets.

Shin Issei women talk about their disappointment—at the very least—in not being able to find jobs at home or jobs that paid enough to survive. They also had anger, determination, and courage, in common with generations of migrants, to pick up and move alone with few skills and no guarantee of a better life in the United States. Their movements can be labeled agentive resistance—that is, ways in which women struggle to overcome the tension and ambivalence inherent in the creation of new, quotidian lives at home and elsewhere (Rosenberger 2013). These are their stories—not single-sited examinations fixed in time but history as a social process that spans nations and states and does so through both a temporal and a geographic lens, tacking back and forth to further analyze key sociocultural changes in Japan and the United States (Trouillot 1995).

A brief word about nomenclature. I use Japanese American, American of Japanese ancestry, and Nikkei interchangeably. In Japanese American studies, Nikkei is most often employed in reference to those Americans of Japanese ancestry who were born in the United States.[3] However, I also pay attention to more recent and inclusive definitions of the term.

> We're not talking about the Japanese Stock Exchange. We are talking about Nikkei *people*—Japanese emigrants and their descendants who have created communities throughout the world. The term Nikkei has multiple and diverse meanings depending on situations, places, and environments. (JANM 2012)

In other words, Nikkei may refer to any individual who may have been born in Japan but who no longer lives there. The diaspora may also define Nikkei as those who were born elsewhere in the world, such as Latin or South America, but who either return or make their first visits to Japan (Adachi 2006). I also prefer to use Nikkei rather than *Nikkeijin*. Nikkei is a self-appropriation, while the addition of *jin*—people—is used primarily by Japanese to denote those of Japanese ancestry living outside Japan (Creighton 2017).

Issues of identity have, in recent years, shaped fundamental discussion about the future of Nikkei America. "Where is the Japanese American community heading?" and "What is Nikkei?" (L. Hirabayashi 2016: i; JANM 2012). These topics imply concerns that Nikkei, particularly in the United States, are disappearing (Navarro 2004). Hence, part of the effort to recognize varying other diasporic experiences is a political project to claim wider membership. By this newer definition of diasporic Nikkei, shin Issei also qualify as Nikkei because they are living outside Japan. However, to avoid confusion, I maintain shin Issei as definitive of a specific cohort of Japanese women migrants who arrived in the United States in the latter part of the twentieth century.

I also consciously choose to apply the term *migrant*, rather than *immigrant*. *Immigrant* implies a permanent uprooting—a jettisoning and forced shedding of all former identities, affiliations, and ways of being for a newer assimilative self, a process that has been labeled symbolic violence (Portes 1997). For contemporary movements of people, *migrant* or even *transmigrant* better describes a social process that is a continual project of both displacement and a rearticulation of being, "an important transnational process that reflects and contributes to the current political configurations of the emerging global economy" (Glick Schiller, Basch, and Blanc 1995: 48). For many migrants, their modern lives demonstrate a simultaneity of existences and ways of being and belonging (Levitt and Glick Schiller 2007). Moreover, shin Issei are often continuous *physical* travelers between Japan and the United States. They reveal diverse modes of movement and a confusing assortment of social terms and classifications in their undertakings, not all of which are legal. "People often shift between these categories, they may enter as students, tourists or visitors . . . then illegally overstay" (Van Hear 1998: 40). This mode of simultaneity in life is not a new phenomenon (Foner 1997).

In addition to definitions, one of the main projects of this book, as stated previously, is uncovering the tensions wrought by new migration in extant American communities and, at the same time, going a step further to investigate possibilities of common purpose or integrated action on social issues that are inclusive of both Nikkei and shin Issei under a larger, encompassing umbrella of belonging. What this may signify for a reconfiguration of the parameters of membership in a broader Nikkei collective is still being worked out. In fashioning new lives for themselves in their American homes, contemporary Japanese migrants are accomplishing this within shifting social spaces constructed not necessarily against but alongside second-, third-, and fourth-generation American-born Japanese. As each group becomes aware of, recognizes, and assesses the other, beginning overtures of possible action on shared goals are not so much collective productions as they are, instead, parallel endeavors with the result that intragroup values and beliefs are strengthened. There is a reinforcement of distinctive identities—shin Issei remain Japanese; Nikkei remain American. Despite a hardening of identities, this does not mean that a wider collective cannot be built. While there are intergroup misunderstandings, it is also, mostly, a case of lack of understanding. These processes of action are not entirely cooperative or collaborative. I use the word *collaborative* carefully and stress that its use is not in the sense of an assumed or positively shared experience. Instead, this project of communality is a collective of individuals with vastly differing histories and cultural processes. Nonetheless, as Nikkei have always understood, and as shin Issei are also coming to realize the longer they live in the United States, the more working toward a broader Nikkei identity and community is deeply influenced by subjectivities of race and racism as well as co-constitutive of gender and class in the United States (Winant 2015). These larger discourses supersede community space and further fracture possible ways of belonging and membership.

While the Nisei, Sansei, Yonsei, and Gosei (fifth-generation Nikkei) who populate today's Nikkei community are familiar to me, shin Issei are far less so. At the end of the day, that is perhaps both the simplest and most complex reason for my interest in this book's subject. I'm reminded that for sociocultural anthropologists, this is one of our mandates—to investigate complex, rapidly changing societies by focusing on people caught up in sweeping global economic changes (Gregory 2007; Chavez 2013).

The fieldwork in this ethnography began in the latter part of 2008, with the bulk of the research ending in 2017, though if one lives and works in the area of research, "leaving" the field is impossible to accomplish. This proved to be the case as the result of a contentious community issue in the Southern California area affecting both shin Issei and Nikkei. It came to a head in 2014 but continued after 2017. A brief period of reimmersion in the field in 2020 was important to document this continuing example of activism among a number of shin Issei and Nikkei where commonalities of purpose were attempted. Because transformation of community and processes of investigating dissimilar groups—American born and foreign born—is one of the putative goals of this book, I believed it was important to follow additional social action regarding activism.

A modified snowball technique was utilized, with more than sixty foreign-born Japanese and native-born Americans of Japanese ancestry who either reside or work in and around Los Angeles' Westside and frequent the longtime Japanese American area of Sawtelle. Other interviews and narratives took place among people involved in Little Tokyo and South Bay activities. None of those individuals who are active in the Little Tokyo area live there.

Forty-five of the women who participated in this study are shin Issei. The remaining are Nikkei who are split between Nisei (primarily in their midseventies) and Sansei (in their early to midfifties). The reasons for researching these two Nikkei generations and not, say, younger Nikkei was their grasp on Nikkei history and changes they had witnessed in their communities because of contemporary migration. Of the shin Issei, forty-two were in their twenties and three were in their early thirties when they left Japan for the United States in the 1980s. Almost without exception, none had personal contacts in the United States. For them, migration was a solo undertaking.

The majority of the women migrants do not have four-year university degrees. Rather, they possess high school diplomas, two-year junior college degrees, or education from smaller Japanese colleges where they majored in subjects like homemaking or arts. None of the women was married at the time of migration, and only one was already engaged to an American citizen living in the United States. Thirty-eight of the women eventually married or had domestic partners, but none of the partners was a Japanese citizen. Thirty-five shin Issei women are mothers who have multicultural, multiracial children (*shin Nisei* and American born).[4] Japanese is still the primary language for shin Issei mothers, though their children, like early twentieth-century Nisei, are bilingual and bicultural. At least ten of the women are separated or have been divorced. By the mid-1990s, many of the women had children in high school and, regardless of their partner status, worked part-time outside the home. Without professional skills or facility to speak fluent English, their jobs were not dissimilar to those they had in Japan. Working in positions such as restocking clerks, saleswomen, office greeters, secretarial assistants, teachers' aides, and food service preparers, they were employed by Japanese and Nikkei businesses. Many of these part-time jobs were near their homes, but commuting in Los Angeles is a way of life, and many shin Issei women drove to work.

Finally, there are four additional shin Issei in this study who are not the norm among the other Japanese women in that they hold degrees, including doctorates, from top-ranked universities in Japan and the United States. Two women came to the United States as children accompanying their parents in the early 1970s. Two others migrated after 2000, symbolic of continuing migration from Japan. Their stories are notable in that they all became quite active in shin Issei issues that also brought them into contact with Nikkei. They also demonstrate the diversity of life experience among shin Issei, a subject that warrants further investigation.

All the shin Issei viewed the United States as a means to expand social capital, thereby increasing opportunities and economic survival. All the women had thought about permanently staying; some were sure of their intentions to stay, but others made that decision shortly after arrival. While all of the shin Issei women entered the United States legally on various short-term visas, the majority immediately lost their status when they looked for a job and began working. Some were able to rectify this through various more permanent education or employment arrangements later, but others were not. There is great reluctance to admit or discuss it, but many have remained undocumented for years. Perhaps as many as one-third have no legal documentation. Nearly two-thirds of the shin Issei women are longtime green card holders, with some in the process of renewal. A green card means they are permanent resident aliens with the ability to work, but they not U.S. citizens. They remain Japanese nationals. Less than half a dozen women are naturalized.

Interviews were conducted in English or occasionally with a shin Issei translator (often an acquaintance or friend of the individual interviewed). Community events, meetings, and informal get-togethers were often recorded for transcription. Shin Issei and Nikkei who appear with first names only are pseudonyms. The use of full first and last names denotes individuals who did not desire anonymity or are public figures. Many people requested total confidentiality because they wanted to speak freely about people they knew or with whom they worked. They were particularly concerned about openly discussing intergroup differences. In addition, many shin Issei women voiced concerns about their citizenship position, their various routes of migration, and their ongoing migration status—or its lack. Some women did not want to be identified even with a pseudonym. Unless stated otherwise in the text, the actual names of organizations and other community entities are used. I have respected everyone's desire for privacy.

For the most part, I have relied on sources by English-published scholars on subjects such as gender, race, migration, and economic transformations and on English translations of Japanese scholars on similar subjects. To contextualize continuing migration from Japan, to position contemporary Japanese women migrants as part of worldwide migration, to tell their stories and situate them in history, and to make them human as migrants who have chosen to settle in the United States—this is what their narratives reveal.

Precarious Lives

Shin Issei are migrating to the United States because of a lack of economic opportunity and security in Japan that underscores the precarity, inequality, and risk that negates their life chances (Giddens 1979). The majority of young Japanese women like Rieko are cheap, unskilled labor. However, the nature of their labor has changed dramatically in the last century. Shin Issei are a group of migrants whose work no longer requires agricultural skills. By contrast, nineteenth-century Issei men, migrating primarily from Japan's countryside, were desirable as cheap labor because of their ability to farm the land. Young shin Issei women are not rural but highly urbanized. They no longer come from the countryside but from major global cities like Tokyo and Osaka. Like that of earlier Japanese migrants, however, their search for economic sustainability and viable lives unachievable in Japan remains (Commerce 2000). The beginnings of this more contemporary migration were the unprecedented strength of the Japanese economy and the rapidity with which this occurred post–World War II. That economic growth ended with seemingly equal speed when the "Bubble Economy" burst in the late 1980s and early 1990s (Kambayashi and Kato 2011).

While it lasted, the Bubble did not benefit all Japanese workers. Structural alterations in the economy, such as a switch from manufacturing to service, government deregulation, the privatization of welfare, and urban gentrification led to "broader changes that have placed a growing proportion of the Japanese at risk of unemployment, poverty, and homelessness" (M. Hasegawa 2005: 990). Homelessness, a term that had no official government definition until 2002, spread in urban areas like Tokyo (Okamoto et al. 2004). Unhoused individuals, including many young women and men who were not clearly visible on the street as homeless but, instead, inhabited public/private spaces, were dubbed "internet café refugees" (M. Hayashi 2014: 1215).

All Japanese workers were subject to increasingly massive economic restructuring and attendant changes in social structures in the 1980s, but these upheavals unequally affected women who "suffered the costs of labor-market 'flexibility' in their function as an easily accessible and disposable 'buffer stock'" of employees (Burkett and Hart-Landsberg 2003: 351). Women's life chances were embedded in gendered structures that circumscribed their participation, not only in the labor force but, as will be discussed, in other aspects of life as well. More than three-quarters of all Japanese women seeking work in Japan have been unable to find full-time positions. Instead, women are consigned to *paato*—part-time jobs. By the first decade of the new century, more than half of this majority were not yet twenty-five years old (Allison 2013). Gendered discourses about who gets work, the kind of work, and the ineffective protections of Japanese equal opportunity laws are behind an especially marked growth of transnational flows of Japanese women searching for employment (Yamashita 2008).

Although Japan's official unemployment levels appear low, these figures mask major transformations in job market classifications. Part-time, temporary, and contract work proliferate, with obviously lower wages and little job security. Japan has no official poverty line; minimum living standards are based on those who may qualify for public assistance (Sekine 2008). Japanese workers might not be thought of as impoverished, but since the 1970s, what has been labeled as the "new urban poverty," including homelessness and joblessness, has ballooned (M. Hayashi 2014). The disintegration of the much-touted lifetime employment system and the subsequent casualization of labor mean that salaries have fallen to well within official poverty standards, though the preferred term is *working poor* (Komamura 2008). This state of insecurity in Japan was inconceivable when local and global narratives were rife with the idea of the Japanese economic juggernaut (Addison 1992).

An individual's response to a lack of a contributory social life and suitable labor lead to conditions of marginalization that are manifest as something beyond the material—affective reactions that encompass one's entire existence:

> a state of desperation, of panic over debt collectors and rent, a life lived on the edge. And by this definition, Japan is becoming an impoverished country. A society where hope has turned scarce and the future has become bleak or inconceivable altogether. (Allison 2013: 6)

Life on the edge becomes an uncertain and insecure circumstance of precarity:

> a multifaceted condition, encapsulating not only legal and economic deprivation but also moral, spiritual, political, and health-related uncertainties. (Campbell and Laheij 2021: 283)

This social marginality is exemplified as a disbelonging, disconnection, and discounting of personal worth and value (Allison 2015). Shin Issei women's desires and decisions to leave Japan are rooted in these social constraints. However, their attempts to evade these limitations in Japan did not end in migrating where "everything looked free." In escaping structures of economic insecurity and of ensuing social precarity centered on gender relations in Japan, shin Issei women did not anticipate encountering other forms of marginality in the United States. They experienced, instead, the co-constitutiveness of new gender inequalities in work and personal lives and the instabilities of both legal and undocumented positions in their relations to the state. Moreover, for the first time, shin Issei women found themselves racialized individuals within both Nikkei communities and wider America.

What emerges, then, as the central argument in this book is that contemporary shin Issei migrants' narratives are stories of continuing marginality, first in Japan and later in the United States. Restrictions on gendered work and life as aging women in Japan, solo journeys to the United States, risky legal status, and marginalities of membership among other corporate Japanese nationals as well as Nikkei define new shin Issei women's lives of precarity within unequal power relations. Despite these limitations, Japanese women have, nonetheless, become active and resilient agents in circumventing social strictures to fashion new lives of meaning. I employ *agency* not narrowly to refer only to acts of overt resistance against domination but also to signify a "creativity, relocation, reinvention of self, leadership" (Pearce 2011: 10). In this sense, shin Issei women vigorously utilize resourceful actions and activities in defining themselves, and in so doing, they have found common belonging and purpose among other Japanese women migrants. The social actions shin Issei undertake are embedded in their precarity—the agency with which they confront, perform, and accommodate themselves to new challenges does not exist in isolation of larger, hegemonic forces. Therefore, their life strategies cannot be limited to spatially discrete global or local spaces but "must be understood as complex and contingent results of ongoing historical and political processes and that while participating in dominant culture flows and processes, [people] are, at the same time, imposing, inventing, reworking their positions" (Gupta and Ferguson 1999: 4).

Mediating Conversations on Contemporary Japanese Migration

In telling the stories of shin Issei, I want to make in the literature several interventions, and perhaps caveats as well, that I hope can better illuminate and frame discussion about the parameters of this specific phase of contemporary Japanese migration.

First, contemporary women's migration from Japan may be contextualized within more recent directions in research on the so-called feminization of worldwide migration (Ruyssen and Salomone 2018; Morrison, Schiff, and Sjoblom 2008; Simonen and Ndiaye 2006; S. Martin 2004; Yamanaka 2003). By 2005, women constituted *half* of the world's migrants (P. Martin 2007). Women migrants are now seen as "a mighty but silent river" of those seeking to improve their life chances (Alcala 2006).

Previous emphases often positioned women as following or reuniting with the majority of migrant male breadwinners; however, because of current migration patterns, that is now being challenged (S. J. Mahler and Pessar 2006; Kanaiaupuni 2000). Those studying Asian migration to the United States have critiqued these prior approaches and the "unmistakably masculine cast" of migratory flows where women are "pushed to the margins of the collective past" (Yanagisako 2002: 183).

> The pedagogical privileging of a masculine, working-class past along with the earliest period of each immigrant group's experiences molds a uniform ethnic, gender, and social class consciousness out of more divergent historical realities. (Yanagisako 2002: 183)

Shin Issei take their place as participants in this recalibrated conversation about women migrants worldwide. Moreover, since the 1990s, female Japanese migrants can also be analyzed in the context of women migrating from other Asian countries who are seeking better means of economic survival in more developed areas of the world. "Feminization has been most pronounced in Asian international labor migration . . . Asian women are moving in their own right as autonomous economic migrants, rather than as dependents of male migrants" (Lim and Oishi 1996: 86). Female Asian economic migrants often find themselves in segmented gendered and feminized labor—vulnerable positions of risk involving domestic work, caregiving, eldercare, and unskilled trades (Estévez-Abe and Caponio 2022; Nurchayati 2011; Constable 1997). Globally, unprecedented female migration *into* Japan is also part of this labor scheme. Women migrate from other Asian countries, such as the Philippines, enlisted to marry rural farmers, become "entertainers," or fill labor shortages (Suzuki 2008; Nakamatsu 2005). From Latin and South America, women migrants who are Nikkei by ancestry are also recruited to work in Japan's unskilled manufacturing markets (L. Yamamoto 2010; Ishikawa 2009; de Carvalho 2003; Yamanaka 2003).

Contemporary Japanese women migrants to the United States are participants in this trend of movement to seek better opportunities. Most significantly, during the period of this investigation, they were the overwhelming majority of those individuals moving *out* of Japan. In fact, Japan led all nations in Asia in terms of gender imbalances in migration (Batalova 2011). Japanese migrants have morphed from a majority of rural young men in the nineteenth century to a majority of young women in the late twentieth century, but the phenomenon of Japanese women in movement is also not new. By 1920, just 14 percent of all immigrant labor in Hawai'i consisted of women. However, of this figure, 80 percent were Japanese women (Takaki 1989).

By the 1980s, the percentage of legal Japanese women migrants in relation to Japanese men was quite remarkable. Between 1970 and 2000, more than 260,000 women and men arrived. Of this figure, about 102,000 were men and more than 158,000 were women—almost triple the number of women, including so-called war brides, who emigrated prior to 1970 (Commerce 2000).[5] This gender imbalance continued to expand in the 1990s. Shin Issei women arrivals far exceeded numbers of men by more than three to one (Commerce 2000). By 2010, shin Issei women in the United States constituted 65.5 percent of the foreign-born Japanese population, far outnumbering the presence of foreign-born Japanese men at 34.5 percent (Commerce 2010). Equally revealing is that by 1987, the median age in this large demographic group of shin Issei women was just 26.9 years (Commerce 1990). Moreover, percentages of contemporary Japanese women surpassed migrating women from all other nations entering the United States. The top countries in second and third positions were Mexico, with 59 percent of all migrants being women, and the Philippines, with 58 percent women (Ruppenstein 1993). It must be pointed out that these are figures for *legal* migrants.

Thus, the majority of shin Issei women were young, born after World War II, unmarried, and deciding on emigration in the 1980s. Put another way, to say *contemporary Japanese migrant* is to say *female migrant* or to simply refer to them as *shin Issei* in much the same vein as a nineteenth-century Issei migrant was assumed to be male. Unless otherwise made specific, and to avoid redundancy, references to shin Issei in this book will denote shin Issei *women*.

Second, the emphasis here is placed on labor and the economic disadvantage (rooted in gendered structures) in Japan that motivate shin Issei movement.

The shin Issei who populate this book do not come from destitute families, nor is there wealth. They do not classify themselves as part of the poverty class or working poor as defined by Japanese government calculations (Komamura 2008). Instead, with some vigor, they refer to themselves as members of Japan's broad, seemingly undifferentiated middle class, a label rooted in the late Tokugawa period.[6] They are not alone. By the early 1970s, 90 percent of all Japanese described themselves as middle class (W. Kelly 1986). The concept of the middle class was championed by the Japanese government post-Meiji and after the official elimination of class distinctions like *daimyo* (land-owning lords and vassals of the military-ruling shoguns) and samurai (military troops under daimyo; Silverberg 1992; Vogel 1967). Japanese policymakers further concentrated on building up more undifferentiated social categories after World War II and the U.S. Occupation (Kawano, Roberts, and Long 2014). Some preferred to jettison *class* altogether with a less stratified term—Japan's *middle mass* (Y. Murakami 1982). However, class as a powerful ordering system in modern Japan has never disappeared. Status in Japanese society continues to be defined around family position, education, and, of course, employment. Middle-class designations still have resonance, but growing social disparities and inequalities that have characterized Japan since the 1980s underscore motivations for shin Issei migration (Chiavacci 2005). Shin Issei see existence in Japan as one of social disadvantage, a lack of opportunity, and economic deprivation. They are highly cognizant of ideologies of gender that contribute to their marginality in Japan, especially as they apply to their positions in current economic restructuring. This awareness of the consequences and realities of the migration experience cannot be minimized or ignored (S. J. Mahler and Pessar 2001). More fully recognizing these inescapable facts allows a reformulation, or at minimum a better understanding, of the circumstances faced by contemporary Japanese women who are choosing to leave home.

However, although there may be acknowledgment about the shift in sexual ratios among those Japanese migrating, young women's reasons for leaving are elided and not categorized as labor. Rather, such women are characterized as those searching for other means of self-fulfillment.

> Like many other contemporary migrants, the shin-issei are, so to speak, adventurers in the globalised environment, seeking socio-psychological satisfaction, placing themselves in ongoing, self-adjusting processes.
>
> Akogare [longing or desire], a primary pull factor for their overseas journeys, may be illusionary; in turn, nevertheless, it does help generate a reality, a social reality which one can call "the era of dual life" between the land of akogare and their mother country. (Hyodo 2013)

Those seen as longing for different lifestyles are described as pursuing new identities outside Japan through novel cultural practices, new kinds of self-fulfilling experiences and excitement. These "adventurers" and "cultural migrants" move "purely for cultural or symbolic reasons" (Y. Fujita 2009: 169). Authors point out that since the economic ascendancy of Japan beginning in the 1970s, there is "a new breed of overseas settlers, people who display a distinctly different set of lifestyle orientations" (M. Sato 1993: 1). In other work, contemporary migrants are portrayed as fallout from postcapital situations or as a "constellation of problematic youth" with adjustment difficulties (Sooudi 2014: 10). The clear inference is that migrants are social misfits and that these so-called "motivational migrants" have the ability to exercise an independent sense of choice and freedom to pack up and leave (M. Sato 1993: 5). Not everyone agrees: "Calling these Japanese youth 'cultural migrants' instead of economic or political migrants may be slightly misleading" (Sakai 2011: 478). Celebratory and romantic discourse of mobility among Japanese women ignores the reasons behind their movements, and the ensuing effects of marginality and social exclusion (Takeda 2013). To reiterate my earlier statement, shin Issei are gendered labor migrants who are not successful economically in Japan. They come to the United States with few skills and an overall lack of human capital (Alba and Nee 1997). Their "choice" to leave must be more critically examined. It is more than simply a search for new lifestyles. By degrees, choice has always figured in a migrant's decision to move elsewhere, but it bears reminding that choice is embedded in larger social and economic circumstances.

> Almost all migration involves choices. Economic migrants make choices, but they do so within constraints. . . . Moreover, many if not most migration streams involve migrants with varying degrees of choice and who experience varying degrees of compulsion. (Van Hear 1998: 42)

Of course, there is no singular migrant experience, and while some shin Issei women may opt for a lifestyle change, my objective is to uncover a multidimensionality to the contemporary Japanese migrant experience. I center the current gender imbalance and further probe the circumstances beyond the desire for new lifestyles that is masquerading as and embedded in structures of economy and labor. Shin Issei are members of an unprivileged, cosmopolitical cohort that may be characterized as transnational and coerced (Cheah 1998). Gendered inequalities are the primary reason contemporary shin Issei leave Japan (Oishi 2007).

Third, shin Issei migration from Japan can be framed in the context of those nations (perhaps more accurately, *the* nation) with which Japan has maintained long-standing affiliations and historical linkages. Moving to countries other than the United States did not even occur to shin Issei in this book. Their movement is directly related to strong social and economic ties to the United States, especially post–World War II. The overpowering presence of the U.S. Occupation influenced and upended every facet of "the traditional social order" (Berkofsky 2010: 5). Recovering Japan and its citizens "embraced this culture (American) without restraint" (Gordon 2007: 16). The generation in which shin Issei reached adulthood was recipient to the consumption of America. "Migrations do not just happen; they are produced. And migrations do not involve just any possible combination of countries; they are patterned. Furthermore, immigrant employment is patterned as well" (Sassen 1994: 74). The relationship between Japan, as the sending nation for goods and services, and the United States, as the receiving nation, was key beginning in the 1960s. These links continue in the twenty-first century in the way both nations have restructured their economies to more fully compete in a global economy, which in turn has influenced the parameters of migratory movement.

The possibilities of life in the United States are especially appealing to shin Issei. Young women believe it is conceivable to achieve not only a more gender-balanced life but also a more unfettered life where they are accepted as individuals and where they find social inclusion in the United States. However, this does not often come to pass. As they seek employment and new ways of local living, perhaps decide on marriage and children, and mature in age, their struggles against unanticipated inequalities in the United States produce new marginalities that necessitate the creation of new life strategies.

Fourth, to further differentiate the shin Issei experience from that of other migrants who come to the United States is the much-researched subject of chain networks. Individuals and groups who maintain social ties linking their home country with cross-border destinations and who can provide access to and utilization of valuable migrant information are instrumental in the creation of so-called migrant networks (Massey, Durand, and Pren 2014). For example, at the close of the nineteenth century, dense, transpacific connections were evident among Issei migrants to the United States and Hawai'i (Konno 2012; Dresner 2008). Contemporarily, other Asian Pacific migrants are also reliant on network connections to help ease the migration process, especially since 1965, when U.S. immigration law changed to favor family reunification (J. Liu, Ong, and Rosenstein 1991). This is not the case among shin Issei migrants. For Japanese moving and settling in the United States in the 1980s and 1990s, personal social networks and linkages did not exist or were extremely limited in scope. The majority of the shin Issei in this book did not have family members already resident in the United States, nor any close friends. They arrived unaccompanied. Access to information and assistance did not come from individuals but via more global means of procurement, such as diasporic knowledge through media and internet discourse (Nagatomo 2017; Y. Kim 2011). More often, the happenstance of "serendipitously hearing about places . . . and opportunities" occurred (Amit 2014: 406).

Moreover, shin Issei's migratory experience should not be confused with the tens of thousands of temporary, multinational Japanese male employees (*chuzai-in*) and their families who began arriving in the United States in large numbers in the early 1980s. Shin Issei had little to nonexistent personal relationships with chuzai-in, the majority of whom were transient global representatives of overseas Japanese corporations. They entered with short-term work visas and usually returned to Japan within three to five years. These company (*kaisha*) workers were part of a transnational and transplanted network whose employers had already established full amenities for all their employees' family needs. Shin Issei women's solo experiences were of settlement and thus were vastly different. However, the appearance of chuzai-in employees who were visible manifestations of postcapitalist labor regimes also allowed for a shin Issei presence. In their early years of residency in the United States, many shin Issei women's labor in jobs such as restaurant and bar hostessing propped up and reinforced newer transnational labor schemes. In Japan and then in the United States, this reproduced a range of stratified, gendered, racial work experiences and histories that contributed to the continuing social regulation of young Japanese women (Ong 1991).

Fifth, this ethnography focuses on contemporary migration *from* Japan and must be seen in the context of movement that has *always* existed, despite attempts by the United States to curtail it. The lacuna of research on this contemporary phase of out-migration has left the subject often absent from discussion or minimized as too insignificant to warrant further investigation (Frey 2018; Oishi 2007; Scholars 2002). The fact that there are still Japanese settling abroad in some numbers apparently strikes many people, academics included, as something of a revelation. It should not.

Much more attention has been paid to studies of contemporary migrant movements *into* Japan. Over several decades until the late 1980s, the majority of this new migrant labor pool was largely unskilled, young women from abroad who were enlisted to fill labor shortages in certain industries. Although Japanese immigration policy underwent major changes in the early 1990s, the laws still do not favor the admissions of unskilled labor and foreign employment, though many backdoor entries exist (Tajima 2000). As indicated previously, foreign female migrants include those recruited as entertainers in the Japanese sex industry, brides from throughout Asia who wed rural Japanese men in villages where young Japanese women have fled to urban areas, or Nikkei women imported from South America to work as factory *dekasegi* (temporary foreign labor; Azuma 2008; Douglass and Roberts 2000; Brody 2002; Takenaka 2003; Tsuda 1999). Again, however, studies that investigate women's labor migration *out* of Japan and their reasons for leaving are few. When out-migration is mentioned, it is with some surprise that "even" single Japanese women have gone abroad in search of work (Lim and Oishi 1996: 88).

While contemporary movement is now heavily skewed toward women, it is not anomalous in terms of the long *durée* of Japanese out-migration historically, though its current circumstances may be unique. This contemporary moment is just the latest chapter in the continuing diaspora of Japanese outbound from Japan for Hawai'i and the United States. Since the mid-1800s, with the exceptions of the 1924 Immigration Act, which halted migration from Asia, and the years surrounding World War II, Japanese emigration to the United States has been of both short- and long-term duration. It has been an ongoing, persistent, and expanding social phenomenon. Approximately 270,000-plus Issei left Japan during a seventy-eight-year period from 1861 to 1939—just prior to World War II. The first group of contract laborers sailed to Hawai'i in 1868, and by 1894, nearly 30,000 others had arrived. However, the vast majority of Issei, approximately 240,000, emigrated to the United States mainland and California (Takahashi 1997). This group was foundational in the establishment of five generations of Nikkei. These mostly Issei men are often assumed to be the largest group of Japanese to migrate to the United States. In fact, they are not. From 1950 to 2015, a somewhat briefer period of sixty-five years, 369,623 Japanese were admitted as permanent residents of the United States (Security 2015).[7]

Though Japan is arguably one of the most highly developed postindustrial nations in the world, it should not be presupposed that its citizens are disinclined to move across borders. Nor should it be assumed that the more modern impulses of Japanese citizens are any different from what drives 232 million migrants from around the world—now more than 3 percent of the world's population—to leave home in search of better opportunities and economic survivability (Division 2013).

Sixth, I would like to initiate further discussion not just about their presence but about the ways in which shin Issei have changed the communities they inhabit—areas where they work, live, and raise families—within traditional Nikkei neighborhoods. By the 1980s, the additions of both transnational, kaisha employees and shin Issei had forever altered what had been places and spaces for generations of Americans of Japanese ancestry. Investigating the effects of post-1965 contemporary migration on other long-standing Asian Pacific American communities has also been well researched by scholars (P. Yang 2011; Toyota 2010; Võ; Saito 1998; Basch, Glick Schiller, and Blanc 1994).

Emphases in Japanese American cultural and ethnic community are well documented and researched, with much valuable work placed on generational belonging, the continuing pursuit of social justice issues within racialized frameworks, and the tenacity and practice of identity among Nikkei (Yamashiro 2017; V. Matsumoto 2014; S. Kurashige 2008; L. Kurashige 2002; Yoo 2000: 1553; Fugita and O'Brien 1991). Additionally, Nikkei community is well researched in areas such as Little Tokyo in Los Angeles (Simpson 2012; Jenks 2011; Shichinohe-Suga 2004; Toji and Umemoto 2003; I. Murase 1983). However, there has been less attention paid to the significance—the meanings and implications—that contemporary shin Issei migrants have created within Nikkei communities and Nikkei responses to these transformations. "The neglect of Japanese Americans by scholars studying contemporary Asian American populations is quite puzzling" (Tsuda 2016: 7). The phenomena of contemporary Japanese migration and its effects within Nikkei community remain a largely uninvestigated topic.

> I am not convinced we need more studies of the concentration camp episode, despite its obvious attractions. Perhaps what is needed most at this moment are studies of the half-century just past, and especially of the new, large wave of Japanese immigrants who have come since 1990. Their story is thus far untold. (Spickard 2009: 207)

A few researchers *do* acknowledge the presence of contemporary Japanese migration to urban areas such as Los Angeles and Southern California (Yamashita 2008; Machimura 2003).

> Shin-Issei, or new first-generation Japanese migrants are bringing transnational ties into the enclave and sharpening its identity as a place materially and socially linked to Japanese cultural forms. (J. Smith 2006: 189)

While these contributions are valuable in their recognition of newer migration, there is little that examines the everyday lives of shin Issei as they inhabit so-called enclaves and Nikkei spaces.

Furthering the argument about shin Issei women's marginality is their recent proximity to and contact with Nikkei. As shin Issei women populated and shared space and place with Nikkei, both groups experienced varying levels of discomfort and misgivings about the other. In long-standing Nikkei communities such as Sawtelle, where roots extend back to the early 1900s, not much is known regarding the impact of new migration, but its presence is there. To reiterate, shin Issei *are* transformative actors, creating new socialities for themselves in a new country. Shin Issei have added diversity and polycentric multiculturalism to the assumed hegemony of Nikkei identity and history (Ribeiros 2006). However, while there might be expected degrees of social affinity with Nikkei because of presumed similarity in social and cultural patterns, there is, in fact, dissimilarity. And while there may be some resemblances and commonalities to the past 150 years or more of Japanese American presence in the United States, contemporary migration from Japan is its own imprint. The new additions to the neighborhood arrive with vastly differing life histories and ideological practices of membership, identity, and belonging.

In Nikkei communities, the presence of new Japanese migrants is, at the very minimum, unsettling to those who claim at least four generations of U.S. citizenship. It is "the periodicity of their history, which has rendered the stages of settlement relatively unambiguous and given rise to distinct generational cohorts" (Nakano Glenn 1986: 7). Theirs is a racial identity—a highly politicized racial and ethnic group consciousness born of generational struggle against social inequality and racism in the United States (Yamashiro 2017; V. Matsumoto 2014; P. Yang 2011; Fiset and Nomura 2005; Yoo 2000; Security 2000).[8] Nikkei who are activists among Japanese Americans display an unwillingness to jettison this racialized identity. They persist in their commitment to participating in democratic processes and in the maintenance of a specific American identity as a community of color.

For these American communities, this is another pivotal moment of social transformation in Japanese American identity and history. Though Nikkei have been characterized by some as fully assimilated into mainstream American life, what emerges instead is the depth and persistence of a racialized citizenship. It is a specific identity clearly demonstrated through continuing networks, organizations, and activities benefiting Japanese Americans (Nikkei for Civil Rights and Redress 2018; Fugita and O'Brien 1991). This retentive agenda remains a highly politicized manifestation of an American historical project. In this activism, macro and micro manifestations of power and its (in)visibility in constructing the materialities of everyday life are not forgotten in the social production of new histories (Trouillot 1995). Nikkei do not see shin Issei as participants in this ownership.

For their part, shin Issei do not seek full incorporation among Americans of Japanese ancestry. Rather, they are mostly active on issues specific to shin Issei. Even after decades of life in the United States, they remain, simply, Japanese. This isn't to say that activism on the part of either group is unproductive or destructive to working toward more beneficial goals for everyone. There are emerging issues of common purpose among the two groups and a nascent appreciation for what the other can offer, but for the most part, these instances are the exception, not the rule.

It may be argued that new Japanese migrants have not produced any significant changes in the structure of communities, say, in the same way as have large numbers of post-1965 Chinese, Korean, or Vietnamese migrants to the United States. To be clear, in comparison to other migrant groups from Asia and the Pacific, figures on contemporary Japanese migration may be considered small in absolute numbers. However, this is *not* the same as insignificant, nor does numerical size bear relevance to transformational changes within Japanese American communities. Perhaps three times as many Japanese are living in the United States now as compared to before World War II (Hyodo 2013).[9] By the 1990s, numbers of foreign-born Japanese grew to more than one-third of the Nikkei community (J. Yamamoto 2011; U.S. Census Bureau 2000). Furthermore, the numerical size of a group most assuredly has never been, and certainly should not now be, an obstacle in the objectives, scope, or validity of any investigation of human populations. Postmodern ethnographers who continue to study smaller communities of people critique and challenge the lack of information and the ineffectual guesswork that still passes as knowledge about those considered less worthy of inclusion and research focus (McGarvey and Seiden 2010: 215).

The question of what inspires contemporary Japanese to migrate in the first place is part of a larger life puzzle whose many pieces are still being rearranged. None of the pieces is yet a neat fit or an ordered picture. This latest stage of migration has occurred only during the last quarter century—is *still* occurring. Emergent are shape-shifting images, materializing fragments of newly constructed everyday lives outside Japan that are geographically beyond borders but still very much of Japan, interpellated on past histories and future hopes.

Finally, a caveat of sorts, or at least a cautionary prelude about what follows. The stories shin Issei tell about themselves and others are experientially real. However, bringing to light their lives and motivations also focuses attention on my own positionality as a researcher and what I would like the reader to also consider. This is a study of migration and community incorporation enacted around cultural differences and processes, but even using the word *culture* can inadvertently construct the Other. I am wary of unspoken cultural binaries that seem inevitable in their constructions—here and there, modern and traditional, the United States and Japan, the West and the East. To me, a key objective for anthropology and social science is to reject concepts of culture as homogeneous, coherent, or timeless. Rather, individuals are confronted with choices, struggle with others, make conflicting statements, argue about points of view on the same events, undergo ups and downs in various relationships and changes in their circumstances and desires, face new pressures, and fail to predict what will happen to them or those around them. (Abu-Lughod 1991: 154)

Cultural frameworks demonstrated through difference are not inherently useless or suspicious as long as there is a continual questioning of "a discursive field where the issue of 'cultural difference' easily reduces to an essentialized notion of different cultural values versus westernization and modernization" (Hirakawa 2000: 50). Culture *is* change and process—fluid and malleable. Two points of Hirakawa's I have tried to keep in mind for what follows: one, the multiplicity and complexity of both shin Issei lives and Nikkei with whom they interact, and, two, migration and its consequences as a postcapital global problem no matter what its cultural context. The contemporary, global political economy has created widespread insecurity, precarity, marginalization, and struggle with profound effects on individual lives (Paret 2016).

Outline of the Book

This investigation takes a twofold approach. In a somewhat diachronic and geographic timeline, I chart the experiences of shin Issei lives—their existence in Japan prior to migration, their motivations for moving to the United States, their settlement, and their growing awareness of who they are in American society. This gives perspective and context for better understanding how their lives intersect with the second approach in this book, which is looking at the continuing meanings of a specific racial and ethnic belonging still practiced by Nikkei in longtime areas of settlement and places where shin Issei are now a new admixture. The relations between the native born and foreign born are often fraught with social tension as each group negotiates place and space for itself.

Chapter 1 introduces shin Issei in Japan and their memories of growing up in the 1960s, reaching young adulthood in the 1970s and 1980s. As the first generation born in postwar Japan, they did not suffer the devastation of war but, instead, were recipient to a surging consumer economy as well as Japan's bid to achieve global parity through massive economic restructuring. This transformed social and economic conditions and came at a time when young Japanese women were attempting to enter the workforce. They now found themselves participants in a very different social and global ecumene (Hannerz 1996). Extant gender imbalances in Japanese social life increased, as did divisions in labor—most significant, a rise in part-time and temporary jobs defined as women's work. A sense of precarity ensued for shin Issei who could not find remunerative employment and who faced additional pressures not just from parents and family but from wider discourses about women's assumed roles in Japanese society. They were encouraged not to seek more education but rather to find suitable marriage partners as quickly as possible before socially imposed expiration dates. Shin Issei looking for jobs and careers in their midtwenties found they were no longer marketable—past their useful shelf life.

Chapter 2 reveals the routes of shin Issei travel and their arrivals in Southern California, paths buoyed by a period of unfettered economic expansion in Japan that spilled across the Pacific. Without a globalizing Japan and its economic reach, a platform for the building of a shin Issei population would most likely not have occurred. Young Japanese women came with few concrete plans for surviving in new homes. They were not assisted with personal networks, but nonetheless, in this mission of movement, they were inadvertently aided by both the Japanese and U.S. governments. Each nation-state sought to foster internationalism and further economic ties, not through schemes of recruited cheap labor of the nineteenth century but through schemes nonetheless, in the promotion of foreign capital investments, foreign tourists, and students. Landing in the United States in the 1980s, shin Issei utilized short-term visas to tour the United States or perhaps enroll in trade schools or junior colleges. Their hidden agendas were more fundamental—to find employment. In their job search, they piggybacked on the presence of multinational Japanese corporations and the thousands of transferred Japanese employees and their families. Over a few brief years in Southern California, a transpacific Japan was created. In this global arena, shin Issei were able to carve out unskilled employment niches for themselves. Shin Issei flouted immigration rules and, instead, became out-of-status migrants with no intentions of returning to Japan. Undocumented positions quickly became flexible, feasible, and invisible.

Chapter 3 uncovers the migrant statuses shin Issei have utilized in settling in Southern California. In particular are the lives of undocumented shin Issei: how they became visa overstayers and how their lack of legal status has evolved into a long-term, liminal condition. There were avenues in past years to adjust their position, but it is doubtful shin Issei would have qualified. In any case, the window of opportunity has closed, and they would mostly likely be deported if discovered. Although the majority of shin Issei migrated to the United States with no prior fiancé or spouse attachments, many do eventually marry to adjust their migrant status, though this is also a fraught process. Regardless of documentation, however, there is a continuing precarity and tension surrounding a constrained daily existence. Even legal residency, if possible, does not diminish this liminality. Furthermore, in many cases there is resistance to naturalization. Shin Issei rank among the lowest of migrant groups to become U.S. citizens. Social identities endure firmly as Japanese and the practices surrounding naturalization are not prioritized.

Chapter 4 takes a closer look at how shin Issei lives have evolved specifically in Southern California. In particular, it builds on the effects of the larger economic imperatives a transplanted global Japan and its massive corporate investment in and around Los Angeles—factors of which shin Issei took advantage. Where foreign capital (and the presence of both chuzai-in and shin Issei) was most visible, the result was often rising tensions in longtime Nikkei neighborhoods—tensions over belonging and a specific American identity. Young migrants working in this transnational arena may have envisioned lives of freedom and opportunity, but in many cases, this did not occur. The types of unskilled employment they were able to find, such as bar hostessing and waitressing, reified structures of both gender and class, with the addition of racialized discourses. Approaching middle age after a decade or more of life in the United States, shin Issei have been stuck working marginal jobs. Some have improved their job skills, but most have not. A few are still single, but most have married (or divorced) and have children. Non-Japanese partners and biracial children who are American-born citizens do not lessen the mothers' marginalities but often seem to exacerbate liminalities. At the same time, however, this continuing social precarity motivates shin Issei to become active among other migrants like themselves. Their social participations mitigate isolation, but the spaces they create for themselves also reinforce being Japanese and, in turn, generate tensions in raising biracial children. Shin Issei mothers who want their children to value their Japanese heritage find themselves inhabiting Nikkei spaces at community schools in neighborhoods like Sawtelle.

Chapter 5 employs Sawtelle as a site of community transformation fueled by the presence of shin Issei. Nikkei and shin Issei may share common places and spaces but not intergroup commonalities of purpose and identity. Maneuvers are choreographed between the two groups as they metaphorically assess each other from opposite sides of the neighborhood street. Each views the other with curiosity and suspicion, which underscores historic class and cultural dissimilarities. Most revealing among these differences are the symbolic and historic perceptions of racial variances. Supposed skin-color differences, in fact, emphasize wider implications about gender, citizenship, and nation. Shin Issei remain Japanese as new additions in the neighborhood while Nikkei continue to claim and act on a racial and ethnic American identity nearly a century old. Emblematic of this divide is a Nikkei project to designate Sawtelle a historic Japanese American community—something shin Issei do not understand. Nonetheless, individuals from both groups begin to tentatively search out possibilities of utilizing intergroup commonalities.

Chapter 6 shares stories of some shin Issei who have begun to work in tandem with Nikkei toward similar, albeit broad, instances of community activism that may allow the building of space for both groups. *Activism* may yet be too strong a word in branding shin Issei involvements, but these embryonic participations can be characterized as contributing understanding in significant ways to the racialized history of Japanese—native and foreign born—in the United States. In particular, I relate shin Issei and Nikkei working at Sawtelle's supplementary school, where intergroup activities have included the subject of Nikkei incarceration in classroom curriculum and, by relation, an acknowledgment of social justice and equality issues that have been longtime objectives for Nikkei. Ad hoc alliances within established Nikkei communities around Southern California have also given Nikkei additional insight into important shin Issei issues of health care and immigration. In prioritizing their own issues, shin Issei and Nikkei do see a degree of common purpose as communities of color in the United States. However, more permanent collaboration or partnerships remain elusive. Whether in Little Tokyo, Sawtelle, or the South Bay, these fluid alliances manifest as a spatiality of cohabitation, each with its own layered borders of belonging within the racialized geography of Southern California—a geography that is a historic and socially produced landscape.

There will most likely always be some level of tension intergroup, but I believe that many Nikkei have faith in this project of inclusion of new Japanese migrants and that it is critical to a larger, reconfigured Japanese American identity. As for shin Issei women, within a small number who are becoming active among their peers, there *is* a desire to participate with Nikkei, but with continuing parameters and borders of intergroup belonging. Recognizing and accepting these group differences means that mutual support between Nikkei and shin Issei is necessary and can be beneficial for both groups working within dominant racial projects in the United States that subsume differences among communities of color. The overarching conundrum is how this will be accomplished.

1

Wilting Office Flowers

At my age, to find a job in Japan is very difficult. After thirty it's hard. Women have to marry before thirty. [When you get a job] you have to write down your age, if you're married, how many kids you have. They ask if you have a boyfriend.

Hana was born in Osaka in 1963. After graduating high school, she did not have money to enroll at a junior college and was able to find only part-time work in a midsize company. She watched many of her women friends in comparable circumstances follow a well-worn path from high school graduation to "OL" (office lady), marriage, and motherhood.

> I didn't want to be an OL. That's what all my friends did after high school. They went to work immediately, at a bank, department stores. This is what women do.

In the early 1970s, the term *OL* became pervasive in describing young women. They were fresh out of high school or some post–high school education, looking for first jobs as OLs or BGs—business girls.

> As suggested by the use of the word "girl," these women were almost all single and young, and they uniformly quit their jobs upon marriage. Some companies routinely set the retirement age for women separate from that of men, sometimes as early as age 35. (Iwao 1993: 155)

Even more descriptive was the slighting term *flowers of the office*—pretty to look at and decorative but insubstantial and transient (Iwao 1993: 155). In their late twenties and early thirties, they are no longer youthful, no longer considered fresh flowers. A Nikkei who traveled frequently to Tokyo on business trips remembers the ubiquity of OLs.

> If you go to Japan, and in the early evening you go past a coffee shop where they have seats in the window, all you see are women clerks. Maybe they feel that this isn't what I'm looking for . . . there's a lot more opportunity for them here [the United States].

This chapter analyzes the lives of shin Issei coming of age in 1970s Japan. Their maturations were personal projects to be sure, but at the same time, they were deeply embedded in larger global schemes of economic and labor reorganization in which Japan participated. The germination of this restructuring was visible beginning in the late nineteenth century but sprouted fully during the postwar U.S. Occupation as a "shared, increasingly global modernity in the 20th century" (Gordon 2007: 1). There were not only altered restrictions on employment opportunities but additional social limitations that led to a discounting of women's worth and value—the consequences of this marginality permeating other aspects of daily life. A brief analysis of social changes in postwar Japan can provide a valuable tool by which to understand not just the alterations that affected Japanese women but the ways those changes eventually transformed shin Issei into contemporary migrants. This is not a discussion of Japan's postwar social history or of Japanese economics per se, but it is still worthwhile to reconstruct some of the details of the Japanese "miracle" following World War II that specifically affected young women's lives.

From Militarism to Consumerism

Japan underwent not just total wartime defeat and devastation but a major social reformation in the years after the war that also saw key changes in the place of a "modern" Japanese woman. With the implementation of Occupation policies, America was positioned as both colonizer and postwar model. The immediate goal was to rid Japan of its militarism by paving the way for American-style values (Kensho 1998).

> The postwar phenomenon of "Americanism" in Japan was seen not just as the result of American military and political imposition, but as a process of deep structural change involving the emotions and desires of Japanese people. (Yoshimi 2003: 434)

Writ large was a wholesale American soft-power cultural project aimed at ridding Japan of what were seen as its feudalistic proclivities (Nakao 2007). Moreover, Japanese women were singled out for democratizing reform but in roles subservient to the home and family, with rigid gender roles between breadwinner and homemaker. American occupiers "actually undertook to implement American Cold War family ideology under the guise of women's liberation" (Takeuchi 2017: 114).

As children of the postwar period, shin Issei were exposed to this portrait of gendered family ideology, which also captured a sexualized female modernity.

> As the pièce de résistance of their gendered interventionism, the occupiers consistently set up a glamorous white American role model for Japanese women and girls to emulate. This idealized female was portrayed as a beautiful, cosmopolitan, and progressive individual who took an active role, not only in the home, but in society as well. (McAndrew 2014: 85)

The American military newspaper *Stars and Stripes* reported on American-style beauty contests featuring Japanese candidates vying for the crown of Miss Nippon (McAndrew 2014). In 1959, when Japan's Akiko Kojima became the first representative from Japan (or any Asian nation) to win the Miss Universe beauty title, Japanese were jubilant. Here was proof positive of postwar progress and acceptance that Japan and, more specifically, Japanese women, could compete and win against white women's Western beauty parameters (Bardsley 2008). Nonetheless, the limits of this supposed emancipatory project exposed continuing systems of gendered inequality in Japan. Japanese male journalists lauded Kojima's ambition—not in becoming Miss Universe but in her aspirations to become "a lovely wife" (Bardsley 2008: 377).

Translated American magazines and books were widespread. Women's magazines touted the new Japanese *mōdan garu* (modern girl) based on images of blond American women dressed in the latest fashions from America and Europe. Imported American films filled lifestyle sections. Hollywood actors such as Doris Day were photographed clad in capri pants (Ochiai 1997). Actors Elizabeth Taylor, James Dean, Ronald Reagan, and Fred Astaire were familiar faces in Japanese media (*Asahi Shinbun* 1956).

A new consumer society with its attendant material manifestations was a guide in the ways of modernity (B. Sato 2003). Washing machines and Coca Cola were marketed for modern housewives. John D. Rockefeller III, who was heavily involved in postwar U.S.-Japan relations, believed that "politics, economics, and culture were the three major components of American foreign relations"—with culture being the most important (T. Matsuda 2007: 4).[1]

American businessmen successfully convinced Japanese consumers to associate consumerism with democracy by using high-pressure salesmanship to promote American goods and services. (T. Matsuda 2007: 14)

No matter that in an early postwar Japan, where surviving on a daily basis was itself not assured, most women could only imaginatively consume the images, not actually afford to live them. The end of the Occupation in 1952 did not terminate American influence, nor did unequal power relations and domination disappear. The politics of everyday Japanese life and culture had become suffused with the American presence.

"America" was more than just an image of new lifestyles and culture. It was an ever-present force intervening in people's daily lives, whose word could not be challenged. (Yoshimi 2003: 435)

The consequences of cultural imperialism produced profound and lasting changes in Japanese society (Tomlinson 1991). The ubiquity of American representations became part of the fabric of a reconstructed Japanese life. For young shin Issei women, these images and products ceased to be wholly American and became woven uncritically, embedded in their everyday local Japanese lives (Ohnuki-Tierney 1997).

Postwar Japan also ushered in significant changes in education opportunities for women. Teaching missions arrived in Japan, with new ideas about classroom curricula and parental participation (Kensho 1998). By the mid-1950s, there were more than thirty-six thousand chapters of the American-led Parent Teacher Association with more than fifteen million Japanese parents claiming membership (Morito 1955). American studies classes were incorporated into courses at Japanese universities. American social scientists were deployed in redesigning Japan area studies for Japanese academics, importing such subjects as American cultural anthropology, which, more generally, aided in the adoption of Occupation policies (Nakao 2007).

Democratization of Japanese education meant reform, with the American system serving as example. Adopted reforms were initially met with resistance from the Meiji bureaucracy—now the postwar Ministry of Education. At least publicly, the government promoted parity and egalitarianism in educating both girls and boys (Morley 1999). New enactments included compulsory school attendance for girls, common curricula for both girls and boys, and the ability of women to attend the same schools and universities as men (Takeuchi 2017; Hara 1995). This is despite the fact that an analysis of the new reforms displayed "vast cultural differences between the system that evolved and the

U.S. system it emulated" (Kempner and Makino 1996: 34). Nonetheless, by 1955, students going to high school instead of directly entering the workforce rose to more than 50 percent (Sakurai 2004).

Almost unheard of before the war, young women began entering post–high school institutions in ever greater numbers (Sasagawa 2004). The sea change in higher education for women is most clearly observed in junior college enrollments. In 1960, just 3 percent of young women went to junior colleges. By 1980, that figure had grown to 21 percent, with women outnumbering men in junior colleges tenfold (Fujimura-Fanselow and Kameda 1995). Nearly every shin Issei woman in this book was afforded a post–high school education—primarily junior college of one to two years. Women attending four-year colleges and universities grew as well, though by smaller rates. In 1980, university men still outnumbered women students by nearly four to one (Fujimura-Fanselow and Kameda 1995).

More critically, whereas it may appear that women were beneficiaries of dramatic social changes in both historical and contemporary contexts, "education wears two faces" (Morley 1999: 55). Nearly a third of the women in junior colleges were majoring in home economics, while at four-year colleges, more than a third of women students took courses in humanities (Fujimura-Fanselow and Kameda 1995). For young women, the educational system was still highly gendered and aimed at producing wives and mothers. As an unintended consequence, the transformative American example created new ways of viewing a world beyond Japan. These new perceptions became an unconscious tutorial in future decisions made by shin Issei women like Chisa, whose Japanese schooling virtually preordained her eventual move to the United States.

Everything I heard and learned in school, the United States is the place. It's the best. In junior high, high school—we all learned English and we learned about America.

Economic Boom Times

During the Occupation in the early 1950s and continuing afterward through the early 1970s, jobs were plentiful, and Japan recorded an era of high economic growth, which was accomplished through rapid industrialization and manufacturing innovation. Personal incomes rose along with the annual gross domestic product (GDP), which increased by 10 percent annually (Burkett and Hart-Landsberg 2003). As the nation recovered, the Japanese government encouraged policies aimed at resurrecting domestic consumerism. After years of severe deprivation, Japanese eagerly embraced social and economic improvements.

The government's 1977 White Paper on National Life was entitled "Towards New Affluence of Living" (Economic Planning Agency 1977). Assembly-line production soared in industries such as domestic automobile manufacturing. It didn't take long for the growth of the export market to eclipse domestic consumption. By 1973, more than two million cars were already destined for foreign markets (T. Nakamura 1994). The government began keeping statistics on social expenditures such as dining out and purchases of the trinity of affluent consumer life—the "Three New Sacred Treasures"—car, color TV, and air conditioner (Economic Planning Agency 1981; Kumazawa 1996). At the same time, with manufacturing climbing, new categories of employees were produced. This resulted in the strengthening of gendered division and segregation in labor markets.

The most well-known example of gendered labor in Western media was the *sarariman* (salaryman), who was held out as Japanese society's perfect representative of waged work (Iida and Morris 2008). The sarariman became a stereotype evocative of Japan's economic miracle. Depicted as a drone wearing a white shirt and dark suit, marching in lockstep to the subway each morning, he toiled for the good of the nation. The lure of lifetime employment with its rewards of permanent pay, guaranteed benefits, and bonuses became a strategic component in hiring and retaining career-track male employees at major companies. Less acknowledged was the cornerstone of this formula's success—the requirement of women's bodies to nurture the interior family while the male breadwinners gave their bodies to the exterior company.

> Within the context of this discourse, disseminated and reinforced very effectively through the instruments of state and society, women were relegated to the private/household sphere as "good wives, wise mothers" (ryosei kenbo) and men to the public/work sphere as "corporate soldiers."[2] (Dasgupta 2000: 192)

In reality, midlevel managers and others typecast as the sarariman were never a majority of male employees (Bishop 2000; Burkett and Hart-Landsberg 2003). In the 1960s, perhaps around 30 percent of white-collar male workers fit this role, and though the percentage increased into the early 1990s, many sararimen were employed at smaller companies that offered far fewer benefits (Miller 1995). Only the largest corporations were able to afford extensive employee benefits, and by the time a sarariman was in his early to middle fifties, he was either coerced into retiring or shunted into lower-paying jobs.

Women in waged labor continued to constitute large numbers in manufacturing into the 1970s, when the Japanese economy was forced to restructure again to meet the changing demands of competition in wider global markets. This was accomplished by fast-tracking into postindustrial manufacturing, new information systems, high technology, and service industries. Gendered divisions in labor were visible in Japan's political economy long before the high-growth period; however, labor opportunities became more circumscribed and increasingly peripheralized for Japanese women into the 1980s (Tsurumi 1990). Postwar discourse still underscored that "wives are more important than jobs or wages" (Kashu Mainichi 1961: 1).

An illustrative example of the rigidity of gendered labor systems occurred in the integrated circuit (IC) industry. At the time, Japan led the world with innovative products like random-access memory cards and silicon chips. Initial stages of this high technology manufacturing required skilled labor in which men were employed in managerial, design, research, and development positions. However, subsequent steps in the industrial process entailed mostly repetitive manual labor with little job training. By the mid-1970s, every major Japanese electronics corporation was employing thousands of young and middle-aged women on the IC assembly lines (K. Fujita and Hill 2005). Younger women were recruited directly out of high schools. Japan also began relying on new infusions of labor in its consumer electronics and manufacturing industries—labor it recruited from among Latin and South American Japanese migrants (Yamanaka 2003).

In the 1980s, dramatic changes occurred in the numbers of women employed in manufacturing. Global market competition and rising yen values made production at home too expensive. Corporations became fully automated, invested capital in robotics, or moved offshore to underdeveloped areas of Asia and the Pacific in search of cheaper labor. In the IC industry, women made up 95 percent of the workforce in 1970; less than fifteen years later, their numbers had dropped to as low as 52 percent (K. Fujita 1988). Women who were able to get jobs found age a more critical factor as employers hired increasingly younger women workers. The younger they became, the less they were paid, with lower pay reflective of both job description and short-term presence in the workplace.

> These young women, after working for five to seven years after high school, are expected to play the socially and culturally imposed role of mother and wife. . . .
>
> State policy does not provide programs to upgrade the skills of women workers, and thus it exacerbated the gender inequality linked to the current restructuring of the international division of labor. (K. Fujita 1988: 53)

Two major oil crises in the mid-1970s plunged Japan into its worst postwar recession but did not result in massive layoffs (T. Nakamura 1994). Instead of jettisoning employees, companies reacted flexibly by shifting male workers to other areas of the corporate structure or transferring redundant jobs to subcontractors. With cooperation among government, businesses, and unions, maintaining employment of core workers was literally achieved at all costs, even if it meant reduced pay for overtime or smaller bonuses (Cargill and Sakamoto 2008). Layoffs and firings were a hard sell, and many companies' adamant refusal to use them continued to reflect the importance of male white-collar workers as linchpins in the well-being and security of not just the economy but also Japanese social life (Keizer 2008).

However, by the 1980s, even the largest corporations began to see the looming economic abyss as the economy began a steady but unquestionable recessionary decline. GDP was down from its double-digit figures, though still at an enviable 4 percent. By comparison, much of the rest of the world was also mired in recession. In the United States, 1980 GDP levels slipped into the red (International Monetary Fund 1980). An important indicator of the decline in Japan's GDP was the drop in personal savings. Domestic consumption and savings were, and continue to be, the purview of married housewives, who oversee all aspects of the household budget. The rate at which average Japanese housewives invested and saved their husband's salaries was crucial to the country's stunning economic growth. Until the late 1970s, annual savings rates were in excess of 20 percent—the highest among postindustrial countries (Yoshikawa and Ohtake 1989). In less than a decade, savings had fallen to record lows of below 15 percent (Bureau 1991).

Bowing to international pressure (from the United States) in 1985, Japan was forced to raise yen rates. Concomitant dollar devaluation sent the Japanese currency skyrocketing (McKinnon 2007). The subsequent appreciation paralyzed the competitiveness of the driving force behind the behemoth economy—the Japanese export market. The result was deindustrialization, layoffs of vaunted permanent workers, and a decline in domestic demand. Japan plunged into severe economic and social stagnation and experienced its highest unemployment rates since the end of the war. Most significant, unemployment began to rise for male breadwinners as more men were beginning to retire (or be retired). In addition, the numbers of women looking for work to supplement family income rose (Agency 1982). Families drew on savings and turned to retirement benefits and public assistance, all of which had major social impacts (M. Hayashi 2014; Atoh 2008). The government responded by increasing unemployment benefits from six months to nearly a year (Kitazawa 1987).

These catastrophic events resonated deeply in the everyday, middle-class lives of both women and men in ways that recast their ideas about themselves and their personal worth as contributing members of society. In what was termed as the "hollowing" of Japan's economy, people's lack of employment undermined their overall sense of security beyond gainful work; their place in their communities became precarious and unmoored (Kenmochi 1987). "Precarity and risk are the fundamental experiences of the global regime of financialization, for people of middle incomes as well as those in poverty" (Susser 2021: 410). Precarity as a system of structured inequality encompasses aspects of race, class, and gender and is a central concern in postindustrial economies at all levels of development (Wright 2016).

Japanese young adults who were entering the job market in the 1980s but experiencing an inability to find work were labeled the "lost generation," with the 1980s branded the "lost decade" (Allison 2012: 356). Their sense of personal security, social affirmation, belonging, rights, and protections were eroded (Vosko, MacDonald, and Cambell 2009; Genda 2005). Young women were caught up in solidifying maternal ideologies that promoted the appropriate "choice" in dropping out of (or not seeking) full-time employment so they could marry and have children. Women who did find work ended up in the fast-growing part-time and service sectors (Gerteis 2009; Sassen 1994). Service jobs at less than thirty-five hours a week were not considered full employment and did not provide benefits, and indeed, to say "part-time work" was to define it as women's work (Shirahase 1995). The halcyon days were ending.

The Paato Revolution

The growth of part-time, *paato* jobs in Japan represents one of the most important changes in women's work since World War II (Nagase 1997; Shirahase 1995). Women workers were never sararimen and never participated in so-called career-track jobs. In the 1980s, they began to populate a new category of employment—part-time jobs—broadly classified as temporary, casual, dispatched, and contract work (Keizer 2008; Weathers 2001; Bishop 2000; Kawashima 1995; Iwao 1993).

Part-time work is the outcome of the casualization of labor that began worldwide, including Japan, in the 1970s. Casualization means increased flexibility—the benefits inhering more to employers and far less to workers. This labor practice "opens up the hiring process, lifts restrictions on employers, and typically lowers the direct and indirect costs of labor" (Sassen 1994: 73). The reason for hiring nonregular women workers is simple: "firms have benefited from lower wage payment for women considerably since it has saved labour costs" (Tachibanaki 1987: 663). Bottom line, the increases in numbers of women working or looking for employment also meant a compliant workforce that did not reap job security, equal pay, or benefits.

> A large part of male-female wage differentials are discriminations against women in wage payment and promotion. They are not receiving the payments that correspond to their contributions to firms. (Tachibanaki 1987: 663)

There are both positive and negative aspects to the rise of the paato worker in Japan's changing economy. For millions of women, part-time work has not only redefined contemporary job classifications but also enlarged women's chances to be at least partially employed. The figures for both women and men who were working part-time in the 1980s are revealing.

Part-time work was a small percentage for both sexes until the early 1970s because there were fewer part-time positions and most women who might work were still at home raising children. Quite abruptly over a period of a few years, women part-timers began to outstrip men. By the mid-1980s, numbers of part-time women workers were more than double that of men (Nakajima 1997; Sassen 1994). By 1990, the numbers had tripled. Into the middle and late 1990s, the number of nonregular working women continued to grow, exceeding that of men in similar positions nearly four to one (Bishop 2000). This did not include the nearly two million women employed as temporary subcontractors doing piecework at home for smaller textile, clothing, or electronics companies. The use of "homeworkers" was another way that companies increased labor flexibility and eliminated employment protections. These workers were officially classified as self-employed (Kawashima 1995).

Part-time workers, of course, are not considered regular employees. To add further complexity to this highly gendered job market in Japan, women workers were segmented into different subgroups of peripheral employees as mentioned previously—contract regular and nonregular workers, part-time dispatched workers, or pieceworkers—in a system that further exacerbated work imbalances regarding wages and job security. Because of the nature of how employers classify their nonregular employees, it is difficult to ascertain specific numbers, but it is still clear that in the 1980s, the majority of women's work fell into nonregular employment, far outpacing men's work of the same type, and that did not mean higher wages (Gerteis 2009; Kubo 2008; Kawashima 1995; Ochiai 1994). Stratification by sex became the norm in labor segmentation. Marginalized women workers searched for lower-paying jobs in other faster-growing sectors of the economy: wholesale and retail sales or the so-called FIRE industries (finance, insurance, real estate), where part-time, non-career-track jobs proliferated. Japanese government figures touted increases in total numbers of women employees, but a closer look shows that nearly 58 percent were in either service jobs or wholesale and retail businesses such as shops, restaurants, and bars (Bureau 1991).

Many women in their late thirties and early forties who were married reentered the labor force to offset the precarious situation of a shrinking family budget. They began returning to work after children were school-age or grown. This is known as the M curve (Brinton 1993; Hendry 1993). The first spike of the M curve occurs when women are in their early twenties and looking for work. The first dip occurs in their midthirties, as they marry, have children, and become what is characterized as the "professional housewife" (Hendry 1993). The second spike follows when mothers are in their forties, children are older and in school, and women begin to reenter the workforce. The final dip in the M curve begins as women age into their sixties and stop working (Yamada 2009; Shirahase 2001). Japan and the United States have similar workforce participation rates over a woman's working life. However, unlike the United States and other postindustrial countries, Japan "has a fundamentally different human capital development system" (Brinton 1993: 2). Young women know they are mandated to quit, forced to do so when they marry and have children.

What is important to the shin Issei story is that the reconfiguring of the job market occurred at the same time that shin Issei women were maturing as young adults, looking for first jobs, and joining the ranks of older women who were reentering the workforce. Because of limited education and few skills, many of the young, unmarried shin Issei women in this study were further shut out and unable to compete in restructured job markets. Even if they were hired as regular employees, they were still expected to quit and get married within a few years and as such were not placed on career-track jobs as were males. Youth and attractiveness were the key temporary-job requirements.

In the mid-1980s, Chisa was approaching her late twenties, still single, and living at her parents' home. Neither she nor her parents favored this living arrangement. They were becoming alarmed about her unmarried status. Chisa had attended a second-tier college and took classes that emphasized humanities and home economics: topics her parents found suitable for their presumed marriage-bound daughter.

> I had graduated from college with a degree in arts, so my parents said it was time for me to get married. I met with an *omiai* [matchmaker] who told me I should move out.

After her schooling, she'd been able to find only part-time work. She was soon laid off from her job at a small office. Chisa needed a job that would allow her to afford an independent life. In conversations, she would often say, "You know when I think about having a good job . . . *yoku dekimashita*" [I want to do well]. She did not want to be looked upon as a burden—someone who is a failure in her family and her community. Chisa was looking for work where her labor would be valued, where someone might say, "Good job!" Her stay-at-home mother and municipal-worker father began to pressure her to find a husband. Several times they tried to arrange marriage prospects from among their family and friends. One vetted candidate came with especially high marks.

> I remember my parents introduced me to some kind of engineer. He was working at designing streetlights and signal lights. I don't want to hear about these kinds of things! [*Laughing.*] I don't care about this! Now when I look at a traffic light, I think somebody actually designs these things.

Nearly two decades later, she recalls these matchmaking attempts and home tensions with no small degree of cynical humor. At the same time, however, she is also quietly reflective about how she interpreted the social constraints under which both she and her parents lived. She sighs and speaks more slowly.

> In Japan they don't care about who's happy; they care about who looks good, who has a good job. If you get introduced to somebody, they want to know who you are working for, if you are making money. They don't care if he's a nice guy.

Aya's work experience reflects her broader life precarity. She graduated from high school, but her junior college courses left her with virtually no job skills. Nonetheless, after rotating among different positions in a midsize company in Tokyo, she was fortunate to be making fairly good money as clerical help and was hoping that her small promotions would lead to something more substantial within the company. However, any future job possibilities ended abruptly in her midtwenties. Aya's male supervisor began making veiled comments that it was time for her to leave. She stayed on despite increasing pressure until her boss finally "let" her go.

> Every year my salary was going up, but he said "There was no more increase, sorry." I thought he wanted me to quit, but he didn't say that.

The atmosphere in the office was not good. It was getting uncomfortable. Nobody said anything to me.

She knew she was at a dead end in finding even part-time work without references. Aya had no marriage prospects, and, in any event, she says this was not a top priority.

The Politics of Reproductive Identities

During Japan's upward trajectory of rapid economic growth, the "wife as full-time housekeeper and mother was the symbol of the well-being and prosperity of the emerging new middle class" (Chiavacci 2005: 110).

> If one juxtaposes a portrait of prewar farm women planting seedlings and carrying rice sheaves with one of postwar housewives tending toddlers, cooking, and shopping, the contrast is striking.
>
> Two key questions for modern Japanese women's history are how this new urban middle-class womanhood emerged as a cultural norm, and how Japanese womanhood came to be defined solely in terms of reproduction—budgeting, buying, housekeeping, and childrearing. (Uno 1991: 19)

The phenomenon of the Japanese housewife began during the boom years following World War I—the brief Taisho period (1912–1926). Restructuring of both urban space and place changed to accommodate a new middle-class social structure. The push to industrialize Japan occurred primarily around the fast-developing urban and suburban areas of Tokyo and Osaka, with millions of people now urban dwellers in millions of *danchi*—massive, multistory apartment complexes. These new social arrangements meant new transportation systems and commuting. In short, for the first time in Japanese society, there evolved a separation of work and home, public and private spheres with women consigned to the home, wherein "the state of being a housewife became so strongly normative that it was practically synonymous with womanhood" (Ochiai 1994: 33). The term *okusan*, which was formerly applied to women married to lower-class civil servants, now defined all stay-at-home wives (Ochiai 1994).

Similarly, "the Japanese state began to see the nation as a big family and the family as the locus of state authority for women" (Tamanoi 1990: 26). The idealized wife-and-mother role did not specifically function to define women's *labor* but was positioned as a role that was preordained and natural to all women. Carried to its "logical" conclusion, this shift in social role meant that female labor was a supplement and secondary to male labor in all aspects. Productive waged work became redefined as an urbanized, male prerogative—a discourse that was especially useful to the new economic goals of the nation even though women's (unpaid) labor had always been crucial in Japan despite its later "supplemental" definition. This corporative family model with male privilege is a pattern that still exists in many aspects of contemporary Japanese social life, and its significance is crucial in understanding gendered ideologies that continue today (Stockman, Bonney, and Xuuewen 1995).

> Social images of work outside the home discouraged women from pursuing careers or long-term employment. Working was considered to be secondary since a woman's place was "naturally" in the home. Marriage was known as "eikyu shushoku" (lifetime employment) and considered to offer the greatest possible security and fulfillment for a woman. (Iwao 1993: 156)

This became a powerfully gendered chip in brokering women's roles to state and nation.

> A reproductive bargain composes an ensemble of institutions, ideologies and identities around social provisioning and care for human beings. The bargain constitutes a hegemonic framework within which actors negotiate rules . . . from different structural positions of power with different resources. (Gottfried 2009: 77)

One of the major ideological underpinnings of this reproductive bargain is the overriding mandate that women marry and have children, all within certain time frames. Sealing the deal compromises women's ability to work and seek careers in the job market. Shin Issei felt this social dictate keenly. The pressure to be married and have children—to virtually anyone as long as he was a sarariman with regular paychecks—was an overriding social decree for young Japanese women of Chisa's generation. Parental attitudes regarding daughters were buttressed by women's education policies that reinforced the *ryosei kenbo* (good wife, wise mother) and professional mother as ideal models. They were ultimate guideposts for a life well lived that subsequently shadowed women in the workplace, not to mention other aspects of life (Matsunaga 2000). Living at home rent-free for too long and refusing marriage despite matchmaking efforts meant young women were subjected to social opprobrium. Those who were still unmarried in their midtwenties were met with derision.

> A common joke refers to them as "Christmas cakes," meaning that like Christmas cakes, they will become too old and stale after the twenty-fifth. (Tipton 2000: 213)

Once out of school, all young Japanese were expected to assume adult roles—to become *shakai-jin*—persons who contribute to society (Okano 1993). Young women who refused age-mandated marriage and childbirth but continued to be single or look for jobs were called out. In mass media, they were labeled as *parasaito shinguru* (parasite singles) and "loser dogs" accused of self-centered motivations, a lack of responsibility, and the cause of the declining birth rate (L. Nakano 2014). "It is no surprise that women think twice about having children and leaving regular employment" (Development 2017: 1). By the mid-1980s, women's mean age at marriage had risen to twenty-six years. Japan's fertility rate fell to what the government regarded as dangerously low levels (Atoh 2008; Brinton 1993). Between 1970 and 2005, fertility rates fell from 2.1 children per woman to just below 1.3 while more women sought divorce, which became marginally less socially stigmatizing (M. Ono 2009). Those promoting stereotypes and blaming single women, however, neither understood nor acknowledged the critical changes in the Japanese economy and the increasing precarity of the labor market for all workers but particularly for women (Kawano, Roberts, and Long 2014).

Mariko was still unmarried and nearly twenty-six, moving from job to job and unable to find a position that offered economic stability.

> I had lost my job in Japan. I had changed so many jobs. I was the oldest employee so [my boss] fired me. I think because I was making too much money. He didn't say anything, but it looks like, yeah, trying to cut costs. Three women; I was highest paid and oldest. Other women [were] younger and were making less money.

Her reaction, interspersed with sighs, was one of dejection, resignation. She was unable to offer solutions that might improve her situation. Like other shin Issei women, she exhausted both energy and money in pursuing employment that could afford a more positive sense of self-worth, not to mention economic survivability.

Kyoko had a series of part-time jobs with no benefits. She was let go at every one of them and finally was forced to move back into her parents' home when she could no longer afford rent. She remembers not being hopeful about her prospects.

> It's not equal, if you want to work. We are so behind in Japan compared to America.
> Changing slowly but still not equal. Maybe working, but the money is different. Maybe only part-time.
> Men go to college. Women get jobs on the floor, sales training, dealing with customers.

Living at home allowed Kyoko to save some money from various short-term jobs. Her parents did not want her moving out on her own until she established her own household—with a husband. In any case, wages from part-time work were insufficient for maintaining an independent life in the major cities of Japan, some of the most expensive urban cores in the world. There were also other compelling reasons for daughters to live at home.

Years earlier, Kyoko's father had relocated the family from his birthplace in a small town to a large city where there were more jobs. He found work at a medium-sized company as a technical manager, but it meant a long daily train commute from their new home in a metropolitan hub where the family knew no one. Until the 1970s, many Japanese lived in multigenerational, coresident families or had other, nearby familial support (Rindfuss et al. 2004). Now, more isolated urban lives were the norm. Moving to the city meant Kyoko's mother was alone the entire day and much of the evening raising children and managing her household. Day-care options were minimal, and in any event, most families could not afford the cost. Kyoko fulfilled this role in taking care of younger siblings.

> My parents were in the city far away from my grandparents. In the countryside, grandparents take care of kids, but my mom had to stay at home; otherwise kids are alone.

Kyoko didn't pay rent, but she helped with household work and running errands. Should her parents have become ill, Kyoko would also have been tasked with caring for them. Even after daughters marry and move out of the parental home, that caregiving responsibility continues. For those who can afford it, retirement homes and nursing facilities are a fairly recent but expensive addition to family social structures in Japan. None of the shin Issei in this study comes from a wealthy family; all were affected by the economic restructuring of the 1980s, and these options would not have been available solutions. Though she found it increasingly difficult the longer she was out of high school, Kyoko did not give up her job search. She was the exception among her women friends, many of whom had simply stopped looking for work.[3]

Younger, recently graduated high school women were the first to be hired, especially as entry-level OLs. However, as the economy worsened in the mid-1980s, increasing numbers of young women and men had become discouraged and had ceased looking for work. Officially, the government did not consider them jobless but simply not in the labor pool. It was a way to keep unemployment figures artificially low and thus did not reflect the real jobless rate (Tachibanaki and Sakurai 1991). Women, in particular, were more likely to stop searching for work and figured heavily among the most discouraged (Genda 2007). Some figures placed women out of the labor pool and thus made them part of Japan's invisible unemployment problem, which was as high as 70 percent (Nobuhito 1995). Rosy economic reports of affluence in the late 1970s turned decidedly glum a decade later. "In search of . . ." became the overriding theme (Economic Planning Agency 1986). Dual incomes in families increased as more women sought employment. However, employed women classified as *full-time* did not increase. Economists warned that this "upward trend" of more women working did not mean economic recovery. For many working women, it did mean job insecurity in all aspects.

Shin Issei living at home experienced daily occurrences of tension and arguments with parents. Quarreling usually began over the lack of employment but fast degenerated into marriage criticism. Kyoko had repeated disagreements with her mother.

> When I was twenty-five or twenty-six, my mom was telling me I have to decide on something. You're not young anymore . . . you know so-and-so who's married; you have to think about it! I say to her, "Oh, you know she's divorced!" What do you think about *that*?

That the "ideal" of marriage was never fully accepted or acted upon by shin Issei women challenged official gender narratives about the role women ought to assume and about their nonconformity in adhering to "accepted behavior" (Dales 2015; Nakane 1974). Young Japanese women began to practice more discrepant modernities to construct new ways of being within existing hegemonies.

> The official truths of the Japanese economic miracle existed along with backstage truths—inequalities and limitations that gradually emerged as the weak underbelly of rapid economic growth. (Rosenberger 2001: 16)

Those who did have jobs had little hope of getting promotions. Expectations and choices shin Issei may have had for their futures were both wistful and uniformly low.

> [In Japan] . . . probably I would have studied English, maybe literature, went to work for some company as a secretary or paper copier—an OL—and then maybe got married. That's all you hear about.

While growing numbers of women found employment in nonregular forms of work in the 1980s, new government mandates were supposedly designed to create more equal opportunity and pay. Instead, women found that gender segregation and age discrimination continued. For several decades prior to the mid-1980s, activist women's groups had begun to push for gender equality in the workplace. In 1986, the Equal Employment Opportunity Law (EEOL) was passed.[4] However, instead of making job discrimination based on sex illegal, the new law stipulated that Japanese employers simply "endeavor to create equality in recruitment, employment, job assignment and promotion" (Nakajima 1997: 8). No employer sanctions were included in the EEOL, and most of the regulations were considered not only toothless and irrelevant but seemingly aimed more at allegedly protecting women than reforming job inequality. Official discourse supported and encouraged equal opportunity in employment, but private polls showed that Japanese men still harbored long-term resistance to workplace equality. A majority of respondents believed men should work outside and women should stay at home (Cargill and Sakamoto 2008).

The response to the EEOL among larger companies was the creation of a dual-track employment system (Rebick 2011; Kawashima 1995). Track one led to managerial positions filled by men; track two were routinized, clerical assistance jobs for women where few skills were needed. A small minority of women, mostly graduates of top-tier, four-year universities, were selected for possible admission to the managerial route, but overwhelming numbers of young women entering the job market did not have that option. Shin Issei saw EEOL promises as hollow.

> No equality in Japan for women, I don't think so. Nobody ever thinks we are equal . . . that never happens.

Some surveys of young women apparently concluded that women made the choice to reject positions with more responsibility because they were worried about increased job demands. "It seems that many women decide the status quo is perhaps all for the best . . . [they] most naturally choose those classified as general positions over managerial track positions" (Kumazawa 1996: 198). In other words, the onus for "choosing" a general-track job was placed on the women themselves, not on any extant, management-formulated employment path for female employees. Part-time work was characterized in similar fashion, with employers often describing part-time work as a choice and claiming that "part-time jobs and service oriented works are preferred by females" because they are more "harmonious" and flexible with women's positions in the home—taking care of children and elderly (Tachibanaki and Sakurai 1991: 1577). Women workers say they are not working part-time voluntarily and that any flexibility benefits their employers, not themselves (Bishop 2000). If the suggestion is that women choose part-time work voluntarily because of convenience, family obligations, or the need to supplement family income, it is also argued that social structures and gender roles for women do not allow for other solutions and make it very difficult for them to rise into the ranks of more responsible, full-time work with benefits (Honda 2005).

What results is that the gendering of structures of work becomes naturalized, normative, and expected (S. J. Mahler and Pessar 2006). Professional work is reserved for men, with the assumption that this category requires skilled, complex managerial know-how, more experience, and more education (Witz 1992). Part-time, clerical, OL work, by definition, implies unskilled or deskilled positions requiring less experience or education and not worth commensurate pay (Steinberg 1990). At job interviews, it was legal to ask young women what was their opinion of the EEOL and whether they thought work and marriage could be combined and how they would do it (Brinton 1993).

> Firms' recent efforts to reorganize the labor market have been more in accordance with economic efficiency than to achieve equality of sexes . . . women are expected to fit into a workplace created by men. . . . Their heavy share of responsibilities at home, however, remains virtually unchanged. (Kawashima 1995: 295)

The gendered wage gap increased steadily during the 1980s; men working full-time were making twice as much as women in comparison to other major postindustrial nations (OECD 2007). Researchers bluntly called the labor market position of women unfavorable.

Working women in Japan face an uphill battle in advancing their careers. Japan ranks among the lowest in the OECD [Organisation for

Economic Co-operation and Development] for women in management positions, and for the share of women on boards of directors, and Japan also fares badly in the number of women in public life.

These gaps can reinforce negative gender stereotypes and inadvertently curtail the aspirations of girls and women of all ages. (OECD 2017: 1)

Young women surveyed about their jobs described their work as "simple-minded, boring, and meaningless because they were not given authority and could not develop their abilities" (Kumazawa 1996: 176). Shin Issei women who couldn't find full-time work echo these sentiments.

> I was working part-time in Japan, data entry on computers. They hired me for three months for data entry, research at an internet office, telephone service. In the office, I was getting about fifteen dollars an hour, sometimes twenty dollars, but still part-time. That's it.

Government policies in the 1980s further stacked the deck against working mothers. If a woman did work to supplement family income, she and her family risked losing significant tax exemptions should her take-home salary be too high (Rebick 2011). Married women who earned more than the tax schedule allowed ended up paying additional taxes separately from spouses; they were penalized and discouraged from attaining higher-paying jobs (Shirahase 1995).

This chapter examined the constraints shin Issei confronted in a restructuring Japanese economy that limited their life opportunities. Gendered discourses of support were largely lacking. Instead, women were labeled as parasites, old, and stale for not accepting roles centering marriage and motherhood. Shin Issei faced an uphill battle with potential employers who rationalized their failure to hire women full-time by saying that "women do not have 'career consciousness' and, moreover, tend to have family responsibilities" (Nakajima 1997: 9). Certainly, none of the shin Issei women in this study wanted to work part-time or at low-paying jobs with limited, if any, job security and benefits. This was not by choice. Perhaps there were better choices to be had elsewhere.

2

Leaving Home

The big factor that made me want to come here—I couldn't stand the fact that women were second class [in Japan] and still are.

I heard that Los Angeles was a dangerous place, so I don't want to go. I was kind of afraid. People told me so many people here have guns [and there is] so much crime.

At that time, you know . . . [in] Little Tokyo . . . there was a lot of money there. There was the Bubble. It was a very wealthy time. Japanese companies were buying buildings here, like the Bonaventure [hotel] was owned by a Japanese company.

The late 1980s was a time of both fear and opportunity for shin Issei migrating to Southern California—opportunity for a better job and career but fear for what they might encounter. Visitors from Japan were advised to learn English words such as *police*, and the majority thought they would likely be victims of crime (Sanger 1993). Shin Issei recall the urgings of family and friends to stay in Japan, where it was safe. One shin Issei had read and heard so many stories of violence, particularly in urban areas, that she opted initially to move to a small town two hours northwest of Los Angeles. She had never heard of it, nor did she have any idea where it was located, but it seemed far enough away from Southern California. Her comments about living in a highly urban area were familiar. "Los Angeles seemed kind of dangerous, right? So I thought countryside would be better." Despite whatever reservations about personal safety these young women may have had about life in the United States, those hesitations were not enough to dissuade them from the belief that they might have better, more fulfilling, and more economically productive lives.

This chapter uncovers the circumstances by which many shin Issei arrived in the United States and opted to settle in California. Moreover, while their transplantation to Southern California may appear to be an entirely individual and independent decision, it was not. As the previous chapter explained, global economic restructuring was the main cause behind their migration. Concurrent with labor alterations as foundational in their migration, additional globalized social and economic transformations were also in play both in Japan and the United States, lending impetus for movement. Some of these changes may be characterized as recruitment schemes by national governments to enlist the participation and movement of young, migrant Japanese women. In this analysis, it is critical to keep in mind larger economic and other social imperatives that provided incentives eagerly sought by shin Issei.

Transnational Linkages

By the 1980s, the Japanese economy was heading into the overheated, so-called Bubble Economy—an unparalleled time of excessive inflation and growth of assets like real estate (Yoda and Harootunian 2006). The Bubble had been slowly inflating for two decades, with Japan amassing vast currency holdings. The country found itself awash in yen, and the United States seemed like a bargain basement. In the mid-1960s, Japan's direct foreign investment in the United States could be counted in the mere tens of thousands of dollars. Barely two decades later that figure was in the billions (M. Wilkins 1990). In somewhat of an understatement, Japanese economists observed, "Japanese firms found it hard to find new places to invest their money" (T. Nakamura 1994: 231). Both individuals and corporate investors from Japan snapped up real estate and other investments around the world.

In perhaps one of the most visible of economic and business decisions, Japanese multinational (MNCs) and transnational companies opened subsidiary headquarters across the United States, including in Southern California. The Japanese found an eager market, and American demand for imports like Japanese automobiles and electronics soared. The selling of innumerable consumer products with the tag "Made in Japan" no longer inspired ridicule. Corporate banking, investment and real estate services, and manufacturing proliferated, and by 1985, Japan had become the world's leading exporter in addition to being the world's number one creditor nation (Watts 1985).

With the infusion of Japanese money and business infrastructure came increasing numbers of overseas Japanese employees reassigned to staff and manage offshore Japanese companies and American workers (M. Wilkins 1990). In the late 1970s, more than one hundred thousand Japanese employees and dependents were living abroad in dozens of foreign countries (Toba 1979). Thousands of chuzai-in and their families relocated to the United States on temporary, nonimmigrant work visas.[1] By 1989, Japanese nationals working temporarily as foreign company transfers, exchange visitors, and other international representatives in the United States numbered more than thirty thousand, with an additional fourteen thousand listed as spouses and children (Justice 1991). Other Japanese nationals who were doing business and investing in the United States as nonmigrants numbered more than sixty-seven thousand. Only citizens from the United Kingdom exceeded these figures.

From the moment they stepped off the plane, (male) employees' requirements for housing, children's education, and other aspects of social life were entirely predetermined and supported by the transnational company structure.[2] Kaisha Japanese were seen as the most noticeable and elite embodiments of the overseas community. A Southern California Japanese business association that began in the early 1960s with a few dozen companies had swelled to more than seven hundred members in the early 1990s (Machimura 2003). In Los Angeles, temporary- and permanent-resident Japanese nationals numbered thirty-six thousand (Machimura 2003).[3]

Japanese-owned supermarkets, restaurants, bars, beauty shops, and language schools further transformed the landscape of neighborhoods in Southern California. Small Japanese-owned businesses supporting the kaisha community needed workers who understood Japanese and were culturally and linguistically competent. It was a chance for shin Issei to embed themselves in this newly constructed transpacific community, and they took advantage of these economic changes. In short, shin Issei found a niche—and easy employment.

> At my restaurants, there were many Japanese customers, so I don't even have to speak English. I was lucky!

In comparison to well-paid chuzai-in employees, young shin Issei constituted a far less noticeable pool of laboring bodies. They were not top of mind as examples of skilled transmigrant employees, but most assuredly, they were also global market labor recruits—their unseen presence part of the continuing persistence of migrant "women's invisibility in national, and international policy, theoretical and historical literature, social science data and even, until recently, the migration studies field" (Hune 1991: 802). Without the manifestations of the highly transnational community of overseas Japanese male employees and their families, the expanding numbers of shin Issei living in the United States may well have been reduced.

In Southern California and beyond, this global Japan was not well received. Until the early 1980s, every major United States domestic automaker manufactured cars in Southern California. Within a decade, the assembly lines had shut down, and tens of thousands of people were thrown out of work (Apodaca 1992). At the same time, in Japan auto production, which had initially concentrated on supplying its own domestic market, pulled into the fast lane. By the early 1980s, Japanese auto exports surpassed American auto production for the first time. The fallout from Japanese exports built rapidly, and Japan was soon seen as a threat to the U.S. economy and especially to American workers.

The "Nipponization" of Southern California was unflattering common parlance in media stories (Davis 1992). Less polite phrases such as "Japan bashing," "invasion," and "economic warfare" made headlines (Sullivan 1992). Japan was well aware of the distrust and anger its newfound economic strength engendered in the United States (Weisman 1991). MNC representatives met with law enforcement and sponsored community talks about hate crimes and increasing racial tensions directed at the Japanese presence (C. Lee 1992).

> Unlike trading companies and banks, which can close their books and return home when emergencies arise in their host countries, manufacturing companies have to continue operating where they are; in other words, though Japanese by origin, they cannot survive without assimilating themselves to local conditions. (Toba 1979: 87)

Despite the growing hostility directed at Japan, the 1980s did not see a lessening of Japanese investment, nor did economic tensions stop the flow of shin Issei migrants.

Familiar Tropes: Land of Opportunity

For shin Issei women who took advantage of wider global transformations, physically visiting the United States was not necessarily a precondition to eventual migration. From childhood, all shin Issei have longtime exposure to America. That the United States has always been among the top preferred destinations for traveling Japanese is no surprise. Affection for the destination aside, perhaps it is more accurate to characterize it as a feeling of familiarity or continuing curiosity and emulation in the sense of what best fits within an experiential Japanese context. The seeds of this awareness were sown early and grew rapidly after the Meiji Restoration. Late nineteenth-century popular press and magazines described migration to America as the shortest route to success (Sawada 1996). For shin Issei, this indoctrination continued with postwar educational reforms that coupled national modernization with American and European ideals (T. Kobayashi 1986). Similar to their mothers who matured in the early postwar years, shin Issei daughters have been habituated and exposed to imagery of life in the United States. However, unlike their mothers, they were able to utilize new global structures to make their imaginings of life elsewhere a reality.

Kyoko always has a ready smile, peering over the tops of her horn-rimmed glasses, oftentimes pushing her straight, blunt-cut hair off her forehead. Her everyday experience in Japan was dominated by American life on mainstream Japanese media. She was an avid consumer.

> I wanted to see what California [was like]. [I knew] about Universal Studios and Disneyland. I saw a lot of TV in Japan before I came here. *Charlie's Angels*, Joe and Ponch in *CHiPs*, Lindsay Wagner in *Bionic Woman*—everything looked fun and cool.

"Fun and cool" for Kyoko was rendered in her imaginings as new opportunities in the United States. One of her last part-time jobs was at a ubiquitous *konbini* (convenience store) near a train station. She flipped her hand outward, a dismissive gesture, and said her work was unimportant. Making a part-time salary, she knew she would never be promoted beyond restocking the shelves or ringing up *o-bento* (lunch) purchases. The only job requirement she ever heard from her boss was, "Sell, sell, and sell more!" Off time from work was spent watching American television entertainment programming and reading about American film stars in Japanese-published fan magazines.

At her last part-time job, answering phones at a travel agency, Kyoko was reading vacation pamphlets when one advertising affordable California trips caught her eye. She sent away for more information.

> There was a brochure selling the trip to go to the United States or England. Two coworkers I knew had gone to school in the U.S., and they spoke English. I asked them, "How's the United States?" "Oh, it's OK!" At that time, it was very cheap.

She knew no one in the United States, but it was easy to find other shin Issei who returned to Japan after study and work. She saw the opportunity to learn English as a way to increase her skill set and enhance her ability to find better employment—not in Japan but in the United States.

> I don't speak English, so I looked around to find someplace to study English at a language school. Cheapest one was in [California]—four-week program. I didn't know anything about [this place]. [I] just chose the cheapest one.

As soon as she had saved some money, Kyoko applied for a three-month tourist visa. Alone, she left Japan, flew to San Francisco, and then took a commuter plane to her final, rural destination away from major urban hubs. It was 1986, and Kyoko was approaching her midtwenties. Her introduction to life in America was like nothing she had constructed from the images she'd seen in Japan—certainly not fun or cool. She was greeted by a hot, dry summer with heat waves shimmering in the distance, dusty country roads, and farmworkers laboring in fields. The tour she'd purchased in Japan included both a quick language-school immersion and accommodations with an American family. Kyoko's hosts were a divorced mother and teen daughter.

> I stayed with a *hakujin* [white] family—they didn't speak Japanese, but they picked me up at the airport, and the next day they drove me to the school. It was just a short time to study English. Like a homestay—like a tourist. Just a short trip to study and live here—just one month.[4]

She found herself sharing a small bedroom with a young woman from Indonesia who had also bought an inexpensive round-trip ticket and homestay tour to learn English. Even now Kyoko finds it difficult to articulate her first experiences in America.

> [This place] was . . . *Oh!* [*Clapping her hands to her face.*] My first American dinner was Domino's pizza! Pizza, yeah, I ate it. Before, in Japan, pizza was like a snack to me; now I understand it isn't here. Mom had only pizza to eat.

Her host family's living habits left her equally nonplussed.

> American family . . . mmm [*tilting her head to one side*]. Daughter was a teenager, and her room was *so* messy! Our room was so clean, just two beds, clean and neat, but daughter's room . . . [*Shaking her head*]. At that time there were cassette tapes—no CDs—there were cassette tapes *all over* her room.

Kyoko's lack of knowledge about her new surroundings and her singularity in traveling alone was juxtaposed with her transnationality before she finally settled in the United States. Shin Issei did not have emplaced familial networks on which to rely in their movements to new homes, but they were far from being totally isolated. They may not have been transnational in terms of physical movement, but shin Issei translocality across national borders was nonetheless constructed through burgeoning socioeconomic opportunities and cultural ties that "are constituted within historical and geographically specific points of origin and migration" (Smith and Guarnizo 1999: 13). Shin Issei actively inhabited numerous transnational circuits, social spaces, and communities before and after their arrival in the United States. Kyoko's reliance on media consumption and a few acquaintances demonstrates that "transnational social spaces are combinations of ties, positions in networks and organizations . . . that reach across the borders of multiple states. These spaces denote dynamic social processes, not static notions of ties and positions" (Faist 2000: 191).

At a macro level are social institutions and structures functioning globally across national borders, what some have typified as transnationalism from above (S. Mahler 1999). Prompted by various U.S. and Japanese government structures that promoted travel, new knowledge, and modernity as desirable, shin Issei women were willing participants in this plan. At a more micro level, transnational activities and ways of being are performed in the everyday lives of individuals, or what some have called a transnationalism from below, out of sight of larger social and political structures (M. P. Smith 2005; Guarnizo and Smith 1999). Shin Issei women have both constructed and acted upon these less observable transborder, transnational links in the frequency of their real and imagined travels between the United States and Japan. Kyoko and her shin Issei sisters were avid consumers of mediated imagery that fed their desire for alternative opportunities. Although not formalized migrant networks, they utilized other, ad hoc means of obtaining information, notably in the acquiring of social media, websites, blogs, and other online avenues (Dekker, Engbersen, and Faber 2015). These links are interconnectivities, and they assisted in building new instrumental relationships once women arrived. A caveat, nonetheless, that "highly transnational" should not conjure images of freewheeling, footloose migrants with unlimited mobility. For shin Issei, transnationality in everyday life is still a practice situated within broader structures of power that define the limits through which identity and belonging are enacted (Y. Kim 2011; Dunn 2009).

Tomoko says just watching what American women wore on weekly television programs aired in Tokyo left her with a sense of frustration. They were images she could not erase.

> In Japan there are so many things you cannot do. Here [in California], you can wear short sleeves; you can wear a tank top even in winter; nobody will say anything to you. Nobody will think you are crazy. In Japan it is different.

Parsing "so many things you cannot do" suggests further insight into women's motivations for migration. The fact remains that the most common reason cited by young Japanese women, and Japanese men as well, who come to the United States is their growing and continuing unemployment (and underemployment) status in Japan (Toivonen and Imoto 2012; Y. Fujita 2009). Young women's agency in leaving Japan must be contextualized within what they believe to be an escape from economic inequality. In new fields of opportunity, they seek to redefine themselves and act upon modes of resistance (Kelsky 1994). Though embodied and nonconfrontational, there is still resistance in the rejection of social norms and expectations in Japan—it is the "cannot do" to *doing* that articulates new lives.

Ten Million Desiring Internationalization

The arrival of shin Issei in the United States, on the heels of chuzai-in, appears timely. However, like many seemingly unplanned and uncoordinated events, increasing migration among Japanese was, in fact, the consequence of specific national discourses, policies, and structural changes in Japanese social life designed to capitalize on Japan's new wealth. Shin Issei took advantage of recently instituted government policies in Japan and the United States that explicitly encouraged international tourism.

The United States did its part in fostering tourism, which in turn brought in more dollars as foreign exchange. In 1988, it announced a worldwide Visa Waiver Program in which invited countries were exempted from the required travel visa to enter the United States. Japan was added to the program list in 1989. The waiver allowed foreign nationals a ninety-day stay in the United States without a visa, though other official documents like a passport were still required, along with a fee.[5] A similar, reciprocal program for U.S. citizens entering Japan as tourists was also begun.

Exemplifying its economic hegemony, Japan began promoting a discourse of national modernity wherein travel was pictured as an exemplar of the global nation. The catchword was *kokusaika* (internationalization). Foreshadowed in the late nineteenth century by the word *kindaika* (modernization), kokusaika became the major theme of Japan's global role, or attempts to achieve it, in the world.

> The alleged failure of the Japanese to internationalize is commonly discussed in the Japanese media, often with lament and sometimes with vexation. The Japanese are constantly prodding themselves to be more international. (Mouer and Sugimoto 1983: 267)

Even though *internationalization* was perceived by many as conceptually vague, the term became rooted in Japanese consciousness to a degree that was, nonetheless, surprising (Mannari and Befu 1983).

By 1980, Japanese tourists were spending $3 billion a year "internationalizing" (C. Johnson 1983). From a little more than one hundred thousand Japanese traveling abroad in the 1960s, numbers grew to more than seventeen million in the following three decades (D. Yamamoto and Gill 1999). Though the Japanese economic "miracle" was winding down in the 1970s, it still took another twenty years for speculation and stagnation to take its full toll. Meantime, consumer spending continued apace (Burkett and Hart-Landsberg 2003). In 1987 the government instituted a national tourist initiative called Ten Million. Its aim was to increase the number of Japanese traveling abroad each year by making travel more desirable and affordable (Sukbin, Mccleary, and Uysal 1995; Polunin 1989). This program exceeded government expectations. In less than a year, Japanese citizens traveling overseas had already reached nearly seven million (Bureau 1989). More than one in every ten Japanese citizens had a passport.

The government urged employers to give workers more time off for leisure activities, which prior to the 1980s was an unheard-of encouragement (Polunin 1989). Major Japanese tourist companies added days to lengthen the duration of tours. In 1978, Japan's new international airport, Narita, was the country's modern hub for international tourists, completed despite widespread civil protest and violence. The airline industry was deregulated, and additional overseas flights, including cheaper charters, became more numerous. Duty-free allowances for items purchased abroad were doubled to more than $1,500 per person (Nozawa 1992). This was tacit acknowledgment that young Japanese women (especially OLs) were big spenders in purchasing foreign-branded European and American goods too expensive to buy at home (Pigliasco 2005). Tourist travel was acceptable and sought after, not just as a means of gaining new life experiences, as it was touted, but, for some, as a route toward realizing economic opportunities beyond borders.

The raft of new regulations, public discourses about internationality, cheaper travel, and the appreciating yen rate all had the desired effect on tourism from Japan. In the 1980s and 1990s, Japanese became the largest group of tourists in the world to visit the United States. In 1981, more than one million visitors to the United States were Japanese. By 1990, that figure had swelled to more than three million (Justice 1991). Increased foreign travel was a desired national goal, but Japanese government officials had not anticipated the travel surge.

> To our surprise, travel services have become Japan's second-largest "import" after oil. With all those yen and dollars being spent offshore as

Japanese "import" hotel lodging, restaurant meals and myriad other travel services, Japan's financial surpluses are shrinking quickly. (Sterngold 1989)

By 2000, despite post-Bubble stagnation, numbers of Japanese tourists had mushroomed to nearly five million a year, and during this period, they continued to supplant travelers from all other parts of the world in visiting the United States (Security 2000).

Gendered Travel Lures

Of all these enticements, the packaged tour was perhaps the biggest change in the way Japanese women traveled since restrictions on overseas movements were lifted in 1964 to coincide with the Tokyo Summer Olympics. For a few hundred dollars, a tourist could buy round-trip group airfare and sightseeing for ten days to two weeks covering Hawai'i and California. A ready travel market mushroomed, with the bulk of new passports issued to those under thirty years old. Numbers of young women traveling outpaced those of young men by almost threefold (Bureau 1989; Japan Ministry of Foreign Affairs 1987). Under the mantle of kokusaika, these managed excursions—everything from fully escorted to semi-independent visits—drew special interest and participation from young twenty-something women, who, by the mid-1980s, were seen as the demographic with the most potential growth (Nozawa 1992).

Travel abroad assumed a highly gendered subjectivity, with young women courted as prime consumers of travel—increasingly independent in regard to their routes, as opposed to their male counterparts (Pigliasco 2005). By the mid-1990s, 48 percent of Japanese women between twenty and twenty-nine years of age had been overseas, many more than once. In the same age cohort, by contrast, just 28 percent of young men had traveled outside Japan (Communications 1997). The skewed gender numbers were not lost on those who profited from consumer travel (Wong 2015; Japan Travel Bureau 2009). Media images specifically aimed at young women touted foreign sites. Japanese televised dramas were shot on location in the United States and Canada with fabricated imaginaries geared to women (Edgington 2014).

Perhaps unsurprisingly, the motivations of young women travelers appeared to have been more directed than those of men of similar age. Women were especially focused on added benefits of travel, such as education and new knowledge about places visited, rather than simple enjoyment (Heung, Qu, and Chu 2001). Shin Issei like Kyoko were visiting with one eye on other opportunities for a more permanent move. There is no doubt that shin Issei were ready consumers of foreign travel. They are the first generation of women to benefit from Japan's strong economic position. Their tourist experience commonly presaged a more permanent move.

Sachiko's junior college degree in Tokyo had netted her only a part-time job and no future in Japan's restructuring job markets. By the time she was twenty-two years old, she'd saved enough money to buy a first vacation to the United States. Most of her friends and family were aghast that she would travel alone. She remembers them warning her about the dangers existing in the United States. Undeterred, she traveled to Hawai'i and then to California—the first in her immediate family to make the transpacific journey.

> I came by myself as part of a tour, but it was kind of independent, so we all went to San Francisco first, and then we could go anywhere we wanted after that. Not [really] a package tour. So I came to LA and went to Knott's Berry Farm—I took the bus by myself.

Returning home, she found herself still working at a series of part-time jobs around Tokyo. Despite objections from her parents, who continued to worry about her personal safety in the United States and thought she should concentrate on finding a husband, Sachiko bought a one-way plane ticket back to Los Angeles in the early 1990s, this time arriving with a four-year student visa.

Chisa became an avid viewer of travel shows on television, read about places to visit, and talked to other young women friends about their experiences. Following a woman acquaintance's advice on a popular tour the woman had taken two years previously, Chisa signed up. Her round-trip vacation included air tickets to Los Angeles from Tokyo and numerous tours to sites in Southern California. Her semistructured trip stipulated just one restriction: on the last day of the tour, she must return to her original port of entry into the United States for departure to Japan. She traveled by bus to Disneyland and stopped off to visit Little Tokyo in downtown Los Angeles. It wasn't all fun and pleasure. Chisa pursed her lips when she remembered trying to hide a local sightseeing map but still receiving hostile stares. She sought to distance herself from essentialized pictures engendered by the seeming overwhelming presence of big-spending Japanese tourists (Woodyard 1995).

Aside from trips designed for sightseeing only, and since many young women were repeat travel customers, Japanese tour companies offered different types of travel products emphasizing ways to acquire new knowledge. Learning English was a top priority. Apart from the obligatory quick trip to Disneyland, sightseeing was not a priority for Kyoko. Instead, she wanted to enlarge her occupational skills by learning as much English as she could on her tourist visa, hence the homestay and brief enrollment in an English language program offered to visitors. Shin Issei women saw their tourist visas and visa waivers as a means by which to build on their social capital and thus enhance chances of better life opportunities like employment. Though most shin Issei women say they didn't have a clear plan for reaching this goal, learning to speak English was considered the first rung on the ladder toward better prospects unavailable to them in Japan. For a brief exposure to life in the United States, a tourist visa, or several, often sufficed. However, many more shin Issei took advantage by becoming full-time international students.

Practicing Kokusaika: Shin Issei Students Abroad

Both Japan and the United States actively sought to promote and attract international students. In 1983, the Japanese government began another program entitled the 100,000 International Students Plan, designed to bring foreign students to Japan to help balance the already large and growing numbers of outbound Japanese students (Umakoshi 1997). During the same period, concomitant programs in the United States put a focus on enticing international students (Cogan, Torney-Purta, and Anderson 1988). American colleges and universities began to feature studies in international relations, global and cultural studies, or business and economic development to appeal to students in Japan who were interested in pursuing post–high school educations abroad. As foreign nationals, those who petition to study for school credits at recognized academic institutions in the United States can qualify for admission on nonimmigrant visa status.[6] A student visa would allow a stay of two to four years, or perhaps longer with visa extensions.

Attracting international students to the United States was part of wider global initiatives to enrich academic programs through diversity (S. Wilkins and Huisman 2012). Foreign students as cash cows were certainly an added benefit. Japanese students signed up. Throughout the 1980s, their numbers grew exponentially. In 1984, barely fourteen thousand Japanese were studying outside Japan, the majority male and most of them in the United States and the United Kingdom (Education 2015). By the early 1990s, thanks to these types of efforts and a sharply stronger yen, the United States was the number one destination, with Japanese student enrollment varying from more than forty-two thousand to figures of nearly sixty thousand (Hanami 1995; Justice 1991).

In tandem with their tourist co-citizens, Japanese students in the United States far outpaced international student groups from all other parts of the world.

As the total number of Japanese students increased in the United States, so did the ratio of women to men. In the 1960s, there were just a few thousand young Japanese studying in the United States, and 75 percent of them were men. Japanese women students could be counted in the few hundreds. By the early 1990s, at least 55 percent were women (H. Ono and Piper 2004). This translates into tens of thousands of Japanese women electing to study in the United States. Like young Japanese women tourists, it also appears that Japanese women students were more active in acquiring social capital than their male counterparts. Those attending community colleges and higher participated in more extracurricular activities, sought out new, non-Japanese friendships, and generally seemed more dynamic in adjusting as foreign students (Toyokawa and Toyokawa 2002). These factors have postschool consequences. Although it may be assumed that a student visa indicates a temporary stay before returning to Japan, accrued social acumen gained from an overseas educational experience can also be a prelude to a more permanent life in the United States. For shin Issei women who enter with student visas, there is, in fact, "a clear link between short and long term movements" (H. Ono and Piper 2004: 102).

The most sought-after postgraduate degree for both Japanese women and men studying abroad in the 1990s was a master of business administration (MBA). However, upon completing coursework, most men returned home to work for companies based in Japan. Not so for women. Once women graduated from professional schools in the United States, they sought employment with foreign subsidiaries in Japan or found jobs and new lives abroad as employees of foreign companies. The majority did not want to work for a Japanese company. In many cases, their degrees penalized them and increased their reluctance to return to Japan (Habu 2000). Career tracks for women returning to Japan were not encouraged by Japanese companies (H. Ono and Piper 2004).

Miki is emblematic of a shin Issei who is highly educated. As well, her route to the United States is dissimilar to those of other shin Issei. In the late 1970s, her father was offered a job in Los Angeles, and the family followed when he was settled. At the time, Miki had just graduated from high school in Japan and was taking English classes at UCLA Extension. A family emergency, however, led to her parents' premature return to Japan. Miki and her younger brother were left behind. The two teens lived alone in an apartment in West

Los Angeles without the benefit of family or friends. She can talk now about those early experiences in the United States, though it is still difficult. The family had no friends or other relations in Los Angeles. Miki remembers her father vainly trying to find someone to watch over his children and finally settling on a stranger. She talks openly about it now, but her seemingly cavalier attitude is belied by her averted gaze and downturned face.

> I was an original parachute kid ... in an apartment building. We had a paper guardian. First, my dad asked our Japanese American gardener who was taking care of our apartment building. My mom had gotten to know him, and they could speak Japanese. My dad asked him to help out, but he said he had a son he hadn't spoken to in two years and he'd failed at child-rearing, and if he couldn't raise his own kid, how could he help out others? So my dad asked an ESL [English as a Second Language] volunteer teacher at UCLA, and she said OK.

Miki spent the next few years attending college, with sporadic visits by the fictive kin who had agreed to "take care" of her and her younger brother. After graduating from UCLA with a degree in engineering, Miki decided to switch fields. A lifelong goal was to become an attorney. In the United States, she knew she had more opportunities to become better qualified for a career. Equally important, continuing her schooling also meant she could extend her visa and wouldn't have to return to Japan.

> I went on to law school so got another student visa in the eighties. Law school gave me more options. I wasn't passionate about engineering. I thought about going back to Japan, but not wholeheartedly.

Neither was she received wholeheartedly by Japanese employers.

> I interviewed with Japanese companies but not really. If I was in Japan, I wouldn't even try to become an engineer or lawyer. I knew I would stay here.

Like most of the shin Issei in this book, Rieko was not highly educated before coming to the United States. In high school, she thought about perhaps going to junior college, but she said teachers were more interested in directing boys toward careers. She remembers never feeling any encouragement to think about a college plan, a long-term job, or a career.

> I was interested in English, but my school counselor asked me what I'd like to *study*. Now English in Japan is a subject, but here [in the United States] it's more of a tool. I realized just learning English wasn't enough.

She began to see that English facility would add to her skill set in a way that was not available to her in Japan. Her most immediate goal was avoiding the OL track as a prelude to expected marriage. Instead of taking the junior college prep courses that traditionally led to OL positions, Rieko went to work part-time, first in the sales offices of a grocery store and then filling orders for a subcontracted pharmaceutical supply company. Neither job lasted long, but living at home, she was able to save much of her salary. She believed an education in the United States would give her opportunities for a better life. Though her English language skills were weak, she took a class designed to help her pass the first test toward becoming an international student.[7] In the mid-1980s, she passed the English test and was issued a two-year student visa.[8] The visa allowed her to attend a junior college in the Los Angeles area. Gesticulating often with her hands, she made it clear that she had given thought to her decision to leave Japan and pursue further education in the United States.

> Here in college you get the opportunity to learn what's out there—in Japan you have to make a choice—meaning office work—and you can't change.
>
> [At junior college] a school counselor suggested nutrition. I took nutrition classes—I did well and liked it. Then I thought [a] hospital would be a number one job for me.

With encouragement from her counselor, Rieko secured an internship at a community hospital. She worked floors picking up meal trays. In the kitchen, she watched a supervisor who managed meal planning. After getting an associate of arts (AA) degree, Rieko transferred to a California state university for three years, earning a bachelor's in nutrition. Eventually, she became a registered dietitian. Rieko says she kept in touch with her junior college counselor, who was always supportive, but few shin Issei have similar guidance from someone who can direct their career paths.

It must be noted that the limited educational research on shin Issei women has concentrated on those, like Miki, who enroll in academic and professional programs at established colleges and universities for purposes of enlarging their educational and managerial skills for long-term career tracks (IIE 2012). Rieko was fortunate to encounter a mentor, but most shin Issei are not as privileged. There is far less research and attention on women like her who have Japanese high school diplomas or perhaps some junior college before entering the United States as students. For many shin Issei, their educational motivations are much more undefined beyond coming to the United States. This sketchiness leads to further imprecision around the types of education they pursue in their new homes.

Two years after her first tourist experience, and now out of high school, Hana returned to the United States. She had two roommates with whom to share expenses in Tokyo but was barely making ends meet. The women were not personal friends, and, in any event, they all worked different shifts and rarely saw one another. At their studio apartment, she says the futons were rolled up and put in a corner when not in use. Working at jobs with low pay and no possibility of either more pay or advancement made Hana's departure a necessity.

> It is easier to get a job here [in the United States]—much easier, especially if you don't have first-rate educations from Japan's top universities. My friends never really intended on going back. They came here to stay. They would never get good-paying jobs in Japan.

For many young shin Issei women who migrated to the United States in the 1980s with few skills, "it is easier to get a job here" became something akin to a mantra. Even those women who possessed degrees from top-ranked universities found themselves shut out of the Japanese labor market and career-track jobs (Tachibanaki 1987). This time, Hana took the English proficiency test and enrolled as an international student at a Southern California junior college. She'd read about many Japanese women choosing to study in the United States after high school graduation and believed that learning English via studying for a two-year AA degree would help her become more qualified in the U.S. job market.

> I wasn't the best student in terms of studying for exams, which is all they do in Japan is study for exams. I knew I didn't want to go to a two-year community college [in Japan], then work as an office lady and have to leave [to get married].

She found a cheap apartment in West Los Angeles with two other young shin Issei she met after reading a notice posted on a Japanese language community bulletin board.

Chisa had failed to secure both a full-time job and a husband in Japan, despite her parents' pleadings. She met their disappointment with no small amount of anger and exasperation. She was vehement about not returning to Japan.

> Why should I go back to Japan? *Why* should I go back? [*Her voice is raised; she is adamant.*] . . . That's my parents' house but not my home!

After her initial tourist visit, Chisa reentered the United States with a student visa to attend post–high school classes. Upon arriving in Los Angeles, she immediately enrolled in an English language school near downtown Los Angeles, but the vocational school did not help her English proficiency. She transferred to a nearby junior college, with incremental improvement in English fluency.

> Even though I took English in Japan, I couldn't speak it well—it was mostly about grammar.
> I went to [junior] college and graduated and finished my AA here, but I still couldn't speak English that well. I had a four-year visa and then got another extension.

After getting fired from her last job, Aya felt she had no choice but to make plans to leave Japan. Initially, she thought about getting a tourist or student visa.

> I saved my money. So maybe I could stay in the United States for three months. My friends told me there were jobs here I could get. I was so stupid. I didn't think anything. Maybe I would go to school to learn English.

Aya's attitude about being "so stupid" is reflective of gendered subjectifications of self-effacement and lack of confidence common among shin Issei. They are quick to point out their shortcomings, apologetic and embarrassed about not working harder or being better students. Aya spent the next several years in and out of the United States on renewable travel permits. This in-between time served Aya well in helping her become more comfortable and familiar with California. While in Tokyo, she worked part-time jobs, saving enough money to reapply for ninety-day tourist visas.

On subsequent solo trips to Southern California, she continued to construct friendships among other shin Issei women, staying in their apartments, sharing cooking and other household chores while they went to work. Two friends had gotten student visas to enroll at a local community college. They encouraged Aya to do the same, but Aya said it was easier to come and go as a short-term tourist. On one trip, she paid a few hundred dollars and enrolled in an English program at a community college. Having heard about the school from other Japanese women migrants, she thought it would be a way to improve her English-speaking skills.

> Everybody goes there. There were other Japanese in my class. But I didn't learn anything. Everybody was speaking Spanish, so I didn't get anything. [I] just paid money.

In the 1980s, while many accredited higher education facilities began to aggressively recruit foreign students who could afford to pay higher tuitions, other, less qualified businesses and educational facilities targeted growing numbers of migrants who wanted to learn English. The proliferation of these types of for-profit courses at all levels of education was seen as a new selling tool to increase profits (S. Wilkins and Huisman 2012; Horie 2002; Habu 2000). For prices ranging from several hundred dollars to a thousand dollars or more, businesses advertising as educational facilities offered classes and supplied information on visa applications, special counseling, and cultural immersion.

> Students are viewed as customers, or as economic units, and are not deemed to be part of the university community.
> In fact, the very concept of an academic community is irrelevant to this vision of globalization, as the university is modelled on a business enterprise in which staff provide a service for fee paying customers. (Habu 2000: 44)

Back home in Japan, Aya decided this time she would follow her friends' advice about applying for a student visa so she could enroll at a junior college in Southern California.

> When I went back to Japan, I tried to get a student's visa, but I didn't get one because I was so old. The U.S. government [in Tokyo] said I couldn't get one.

Though Aya was refused a student visa after applying, she was still determined to pursue new opportunities outside Japan. Undeterred, she got another tourist visa waiver and resumed life in Los Angeles. This time, at the end of three months, she did not return to Japan.

After finishing her first-time tourist homestay, Kyoko returned to Japan and her part-time travel agency job. She worked for another two years to save money. While in California, she had made friends with another shin Issei woman who was also on a homestay. The friend had returned to Japan at the end of her tourist visa and then reentered on a student visa, enrolling at a Southern California junior college. She urged Kyoko to do the same thing.

This chapter looked at the resourceful and creative ways in which shin Issei utilized larger global and economic structures to facilitate their migration to the United States. Without the benefit of extensive personal networks smoothing the passage, theirs was a singular journey. They were abetted by economic regimes, and as recruits of efforts by both Japan and the United States, shin Issei arrived as tourists or students. However, their legal visas were mostly a prelude to look for work, which they did without the legal standing to do so. They took advantage of the burgeoning numbers of Japanese nationals preceding them—imported as MNC labor. The presence of a kaisha community allowed shin Issei to create employment niches for themselves among conationals, but at the same time, their new lives were framed by precarity surrounding their lack of legal status.

3

Precarious Life under the Radar

Well, if they catch me then I have to go back to Japan, but the government here would have to do something different because you know it's not just me who's illegal.

I don't have a green card. I'm illegal. It's hard to get a visa now. It costs money, maybe $10,000 if you use a lawyer, and there's no guarantee, you know?

Both these shin Issei have been in the United States for more than two decades and were in their late forties by the early 2000s. They live alone, and neither is married. Almost immediately after arriving in the United States on tourist visas, they searched for and found jobs. As quickly, their new employment rendered them out of status.[1] Two months later, working full-time, they did not return to Japan. In addition to illegally working, they also became overstayers—individuals who don't leave the United States when legal visas expire. In this liminality, they are circumspect about their status but still not overly worried about deportation. However, they are resigned to probably never becoming documented. For shin Issei who have lived in the United States for more than ten years without documentation, a path to lawful permanent residency (LPR or green card) is most likely not possible because of their prolonged positions as undocumented. They can return to Japan, but most often, returning means being permanently barred by the United States for ten years—or longer.

This chapter uncovers the social and political effects surrounding the migration statuses of shin Issei. It examines how their lives unfold when their legal status in the United States is lost. Undocumented shin Issei are a largely underinvestigated population. There is abundant public policy research on unauthorized individuals living in the United States, including rising rates in numbers from Asia, but comparable rates from Japan are mostly absent. The general assumption is that undocumented populations of Japanese nationals are proportionally high (Rosenblum and Soto 2015; Sooudi 2014). Among those lacking legal standing, such as shin Issei, the precarity that is a daily condition of existence is a "powerful index of social, political, and economic inequality... rendering them available for criminalization, marginalization, exploitation, and even dehumanization" (Thomas and Galemba 2013: 211). But even for those shin Issei who work toward a path to legal status, this still does not guarantee a move to full American citizenship through naturalization, nor does it mean other indices of migrant marginality are eliminated. Legal documentation falling short of full naturalization still carries a marginalized impermanence and liminality in daily life.

Fluidities in Movement: Travel cum Migration

The relative flexibility of renewing tourist visas allowed short-term visitors like Kyoko the opportunity to experience what life in the United States might entail. More to the point, it provided shin Issei entrée for a stay of much longer duration, though not as officially sanctioned permanent migrants. The vast majority of shin Issei enter the United States legally with valid tourist or student visas—and leave the country before their visas expire. For those who don't depart and do not have lawful visas or other resident authorization for staying, this, of course, is not *im*migration in the sense of a legal move. These individuals become undocumented and subject to deportation and possible denial of reentry. Despite these harsh penalties, shin Issei risk apprehension in order to work. While some academics are reluctant to call them economic migrants, I reiterate the argument that shin Issei are labor—women who come to the United States in search of better economic opportunities with the hope of evading constraining discourses at home (Hosler 1998). As graduates of gendered education systems in Japan, shin Issei in this book talk about their mediocre schooling and a lack of interest and motivation from their teachers resulting in the same from them. Instead, the onus for more positive educational experiences falls on shin Issei, who are often considered "not necessarily well qualified, because most of them are dropouts from the Japanese education or corporate systems" (Yamashita 2008: 106). Their interests in tourism and sightseeing do not preclude more hidden economic motivations for circumventing and ignoring immigration laws once they are in the United States. Similarly, student visas were sought, but American educations were not top of mind—finding employment was.

In the United States, definitions of entry between immigrant and nonimmigrant are a clear binary. However, looking more closely at this either-or dichotomy reveals that in many ways, it does not fully describe the shin Issei experience. Metaphorically, migrants may enter a new country via a front door, a side door, or a back door (P. Martin 2007). The front door is for those individuals who enter legally with the specific intent of eventually settling. The side door is open for legal tourists, students, short-term workers, and others admitted temporarily for a specific period and reason with set times for departure. Back-door entrants are those without documentation or individuals who violate the terms of their original entry. Shin Issei women have taken advantage of entering the United States through all three doors. However, among the women in this book, the latter two doors are the most common portals through which they have sought and gained permanency of settlement in their new homes.

Perhaps most significant is the shifting nature of shin Issei movements, the flexibility of temporality and impermanence falling between legal definitions. Categories of legal or illegal, documented or undocumented, permanent or temporary, visiting or staying have become blurred in practice (Inutake 2003; S. M. Lee 1996). Warranting further investigation beyond shin Issei migrant practices are those Japanese corporate chuzai-in families living temporarily in the United States who have also used work visas as a resource to convert into more permanent LPRs rather than returning to Japan (Yasuike 2005).

Among shin Issei who enter on temporary, short-term visits and then end up staying, their intentions for more permanence are not always well reasoned or fully understood by the women themselves, beyond the fact that they have no desire to return to Japan. This processual transition from temporary to permanent becomes a fraught social process (Andressen and the Kumagai 1996). Women do not say, "I will become illegal." More often, staying is simply the result of running out of money and thus, they need to find a job. A legal classification is no longer adequate to describe real-life, on-the-ground practices. However, to be clear, binary oppositions regarding migrant status still exist juridically for nation-states. Therefore the separation of terms between official government definitions of *legal* and *illegal* still serve here as the default framework. Shin Issei women *are* still labeled and circumscribed by state structures at every step of their movement. They are classified as legal—or not. Taking advantage of the two side doors as a means by which to obtain a more permanent stay allows shin Issei women to evade the gaze of legal subjectifications—but of course, not entirely. Evasion lapses into something much more worrisome. At the very least, most shin Issei women who are unauthorized find that a daily life in-between becomes a tenuous, illegal tightrope of precarity. A shin Issei woman who now lives in a suburb south of Los Angeles visited the United States initially with a tourist visa.

> I have an uncle who went to Hawai'i and got married to a Caucasian woman. When I was in high school I had the opportunity to visit him with my grandparents. I really liked it!

Four years later, losing her part-time job selling clothing in Tokyo motivated her to think about better opportunities in the United States. Armed with another tourist visa, she came back, this time to Southern California. Within a few weeks of her return, she found a job working in a restaurant. She did not return to Japan when the visa expired. Thus, her temporary, nonwork permit became contiguous with, and indistinguishable from, what shortly devolved into an out-of-status and permanent nonmigrant backdoor standing. Working without sponsorship from an employer immediately renders shin Issei unauthorized, and as they continue to work, they become embedded in social processes that further assist in establishing their new lives outside Japan. They soon become overstayers as well.[2]

The United States government concedes that figures on individuals who have overstayed a tourist or student visa (not to mention those who are working while on restricted visas) are neither accurate nor reliable (Wasem 2014). In the late 1990s, some reports put the number of overstayers at 40 percent of all undocumented individuals in the United States (Nixon 2016). At the time, the then Immigration and Naturalization Service (INS) budget concentrated primarily on deterring people attempting to enter the United States, not on ferreting out and deporting those individuals already in the country who had not departed when legally mandated to do so. Aside from deporting undocumented migrants, the government was considering removing from the Visa Waiver Program those countries with high rates of overstayers and others without proper visas. One challenge to tracing overstayers was that most arrive by air. The airlines were responsible for passing out arrival/departure forms to all passengers, but not all international air carriers were diligent in this task, nor did foreign air carriers want to act as agents of the United States. Plans by the United States to beef up overstay monitoring met with resistance from both the airline and tourism industries (Nixon 2016).

In the early 1990s, the INS began to collect preliminary estimates of this population, in part by utilizing U.S. Census tracking of the foreign-born population (Office of Policy and Planning 2001). At the time, at least six thousand Japanese nationals were thought to be unauthorized residents of the United States. By 2000, that figure had grown by more than 133 percent, to at least fourteen thousand people (Office of Policy and Planning 2001). However, given that in the late 1980s and early 1990s Japanese were the largest tourist group and the largest international student population in the United States, in all likelihood, the figures of overstayers are undercounts. Government reports make note that whatever statistics are available, the exponential growth of Japanese undocumented workers and overstayers is, nonetheless, notable (Justice 1991). By comparison, these figures are dwarfed by other undocumented migrants in the millions from countries in Latin America, China, or the Philippines. Taken as a whole, Asians are the fastest-growing undocumented group (Rosenblum and Soto 2015).

An undercount of Japanese who are undocumented may also reflect the apparently well-founded fears of many migrants about completing census forms with information that will subsequently be scrutinized and utilized by government agencies. This fear is not without historical precedent. The role of the U.S. Census in the days preceding the mass incarceration of Nikkei shows that government officials "gave direct assistance to the military authorities on the West Coast" by turning over 1940 tract data showing the residential addresses of Japanese Americans (Seltzer and Anderson 2001). Notwithstanding the furor and eventual court decision disallowing a citizenship question on the 2020 U.S. Census, the federal government has a number of other methods by which it calculates its legal citizens (Wang 2019).

Among the reasons for the growth of undocumented shin Issei is the deterioration of the Japanese economy in the 1990s. Shin Issei women who were already shut out of labor markets in Japan would have faced an even bleaker employment picture had they returned. Furthermore, the growth of undocumented workers may also be tied to increased tightening of United States immigration law. The Illegal Immigration Reform and Immigrant Responsibility Act of 1996 (IIRIRA) augmented border enforcement and also made it more difficult for undocumented migrants to become documented (Bibler Coutin 2003). Individuals living in the United States for more than a year without documentation could be deported as well as subject to a ten-year ban on reentry (American Immigration Council 2016). Nikkei community attorneys representing Japanese migrants say many undocumented Japanese *did* return to Japan to avoid deportation and the subsequent ten-year bar to readmission, but many more did not.

IIRIRA had the unintended consequence of forcing individuals to stay and accept the risk of continuing to live illegally. That is, it caused a "discount" formula to be applied in this life decision. Those without documentation discount the chances of being arrested and deported for the greater benefits, both social and economic, that accrue by continuing to live in the United States. "[The] true calculus should include an expected utility of their situation in their home country" (Rocha et al. 2014: 95). Thus, it can be argued that as a result of being locked out of profitable lives in Japan and facing additional negative social consequences that marginalized them, shin Issei opted to remain undocumented because their lives in the United States were socially and economically more cost effective. In these acts of agency, the chances of being caught and deported are minimized.

This infers that many shin Issei live an existence of liminality. In effect, a combination of the lack of economic and social well-being in Japan and the heightened and increasingly restrictive immigration policy in the United States has ended a circularity of transpacific physical mobility. Like other undocumented migrants, shin Issei have become "caged in as long-term settlers" (Massey, Durand, and Pren 2015: 1039).

Since the 1980s, the presence of new shin Issei settlers, both documented and undocumented, has had significant social impacts in long-established Nikkei communities where shin Issei work and live. In 1982, the INS began sweeps at restaurants and other small businesses in the Little Tokyo area of downtown Los Angeles. During one roundup, more than two dozen undocumented migrants from Japan were arrested. Some in the Nikkei community saw racial backlash in the search for undocumented Japanese. Nikkei blamed the raids on the increasing anti-Japanese sentiment in the United States resulting from rising Japanese economic investments (Mathews 1982). The INS defended its actions by saying that Little Tokyo was "inundated" with undocumented migrants and that its agents were only targeting specific businesses after getting citizen complaints (P. Imamura 1982). The INS claimed that the community was overreacting to the raids and that some of the complaints were reported by Nikkei themselves.

> They feel that it was their duty as U.S. citizens to make these reports to us . . . they feel that illegal Japanese in the United States reflects poorly on lawful Japanese residents. (P. Imamura 1982: 1)

Working with Neither Skills nor Green Cards

Like shin Issei on tourist visas who sought employment, international students in the United States are not permitted to work except in limited on-campus related jobs. However, Japanese students enrolled in post–high school coursework in the United States also, invariably, worked.

Hana's first-time experience in the United States as a tourist whetted her appetite to eventually leave Japan for more opportunities. When she returned to the United States, this time with a student visa, she found employment at a Japanese business bar. Working at night left her little time for future academic and career planning. Attending community college during the day in arts classes did not build her skills.

> I remember in the early eighties, Japanese students studied really hard, [but] they all had part-time jobs and they studied, too. By the time I

graduated most of them had gone back to Japan. They didn't have any more money.

Like other shin Issei, Hana had already spent her personal savings and hence began working at the bar. However, after the third time her Japanese employer refused to pay her for overtime, Hana quit. Taking advantage of new economic connections between Japan and the United States, she subsequently found a full-time job in Los Angeles with the help of a Japanese employment agency based in Southern California.

> [The company] was looking for a Japanese-speaking person. It was part of a large rice mill in the States. Our division took the rice and ground it into rice flour for cake mixes to ship [to Japan].
>
> You know [in Japan] it was illegal to import U.S. rice but there are ways to get around it. And during this time Japan opened up more. There were more California companies doing business in Japan and [U.S. firms] needed Japanese employees.

Eventually Hana was promoted to an office manager—still without a work permit—but she was able to begin saving some money again. For a time, she dropped out of junior college, but before her student visa expired, she reenrolled in order to complete her AA degree while still working.

Another shin Issei who entered the United States with a student visa finished her AA degree in office administration at a Los Angeles area junior college. Before her visa expired, she found a clerical position at an employment agency. She said she was doing well, making a good salary, and learning skills to help other Japanese nationals qualify for permanent residency. She had thought her Japanese employer would sponsor her for an employment-based green card as well, but after a year, her boss told her she wouldn't qualify.[3] She quit and started working part-time as a salesclerk, a job without skills or a potential sponsor. She has been undocumented for nearly twenty years.

> I don't think about it too much. Sometimes I worry about it, but you know I have a California driver's license, Social Security [card], I pay taxes, so . . . [*Shrugging her shoulders.*]

Shin Issei often try to find an employment sponsor to begin processing for a green card. However, for those women with limited job skills, this is a difficult task, and not just for women but for their employers as well, who need to prove that the green card applicant's employability is essential for the business.

Since the landmark Immigration and Nationality Act of 1965 (commonly known as the Hart-Celler Act), United States policy has rested on two broad platforms for permanent legal entry and residency.[4] One platform is based on employment preferences (Ruppenstein 1993). These categories are jobs for which American employers seek and sponsor foreign nationals, usually highly trained, to work in the United States. Legal migrants who capitalize on employer-based preferences, for example, may have specifically needed professional skills, extraordinary scientific or academic accomplishments, experience as management-level multinational supervisors, or assets of more than $1 million. There are also categories for temporary nonmigrant workers, such as many South Asian high technology and software engineers who filled critical labor gaps as the United States retooled its economy beginning in the 1970s (J. Liu, Ong, and Rosenstein 1991). Individuals who migrate through employment preferences may not have family ties in the United States, but they often have extensive professional networks and skills, which allowed them to initially migrate and, in turn, enhanced their ability to expand their social capital. Employment gives them opportunities to further network and shape social relationships, though often these networks are considered weak social ties that function only at an instrumental level (Toyota 2010; Avenarius 2002). In the case of some work visas, such as the H1b category, national racialized dialogue continues to create tension for those authorized migrants seeking a path to permanent status and citizenship (D. Yang 2005).

The most frequently used migration platform is family reunification. Family members already in the United States as legal residents or native-born citizens are able to sponsor other family who are overseas. This is referred to as chain migration or migrant social networks (Simonen and Ndiaye 2006; Fouron and Glick Schiller 2001; Hune 1991). The bulk of post-1965 migrants from Asia and the Pacific entered under family reunification. By 1985, 40 percent of all newly admitted legal migrants to the United States were from Asia (J. Liu, Ong, and Rosenstein 1991).

Within the context of Hart-Celler, the example of shin Issei women stands outside this framework of chain migration. The numbers of Japanese nationals who qualified under family reunification have been insignificant in comparison to those of other LPR groups. In 1996, just 183 Japanese were given family LPR status, whereas more than 44,000 from Mexico, more than 21,000 from India, nearly 18,000 from the Philippines, and 11,000 from the People's Republic of China were granted family reunification allowing for green cards (Security 1996). This reflects long-extant migration networks maintained by individuals from the top four sending countries, as opposed to Japanese, who have had far fewer familial networks on which to rely.

In addition to the fact that their side-door, legal entries as tourists or students did not involve applying for legal permanent residency, shin Issei women would also not have had the option of being qualified candidates on either of the two primary immigration reform platforms. Women like Kyoko, Hana, Sachiko, Chisa, and Aya had no specific skills to offer and therefore no employers who might wish to sponsor their entry into the United States. Each knew she would have to find employment fairly soon to survive. Though each had some money saved, none had great personal wealth reserves, and getting a job was the first priority. They also knew that without any family already in the United States, they were on their own. Hana did live with an aunt for a few weeks, but an aunt cannot sponsor a niece.[5]

She is now in her early forties and says she thought about applying for a green card when a legal path to citizenship was offered in 1986 under the Immigration Reform and Control Act but was deterred by stories she'd heard about the application process leading instead to deportation. Moreover, she did not want to risk her well-paid, six-day-a-week job. At the time, though employer sanctions were law, no one at work asked for any legal documentation prior to her hiring. She says her ability to speak Japanese with customers at a small sales office was more important. She lost that job as Japanese businesses in the United States retrenched post-Bubble. Thereafter, she shuttled between jobs at several small restaurants. As is common among other undocumented individuals, her status has defined and confined her precarious existence in Los Angeles. She has spent years hiding her illegality. Even close friends and family in Japan do not know she has been undocumented for nearly a quarter of a century.

> I talked to an attorney a long time ago, but I didn't have [enough] money saved. Not too many people know I'm illegal. My friends say to me, "Oh, you have a green card," [but] they don't know.

She is not overly concerned about being deported, but it is always somewhere in the back of her mind. Life in the United States is not what she envisioned for her future.

> If I had a green card, I would have a different life. I would go to school . . . maybe open a business.

A recent trip to see another immigration attorney about applying for a green card was disappointing. The attorney was blunt.

Are you a chef, an artist; do you have a special talent? You've been undocumented too long. Yeah, you can go back to Japan, but you'll never get back here for at least ten years and probably not after that. You'd have to go for an interview at the American Embassy in Tokyo.

His solution was equally frank. He looked at her from across his desk and said, "Get married!" Since she had never considered this option, she sat mute, unable to respond. Women's singular reason for coming to the United States was to escape the inequality of gendered social structures in Japan that severely limited life opportunities, not to find a husband.

Exogamy among Stale Holiday Cakes

Because of their relative youth (although they are rapidly aging out), it might be posited that shin Issei women migrated to the United States, one, to join fiancé(e)s or, two, to find future spouses. No one had plans to return to Japan; just one woman in this study came to the United States already engaged to be married. None of the other women was married or joining a partner. They had spent years carving out single lives on new social ground, but over time they had also become reflective of choices they had made about career and family. For shin Issei women, migration is a singular decision not contingent on immediate family needs. Even for women who were side-door entrants and whose legal status as temporary visitors had lapsed, there was no overwhelming pressure to find citizen partners, despite the surety of deportation if caught. In the 1980s, overall numbers of Japanese women coming to the United States either to join spouses or to apply for a fiancé(e) visa was just 3 percent. Only women from the United Kingdom migrating to California to join future partners had similar low percentages (Ruppenstein 1993).

Shin Issei statuses as unmarried and unconnected marked them in the minority of women migrants. However, these initial characteristics, which set shin Issei women apart from other female migrants in the early 1980s, may no longer be that uncommon among contemporary women migrants generally. By the late twentieth century, signaling "a major historical shift in the profile of immigrant women," 34 percent of all women migrants were not joining spouses or partners (Pearce 2011: 42). Among countries in Asia where female migration has predominated over the last decades, there were significant numbers of Asian women who moved on their own as economically motivated migrants, not as dependents of males (Lim and Oishi 1996). The nature of global labor, particularly in service-related jobs, has increased employment opportunities for women. These newer employment prospects allow women to send remittances home to family in the same way male migrants have done and to make significant economic contributions (Bretell 2007; Simonen and Ndiaye 2006). Shin Issei are atypical in that they do not regularly send monetary remittances to family in Japan, although they still participate in sending gifts, including money, for various social occasions.[6]

With no great accumulated wealth or connections, for example, to help them access loans from financial institutions, some shin Issei could only aspire to owning a small business themselves. A small business might mean a Japanese restaurant or noodle shop or perhaps a beauty salon, but these types of business would require licenses and proof of documentation. Women eventually did begin thinking about another life step: marriage and children. By their early to midthirties, marriage was perceived both as a way to parenthood and as another route to avoid returning to Japan. Nearly three dozen shin Issei in this study did marry and have children. A few remained single, and others had already become divorced mothers. All had worked outside the home until they had children. Those who had divorced continued to work to support themselves and their children. The women's life partners had been overwhelmingly not Japanese but American citizens, including naturalized citizens of various ethnic and racial backgrounds. The women met future husbands while they were students or perhaps at their jobs.

Masami wanted to work in an advertising job that would give her the opportunity for career advancement. She knew she would not be given that chance in Japan. She entered the United States on a student visa, which she renewed twice to finish her AA degree. Upon graduating, she knew her life would remain in the United States.

> I really wanted to stay here. I went through that green card lottery. I paid an attorney several hundred dollars to get my name in. He told me, "I know how to get you a green card, but it will cost you." I was trying to find a way to stay here.

In the early 1990s, the United States instituted a lottery system for millions of potential permanent migrant applicants from around the world (Daily Yomiuri 1994). The lottery was not open to those nationals already living unauthorized in the United States. Except for the fees the attorney charged her, Masami's chances of qualifying for the lottery ended up like other games of infinite chance. Another solution presented itself.

> I happened to meet my husband—a hakujin guy—it came at the right time. I was graduating. He said, "Well, we're going to be together, so

why don't we get married and you can get a green card?" So I gave up on that lottery thing.⁷

On her wedding day at a banquet venue in Los Angeles, Tomoko made quite an entrance. In traditionally applied white makeup and dressed by a professional Japanese wedding consultant, she was fully attired in bridal kimono. The professional was required to properly robe her in customary wedding kimono, which included a heavily embroidered *uchikake* overcoat and white *tsunokakushi* headdress. Both had been rented at considerable cost. Tomoko's new husband is a white American. He, too, was similarly dressed in traditional Japanese wedding clothing and carried a closed fan. His relatives looked rather nonplussed during the ceremony and festivities. Tomoko's immediate family had flown in from Tokyo. It was their first visit to the United States, and they seemed uncomfortable through most of the celebrations. Neither the bride's nor the groom's side was fluent in the other's language, and conversation was minimal. As is often the custom in contemporary Japan, Tomoko changed from kimono to a Western-style wedding gown for the sit-down dinner reception.

In the late 1980s, Tomoko was in her midtwenties. She'd grown up in a suburb of Tokyo. She is tall with expressive eyes and exudes a confidence and an outspokenness some would say are atypical for a Japanese woman. After she graduated in arts from a small junior college in Tokyo, her first job at a small company did not last long. With no income and no new leads for work, she was still living at home with her parents. Her father, a midlevel supervisor in a city office, tried to set her up with the son of one of his coworkers. A dismal dinner was followed by an even more depressing evening spent at a noisy bar. Tomoko decided she had to find work and a life elsewhere.

By any measure, marriage is a life-changing event for individuals. Although shin Issei migrated from a country where there are highly gendered social systems, in choosing partners outside the homeland, shin Issei women like Tomoko soon encounter other, additional asymmetries of power. Her marriage culminated a nearly ten-year-long struggle to stay in the United States. The decade was a precarious one for Tomoko, unmarried with no family in the United States, a sometime junior college student who worked full-time as a hostess at a downtown Los Angeles restaurant and bar. Her future husband became a regular customer and eventually proposed. Everyone knew about the INS raids in Little Tokyo, and deportation was never far from her mind. Approaching her early thirties and tired of hiding, Tomoko knew her age put her at a disadvantage compared to younger women.

> When I met my husband, I was working at a restaurant. We had a mutual friend who set us up. [He said,] "I know this one guy who wants to get married; you want to meet him?" I said OK.

However, after her years of being undocumented, she said, immigration officials were apparently not convinced the marriage was genuine.

> I had to be interviewed twice by Immigration [the INS]. I had to take my wedding pictures, and other pictures of me and my husband because they want to make sure the marriage was a real one because they were sometimes fake!

When it looked as though the INS might deport her, Tomoko says her new husband spent $4,000 to get her legal residency. It was another year before she was issued a green card.

> My husband got an immigration attorney. The attorney said the pictures were good because they showed me with different hairstyles and different times. Wow! I never thought about those things!

Still not persuaded about the validity of the marriage, and despite her possession of a green card, the INS called Tomoko in for another interview nearly eighteen months later. She was now seven months pregnant with her first child and had been working as an assistant to a preschool teacher. She says the immigration official took one look at her pregnant condition and told her to get out of his office. Evidently, the agent had finally decided hers was not a temporary, sham marriage.

While she admittedly "never thought about those things," her migration experiences were eye opening for Tomoko. She was now a legal resident, yet despite this, and because of her many years of living in the shadows, her sense of unease and apprehension did not end. She continued to feel a precarity about the weight of a government's power to regulate and define her embodied everyday experience. She says she continued to worry about being deported and felt she had no one with whom to talk who might understand her anxiety. Her husband didn't appear overly concerned and would tell her not to worry.

This study is not a detailed discussion about marital interactions among shin Issei per se. Partners of shin Issei were not sought out as investigatory subjects, and it is an area warranting further investigation. However, several observations and inferences may be suggested about how shin Issei wives and mothers position themselves vis-à-vis these important personal relationships in their lives; how they see themselves *incorporating* into an American community; and what this means to them as Japanese women.

Shin Issei movements occurred within highly gendered divisions of labor and social structures in Japan that, in the 1980s, were illustrative of the pressure women felt to become ryosei kenbo (Nemoto 2008). In Japan, they resisted by opting out and leaving the country. They escaped placement of themselves as unmarried women in stratified social roles and accompanying unattractive sobriquets, such as *out-of-date, stale cakes, loser dogs,* or *parasaito*. Women who stayed in Japan were getting married at a later age, if at all. By 2010, women were nearly twenty-nine years old by their first marriage; men were more than thirty years old. Twenty-three percent of all Japanese women had never married by their late thirties, and nearly 36 percent of all Japanese men were still single, leading to another oft-spoken phrase, "women who won't marry and men who can't marry" (Dales 2015: 24). However, young women's lack of desire to marry Japanese men in Japan doesn't mean they don't want to marry or have children with partners elsewhere.

Endogamy declined among all racial groups in the United States in the latter half of the twentieth century. Nonetheless, shin Issei are an exception among other women who marry outside their racial or ethnic group (S. M. Lee and Fernandez 1998). Native-born Asian Americans—Japanese and Chinese—have the highest rates of racial exogamy, with women marrying white men as the most common form of intermarriage (Chen and Takeuchi 2011; S. Lee and Boyd 2008). In particular, this increasing trend of racial intermarriage of native-born Nikkei and white Americans has been noted since the early 1970s. By 1979, racial intermarriages among native-born Nikkei men constituted about 47 percent; among Nikkei women, the rate was nearly 53 percent (Kitano et al. 1984). More recent studies of intermarriage show that Nikkei women and men continue to be most likely to marry whites and that American nativity remains a strong indicator of the possibility of intermarriage between Nikkei and whites (Qian, Blair, and Ruf 2001).

Once again, however, shin Issei women stand outside this example. In general, intermarriage between migrants and native-born white Americans is less likely *except* for Japanese female migrants. Of shin Issei women between twenty and thirty-four years old in 1990, nearly 68 percent married white Americans (Qian, Blair, and Ruf 2001; S. M. Lee and Yamanaka 1990). Comparable percentages of exogamy are nearly identical with shin Issei who have a high school education or less to shin Issei women who have graduated from college and above (Qian, Blair, and Ruf 2001).[8] Some studies also indicate the value of the partner's citizenship as a consideration for migrants in building social capital with partners who have better educations or higher socioeconomic statuses (Chen and Takeuchi 2011). However, this doesn't seem to be a factor among shin Issei in this study. At the time of her marriage, Tomoko was a part-time server at a ramen shop while her husband worked as a salesman. Both had some junior college education. Other couples, like Masami and her American spouse, each had AA degrees; their social positions were not significantly unequal at the time of marriage. Rieko met her white American husband while they were students at a state college. After she finished with a degree in nutrition, her job in food services at a local community hospital and employee sponsorship led to her getting a green card. Her husband's degree in business at the same college enabled him to find work in personnel administration. In her early thirties, she felt time was running out on having children. Her husband also wanted children, so they decided to get married.

No shin Issei woman in this study married a Japanese national. Most women's partners were white Americans. Other shin Issei married African Americans, naturalized citizens from European countries, or native-born Nikkei. Of course, a possible reason shin Issei women chose American-citizen spouses is that they wanted to ensure legal migrant status through partners who were citizens. Tomoko's long undocumented status vied with her age and desire to have children.

The Importance of Being Japanese

Shin Issei are defined—and define themselves—with various migration classifications, but at heart, women still refer to themselves as Japanese. Marrying an American citizen and acquiring a green card may mean a shin Issei is allowed to remain and work in the United States, but individuals are still classified as resident aliens. It is not American citizenship. Even though they may qualify, becoming naturalized citizens is not a priority. This is personal choice, but years of unlawful status is another situation entirely. For those who have been undocumented for several decades or more, avenues on the road to legalization and, subsequently, naturalization are nearly impossible to fulfill. Returning to Japan to present oneself for an interview at the U.S. Embassy in Tokyo or other consular office to explain undocumented status generally shuts the door on readmission to the United States. One Nikkei spoke about the liminality of shin Issei living in the shadows:

> What kind of life is being an illegal? My opinion, if you're young, you live for the day or [for] hanging out with your friends—you don't live for your 401(k). You don't think about getting deported.

Only if they've been here for a period of time do you start to think about it. Then they get depressed. And if they stay here long enough, going back to [Japan] is the worst thing in the world. They can't come back. The question is whether they'll [the United States] let you back in.

Nikkei comments are revealing in that for the first time in nearly a century, questions of who is legal and who is not are once again topics of conversation. Issues of citizenship were at the forefront among young American-born Nisei and their Issei parents who were denied citizenship in the years before and after World War II. Now, for Nikkei who see shin Issei working and living among them, the challenges surrounding the acknowledgment of illegality is a newfound concern.

I didn't realize how big a deal that was until I started thinking about it. Yeah, OK, I go to these Japanese restaurants and there are always these young Japanese girls there, working, serving.

I always ask them, "Are you from Japan?" and they say, "Yeah." Sure, I wonder if they're here illegally or what.

Familiar migrant faces become friends—until one day, the familiar face disappears. A Nikkei talks about a Japanese woman the family had come to know at a restaurant they frequented.

I met a young Japanese girl who desperately wanted to come [and stay in] the U.S. but couldn't get in [permanently]. I find out she's now in Poland!

Maybe part of what we should be doing is helping these people get their legal papers somehow. We've got lawyers in our community. Whatever it is that [they] need, maybe that's one of the ways we can provide something for the next generation of Japanese from Japan.

However, it cannot be assumed that legal status with a green card means American citizenship is an automatic next step for shin Issei. Japanese women, in fact, have the lowest rates of naturalization, not just among all Asian groups but among *all* migrant populations in the United States (P. Yang 2002; Justice 1996). In the last forty years, while the numbers of Japanese nationals living in the United States has increased, those seeking to become naturalized U.S. citizens has dropped precipitously. Before 1980, foreign-born Japanese (both men and women) naturalized at a rate of 70 percent (this included many

Japan-born brides of U.S. service members who settled with their new husbands in the United States). By 1989, naturalization figures had declined to 33 percent. In 1990, only Mexico and El Salvador had higher rates than Japan of recent immigrants who were *less* likely to be citizens (U.S. Census Bureau 1990). By 1999, the rate of naturalizing Japanese had fallen to 14.5 percent. By 2000, the rate was just 2.3 percent, though the population of Japanese in the United States had increased dramatically. Out of more than 130,000 foreign-born Japanese (the majority young women) who entered the United States between 2000 and 2009, just 3,000 individuals naturalized (U.S. Census Bureau 2009). To be clear, part of the low naturalization rates for Japan (and other recent migrant groups) may be attributable to the fact that newer arrivals of shin Issei simply haven't been in the country long enough to qualify for citizenship.[9]

Nonetheless, as shin Issei women in this study show, many have now been in the United States for several decades, long enough to become naturalized if they are in the country legally, but have chosen not to become citizens. A valid LPR does allow international travel. Other shin Issei like Hana and Chisa initially had student visas, which also enabled them to travel to and from the United States. This marks young shin Issei as part of a fluid, transnational, and globalized migrant pool (Rannveig Agunias and Newland 2007). Shin Issei found this circularity of transmigration a preferred means of residence in the United States (Massey and Malone 2002).

In further assessing major factors that determine motivations for naturalization among migrants, it has been noted that "with few exceptions, educational attainment, income and marriage . . . generally increase the likelihood of naturalization for all groups" (P. Yang 2002: 2). However, it appears that Japanese women migrants again prove the exception. Despite the high numbers of shin Issei who have American-citizen partners (native born or naturalized), this group of women is not naturalizing in great numbers. Nor does women's level of education or income have any effect on their propensity to become American citizens. In fact, higher levels of education among Japanese women nationals may actually contribute to lower levels of naturalization (P. Yang 2002). This is not a phenomenon singular to the United States. Japanese women who choose to live in other nations also do not give up their Japanese citizenship (Thang and Toyota 2015; M. Sato 1993).

Chika migrated as a single woman from the north of Tokyo in the mid-1980s and has lived in the United States for more than three decades. She arrived with a student visa, and when she finished school, she soon got legal residence because her employer needed someone who could speak and read Japanese. She explained, "Back in nineties, it was much easier to get a green card." She married, had two children, and divorced her American-citizen husband. Through it all, she said, her long residence in the United States has made her feel both American and Japanese. What she means by this is that she has a level of comfort and knowledge about living in the United States. However, she is unwavering when she says she has no desire to become an American citizen. More succinctly, Chika feels no pressure to do so. She traveled easily to and from Japan for many years, taking her American-born shin Nisei children to visit family. In terms of her personal life, and in particular the ease with which she can visit her family in Japan, Chika sees no added benefits to naturalization.

> It's even easier for me to visit Japan and [her hometown] than it is for my sister who lives in [Southern Japan]! She has to travel by trains, can only take a week off and then go home again. I can go very easily from here to [there], and I can stay a month or more! It's easier [for me] than for her!

Chika's legalized transnational life is common among shin Issei women who have green cards. The relative simplicity of renewing and traveling abroad with an LPR, the cheapness of air travel, and the many ways to keep in touch with Japan make U.S. citizenship optional.

Moreover, in the United States there are no legal conditions against possessing both American citizenship and citizenship from another country, despite the clarity of the Oath of Allegiance to which new American citizens pledge during swearing-in ceremonies.

> I hereby declare, on oath, that I absolutely and entirely renounce and abjure all allegiance and fidelity to any foreign prince, potentate, state, or sovereignty, of whom or which I have heretofore been a subject or citizen. (Services, n.d.)

The subject of dual citizenship has historically—and perhaps even more so since the early 1990s—been fraught with controversy over issues of national sovereignty and security, divided loyalties, and the supposed disappearance of characteristic cultural values and civic institutions (House Subcommittee on Immigration, Border Security, and Claims 2006). Officially, the United States neither sanctions dual citizenship nor prohibits it. The only major proviso is that if a person is a citizen of the United States and another country, the individual must abide by all the laws of *both* nations (House Subcommittee on Immigration, Border Security, and Claims 2006). What has become commonplace among shin Issei women is that those who do become naturalized recipients of a navy-blue, American eagle–embossed, U.S. passport do not surrender their wine-colored Japanese passports stamped with the national emblem—the Imperial Chrysanthemum (Befu 1992). In short, they become dual citizens. Dual citizenship in Japan is illegal. However, in recent years, the Japanese government has unofficially followed a "don't ask, don't tell" policy.

> The nationality law officially obliges those who have multiple citizenships by birthright to choose one by the age of 22. But in fact, possibly hundreds of thousands have maintained multiple nationalities and to date the government has never cracked down on any of them.
>
> Confusion about the legality of holding dual nationalities stems from the opaqueness of the law and the difficulties surrounding its enforcement, causing some to forfeit one of their nationalities while others live in fear of a day when they are forced to choose between their citizenship, identity and family ties. (S. Murakami and Baird 2018: 1)

Thus, while dual citizenship may not be formally sanctioned by nation-states, it nonetheless appears to be a recognition of a transnationalized life in which many people take part (Baubock 2003). Like other shin Issei women, Miki is cautious with whom she shares her status as a citizen of both Japan and the United States. Several months after marrying her American husband, she was granted LPR status, but it was not all a smooth transition. She remembers her first experience using her temporarily approved green card. Returning from vacation in Hawai'i, she was taken aside by the INS and questioned prior to boarding a plane back to Southern California.

> This was on my honeymoon in Hawai'i, and my husband was standing right there! We got married in Japan, and we were coming back.
>
> I had already been approved for a green card—had proof of advance approval—and permission to go outside the country. In Hawai'i, he was standing there saying, "This is my wife"! And they were still trying to stop me! The supervisor finally said I was OK, but . . . [*Shaking her head.*]

Despite this, Miki saw no reason to naturalize. Her husband said it was her choice. Even after giving birth to two shin Nisei children, she continued to use her Japanese passport and resist naturalization. While the children (with American passports) were young, Miki took them to Japan every summer to visit her family—until September 11, 2001.

> [It] changed my whole perspective. I want to protect my kids and that's when I got my citizenship. I decided since I go back and forth, I didn't want to be interrogated [by immigration officials] with me in one room and my babies in another room because we have different status. Something like that could happen with the kids because I travel alone with them.

Her decision to become an American citizen was transformed overnight because of her children—an act of instrumentality rather than one of patriotism. The internal struggle to naturalize was eased by the fact that she never renounced being a Japanese national.

> I had a really big conflict in my head. I really didn't want to become a U.S. citizen because that would mean I would have to give up my Japanese citizenship although I still keep it!

Shin Issei women say being Japanese is simply who they are and will remain regardless of what symbol is displayed on their passports. More specifically, they see themselves as part of a homogeneous majority of the nation-state of Japan that claims membership manifested through blood as the putative carrier of an immutable culture and social identity (Weiner 1997).

> Since a scientifically founded "racial" classification of the Japanese and non-Japanese is meaningless, "Japanese blood" is, first and foremost, a case of social construction of difference. (Kosaku 1992: 24)

Land, people, culture, and language are asserted as mutually equivalent in producing common descent among Japanese subjects (Befu 2001). This ethnonationalist belief in essential characteristics of what it means to be Japanese should not necessarily or always be confused with ethnocentrism—judging another group relative to one's own (Thompson 2021). Japanese ethnocentrism has shifted from nationalist and militarist racial ideologies to focus instead on the primacy of culture and ethnicity as a basis of identity because, it is argued, Japan is an ethnically homogeneous state (Takekawa 2007; Neuliep, Chaudoir, and McCroskey 2001). That Japan has maintained its insularity and relatedly, its homogeneity, is fiction since Japan has always been racially and culturally diverse (Duthie 2014).

Part of this hegemonic notion of identity can be illustrated in how the United States and Japan construct national citizenship and belonging. In the United States, citizenship at birth is a consequence of geography. In Japan, citizenship is determined by blood.[10] Japan is, of course, not unique among nations in tying together blood, race, and nation as key identifiers of belonging (Roberston 2002). Current Japanese law stipulates that those individuals (shin Nisei) born of Japanese parents (shin Issei registered in Japan) can claim Japanese citizenship if they desire. If shin Nisei choose Japanese nationality, they must give up their American citizenship. Shin Issei mothers say it's up to their children.

> My daughter has to make her choice by twenty-two [years old]—if she wants to be [a] Japanese national. She has to decide, but it's her decision, not mine.

Other older generations of American-born Japanese such as Nisei, Sansei, or Yonsei are, of course, citizens of the United States by virtue of geography of birth. Japan does not consider them Japanese nationals. Since the 1980s, Japan has in fact eased its laws on citizenship primarily because of labor shortages. Several hundred thousand immigrants have become naturalized, although public discourse still upholds the view that Japan is a monoethnic nation, not a country of immigrants (Liu-Farrar 2020).

Shin Issei women who do not naturalize as U.S. citizens, maintain dual status, or remain undocumented cite other more contributory reasons for retaining Japanese nationality. While in their twenties, shin Issei women never contemplated returning to Japan. Their goal was to establish new lives in the United States and to take advantage of opportunities that were not possible for them in Japan. Living in the United States for three or four decades or more, they are now aging into their fifties and sixties. Their goal is no longer finding employment, or perhaps gaining more skills through education in the United States. Life's opportunities have assumed different priorities.

> [I have] no green card. I don't want to get citizenship. [But] maybe I'd like to go back to Japan to retire. You know medical expenses are terrible here.

Access to health care and pensions in Japan are among the reasons shin Issei women do not give up their Japanese citizenship. National welfare plans in Japan cover both those who are or have worked full- and part-time and those who are unemployed. Subsidized medical costs are arguably Japan's most successful benefits program. Generally, national health insurance payouts far exceed those available in the United States. In 1990s Japan, major social welfare reforms were enacted—compulsory long-term health insurance, increased parental leave, and childcare—in what was seen as a beginning shift in gender relations both in the workplace and at home (Peng 2002). In the near future, however, welfare programs will be reaching overload because of the high aging population, the low fertility levels leading to fewer future workers, and the economic losses accruing from increased nonregular employment (Kasza and Horie 2011). For now, however, social benefits outside the United States remain an attractive lure, exerting a stronger pull than naturalization for some shin Issei.

> U.S. citizenship? Doesn't seem to be important, although I think about it. The only reason I would get that if it's a financial decision. If you have a house, maybe for tax purposes . . . property ownership. Maybe if I get ill.

No matter how long they live in the United States or whether they are naturalized, many shin Issei still consider themselves Japanese. While being legally Japanese is difficult to jettison, its possession is made more obvious in the small events of daily life in the United States. One shin Issei woman who, after nearly twenty-five years, still has an LPR said:

> It's hard to become Japanese, so it'd be hard to give it up. But sometimes it's strange. When people sing the [U.S.] national anthem and they put their hand on their chest, I notice that I'm not doing that. I'm not American, and I think more and more about that. In a way, I guess I sometimes don't belong. I lost my home.

A migrant transnationalism in a more globalized society that "creates overlapping memberships between territorially separated and independent polities" focuses an understanding of the actions and agency performed by shin Issei women in transnational social fields beyond nation-state borders, though it does not erase those borders (Baubock 2003: 700). At the same time, it illustrates the liminality shin Issei women continue to experience and indicates that for many of them, no matter how comfortable they may feel in the United States, this is not their home. Indeed, the sense of loss of home, of not fully belonging anywhere even if they are naturalized, is an everyday intermediate positionality for shin Issei.

> I do have to renew my permanent residence every ten years. But I hear they are considering dual citizenship. Once my parents are gone, I don't know if I have a place to go, anyway. I don't know if I have a home in Japan.

> I am both Japanese and American. [When] I was watching the Beijing Olympics, I root[ed] for both Japan and the U.S.

In this continuing precarity and inability to be fully *in* the United States are the spaces of discontent and isolation among shin Issei. However, unwilling to accept their marginality has given impetus to some shin Issei to become activists in reaching out to others within their own circles.

This chapter illuminated shin Issei in the multiplicity of their migrant statuses, which often places them outside of more commonly experienced migrant lives. Initially, many women became overstayers without documentation. Over the years, necessity has meant that they have worked, which places them at another level of illegality. They do not seem overly concerned about deportation, but nonetheless, their precarious lives are woven from fabric always on the verge of unraveling should they be apprehended by U.S. immigration officials. Moreover, even among shin Issei who have legal status or are married to American citizens, it might be posited that these factors instantiate a desire for naturalization. This, however, has not been the case, and shin Issei remain among the most intractable of all migrants to become citizens.

4

Surviving around the Neighborhoods

> It's hard to make friends here. In some of my classes I got discriminated especially because my English is not good and sometimes the teacher would say things. And I heard students say things about me, too. That I'm no good.

For shin Issei, beginning life in the United States was an existence of everyday marginalities underlined with no small amount of social isolation.

> I felt people were friendly, but it was [searching for a word]—superficial? On the surface they were friendly, but to become friends, there was difficulty. I was depressed about that. Sometimes I wondered if it was just LA.

While Chapter 2 analyzed larger global events that precipitated shin Issei movement abroad, this chapter takes a closer, on-the-ground look at how those events resonated in the shaping of shin Issei lives as they settled in Southern California communities. This brief historic analysis provides context about how and where shin Issei embedded themselves in this global/local ecumene. Young Japanese women left Japan to escape socially gendered hierarchies, but without skills they often found themselves in virtually the same situation in the United States: working in subordinate positions that reinforced their marginality. This precarity was further exacerbated as shin Issei became wives of white Americans and mothers of children who were biracial. In response to growing social isolation, some shin Issei began to reach out and become active among others like themselves.

She was a young, twenty-something shin Issei when she arrived in Los Angeles on a tourist visa in the 1980s. She never left, and now in her midforties, she remains undocumented. She lives in a studio apartment in Eagle Rock, having moved there some years ago to room with another shin Issei woman who later got married. Next to the front door are several pairs of worn house slippers, a large paper grocery bag stuffed with empty take-out containers and plastic bags, each of the bags tied in a half-knot loop. In one corner a futon is rolled up in a flowered comforter. Opening the refrigerator door to take out a jar of *mugicha* (iced barley tea) releases a strong odor of *tsukemono* (Japanese pickles).

Though she's been here for a while, she still knows no one nearby. The longer she lived in the United States, the more her Prior assumptions about the friendliness of Americans changed. She began to recognize subtler messages.

> People were different here, different type. First, people are very friendly and nice, but then you start seeing negatives. Like the service here, people at banks . . . not really very friendly. Once you start living here, you start seeing negatives.

At first, she was nervous when shopping for groceries near her apartment. Her sense of separation was intensified by her inability to easily converse in English with others she encountered at the supermarket or gas station. In her workday she speaks primarily Japanese and has little need to learn more English, and most likely she will never achieve fluency. She would shop at several Japanese markets near her work in West Los Angeles, where the fare on offer was recognizable—familiar brands and types of foods—or she would make the drive to Little Tokyo.

In any case, she was moving to Gardena shortly, not only because rents were cheaper there but because, she said, "it's easier to be Japanese." The pending move also calls attention to the fact that Gardena is a longtime Nikkei community settled before World War II as agricultural land where Nikkei could farm. However, she wasn't thinking of Gardena's history but rather the influx of transnational capital in the Gardena and South Bay neighborhoods that would provide her with an increased level of familiarity of a transplanted Japan. Adjacent to Gardena are Torrance and the South Bay, which became a hub for Japanese corporate structures and also morphed into a favored area of residence for chuzai-in families in the 1990s. "Easier to be Japanese" was emblematic of her own ongoing social exclusion and called attention to her ethnonational marginality as a Japanese woman (Lie 2001: 238).

Like other shin Issei prior to migration, she was an avid watcher of American television programming in Japan and read American magazines with Japanese translations. She saw America as a place of opportunity and freedom and gathered as much information about American lifestyles as she could. The piles of Japanese language magazines in the apartment are primarily published in the United States and are available free of charge at newsstands around Japanese restaurants and businesses. Shin Issei read them eagerly for their want ads and personals. Only occasionally does she watch American television broadcasting. For many years, she watched televised Japanese programming on Los Angeles' single Japanese language station, but now the existence of the internet has made it even easier to keep ties to Japan alive.[1] Social media and other forms of communication and participation create new ways of networking that bring all things Japanese within a keystroke or swipe (Y. Kim 2011; Mallan, Ashford, and Singh 2010). This has facilitated in easing her re-creation of a Japanese life in Los Angeles and her constructed sense of belonging to an imagined community of other Japanese both in Japan and California (Anderson 1991). Consuming Japanese media in the United States also helps to strengthen and reaffirm both her sense of belonging and self-esteem (Y. Kim 2011; Y. Fujita 2009). Her media habits are now almost entirely Japan based, and she reads very little about Nikkei community news. Before she leaves for the first of her two daily jobs, she sits down at a small table and turns on her laptop to check for emails or anything new posted on *mixi*, a Japanese social media site.

> I'm always on the computer looking at Japanese news, or maybe calling my mother. I can call any time free. I get news about Japan all the time. On computer, [I look at] YouTube, Veoh dot com [a video sharing website], Asahi News. Not too much TV.

Shin Issei women who migrated in the 1980s no longer find that their local lives are totally uncharted terrain. Over the years, they have cobbled together a locality that fosters varying degrees of transnationality to quotidian life. Home is in the United States, but home also exhibits a simultaneity in Japan. Concepts of deterritorialization, however, should be approached with neither exaggeration nor celebration. "Transnational networks are grounded in particular places, even if these places are multiple rather than singular, and they have an impact on localities and regions." (Smart 1999: 60). Shin Issei who can legally travel maintain ongoing physical ties to Japan. However, though a transnationalized life may have some benefits in expanding the means of living beyond borders, shin Issei women collectively remain, for the most part, physically emplaced. Migrant mobility, both physical and imagined, may be fluid, but at the same time, social life is nonetheless local, primarily moored and bounded (Kivisto 2003). For those women who have neither funds nor proper documentation to freely travel overseas, places where the foundations of older Nikkei neighborhoods like Sawtelle exist, layered now by kaisha business, have enabled them to craft a spatialized consumption of global Japan. Nonetheless, for shin Issei women, *furusato* (the nostalgic hometown in Japan) is always on the horizon.

She would like to visit her family in Japan—they have never been to the United States. However, she knows that if she left Los Angeles, she could probably never return. Logging off her laptop, she gets ready to drive to a West Los Angeles ramen shop where she is a waitress and night manager. After her shift there, she will drive to the home of a grade school teacher to help assemble class art projects. She's thinking about going back to school herself and hopes to earn teaching credits—but because she is undocumented, she would most likely would never get a student visa.

Where Nikkei lived and worked, the presence of shin Issei was received with differing degrees of reception: reactions of puzzlement or resentment. Activist Nikkei were initially more focused on resisting the incursion of Japanese capital investment in longtime Japanese American communities. For its part, the transnational kaisha community paid little attention to shin Issei, seeing young women migrants as supplemental workers laboring within the larger corporate arena. In either view, shin Issei found themselves marginalized in both old and new ways.

> They are positioned on the periphery. . . . They tend to live out their lives—on the margins of society and in their own social enclaves. (Ben-Ari and Fong 2008: 82)

However, these various reactions also propelled shin Issei toward agentively carving out new place and space among other Japanese migrant women like themselves, which subsequently also provided grounding for future engagements in the broader Nikkei community. To begin creating place and space for themselves, shin Issei searched for work among those with whom they were most familiar—the Japanese corporate structure. Understanding how Japanese kaisha invested in areas like Southern California where they created transnationalized structures can more clearly explain how and why shin Issei migrants embedded themselves in these new spaces. Theirs was foremost an economic decision, but at the same time, they "live[d] in a social and cultural world that consist[ed] of far more than economic calculations," which enabled them to take advantage of a transnational habitus of social practices (P. Kelly and Lusis 2006: 844). Along with more visible chuzai-in, contemporary shin Issei were also performers in the reformation of urban life (Glick Schiller and Caglar 2009). In this, Japanese nationals benefited from previous social structures built by earlier individuals of Japanese ancestry.

Tensions over Racialized Space

One of the first Issei migrants arrived in Los Angeles in 1885 and opened a small restaurant in Little Tokyo. Soon thereafter, perhaps two dozen or so other Issei joined him in settling around East First Street in downtown Los Angeles (I. Murase 1983). Little Tokyo's economy grew exponentially between 1900 and 1909, mushrooming from 56 businesses to more than 470 (Takaki 1989). These small family enterprises served the rapidly increasing Issei population throughout the Los Angeles basin (Jenks 2011). The creation of *Nihonmachi* (Japantown) enclaves like Little Tokyo was a means by which Issei persevered against severe social constraints.

> During this period, marked by racial segregation and exclusionist policies, Japanese in America had very limited economic opportunities.
> The establishment of Little Tokyo as the hub for a complex ethnic economy based on networks of small agricultural producers throughout the region illustrates their struggle to develop one of the few economic niches available to them. (Toji and Umemoto 2003: 22)

Pre–World War II Little Tokyo was home to as many as thirty thousand people. Though the area was always a multiracial community—the most segregated census tract in 1940 was just 36 percent Nikkei—Little Tokyo was nonetheless the historic heartbeat of Nikkei belonging (Modell 1977). For Issei and their American-born Nisei children, ethnic enclaves were not just safe havens in which to live or places within which to do business with co-ethnics but geographic spaces where identity and everyday lives of marginality might be enacted and reinforced. The preservation of place held meaning far beyond the physical space.

Returning to a postwar Los Angeles after mass exclusion and the Incarceration, Japanese Americans moved back into Little Tokyo, reestablishing residences and businesses. During their absence, the area was redubbed Bronzeville because of the many African Americans who were unable to find housing elsewhere and instead rented white-owned spaces around Little Tokyo (Niiya, n.d.; Jenks 2011). With resettling Nikkei, housing was scarce; living and health conditions in Little Tokyo were criticized by Los Angeles city officials who believed the area "almost require[d] the help of missionaries" (Verge 1994: 306). The less transparent reason for blighted living conditions had more to do with "racist spatial practices by local government" (Jenks 2011: 201).

The City of Los Angeles had already targeted Little Tokyo for extensive urban redevelopment within a few years after the end of World War II. Utilizing eminent domain beginning in 1948, the City of Los Angeles razed residences and small mom-and-pop stores along "two of the most vibrant blocks in Little Tokyo" to build the new headquarters of the Los Angeles Police Department (Fine 2017). The new building "faced City Hall to the west and gave its rear to the diminished community" (Fine 2017). By the 1950s, more than one thousand residents had been forcibly removed (Toji and Umemoto 2003). The battle lines for claiming this space were drawn by the city but were not met with acquiescence by Nikkei. Instead there was active, vigorous, and prolonged opposition. Several decades of fighting for place and space underscored the importance of a preservation of a Nikkei identity within Little Tokyo. This continued into the late 1970s and beyond and became conflated with the incursion of Japanese corporate investment.

Courting Yen

Japan's overwhelming transnational economic investment in the United States did not occur randomly but was assisted by local economic changes in urban areas like Los Angeles where political leaders were especially eager to court and take advantage of so-called Pacific Rim economic power (Jenks 2008). It was an integrative process of foreign and domestic, a product of the forces of utopianized transnational capitalism (Dirlik 1999). Drawn by bargain-priced real estate and the welcoming arms of Los Angeles city politicians, Japanese ownership and investment transformed the urban landscape. In a first-ever move by a local government, the City of Los Angeles took out a loan from a foreign government—Japan (Soja 1996). By the late 1980s, Japanese real estate investments in North America totaled nearly $17 billion, with as much as 25 percent of that centered in Los Angeles office space (Clifford 1994). At the end of a highly publicized two-and-a-half-month period in 1986, Shuwa Investments, a Tokyo-based commercial and real estate giant, gobbled up nearly $1 billion worth of Los Angeles skyline (Broder 1986). Los Angeles Mayor Tom Bradley, a strong supporter of Shuwa (which subsequently gave generously to

Bradley's failed campaign for California governor in 1988) and other Japanese business ventures, liked to promote the (economic) possibilities of the Pacific Rim. He branded as racist the most frenzied reactions against increasing Japanese investments (Davis 1992).

Into the long-established Nikkei community of Little Tokyo, with its complex webs and networks of relationships, came transnational newcomers with money to spend. As had occurred postwar, Nikkei again felt they were being overrun. Japanese investment became a lightning rod for activists who saw little economic benefit accruing to existing Nikkei residents and small businesses and believed that "transnational capital into the neighborhood would become a conduit through which Japantown would be further transformed into a Disney-esque tourist trap" (Lai 2013: 472). Foreign money was perceived as a dilution and negation of local cultural heritage and social identity (Buckley and Graves 2016). Little Tokyo was home turf—not a "beachhead for Japanese corporate investments" (Jenks 2008: 238). Longtime community activists like Nisei Kats Kunitsugu remembered what occurred during an annual Nisei Week Parade in Little Tokyo in the 1970s that turned into an angry protest by Sansei.

> There was a big demonstration during Nisei Week. They actually burned a Japanese Rising Sun flag in [the] street. They were worried about Japanese companies taking over Little Tokyo and kicking out JAs [Japanese Americans].

Resistance among activist groups in Little Tokyo protested global Japanese projects like the New Otani Hotel and the Kajima Building, labeling Japan's investors as "imperialist land-grabbers" (Shichinohe-Suga 2004: 247).

The infusion of Japanese money occurred during a time when Nikkei activists in Little Tokyo and other established Nihonmachi in California were fighting urban redevelopment. However, at the same time, Nikkei-led (primarily Nisei) development projects benefited from Japanese corporate capital. New, major community projects like the Japanese American Cultural and Community Center and the Japanese American National Museum competed for infusions of overseas capital (Simpson 2012). The Nikkei Aratani Theatre project in Little Tokyo raised two-thirds of its budget from Japanese businesses and the Japanese government (Harmetz 1982). As in other redeveloping Nihonmachi, Nikkei often walked a line between courting and critiquing Japanese money and mediating claims to retentive spaces of racial cultural knowledge (Oda 2014; Shichinohe-Suga 2004). These claims were mostly ignored by local politicians and Japanese corporate investors.

All these actors took up more competitive positions than the traditional Japanese Americans because they had more ties with current Japanese culture and therefore could reproduce conditions that were more similar to those of a "real" Japan. (Machimura 2003: 148)

Whatever "real" Japan was constructed beyond its national borders, the implications of Machimura's argument are clear and were echoed by city planners who desired an "authentic" Japan that more accurately envisioned Pacific gateways (Oda 2014). Historic Nikkei communities were not genuine and needed renovation to make these areas more palatable for a new kind of global Japanese settler. Japanese money and its more observable displays both utilized and elided the historical construction of the local within Nikkei communities. Within this local, there persisted the maintenance of a racial identity hewn on contested sociospatial terrain (Soja 2011). This dialectic resonated far beyond the enclave and was felt throughout Southern California Nikkei communities where new Japanese migrants did not identify with other Nikkei—more specifically, native-born Americans.

These developments marked a turning point in Little Tokyo's transformation, as Japanese businesses envisioned a commercial area for Japanese tourists and for the growing number of Japanese corporate employees stationed in the region. (Toji and Umemoto 2003: 28)

Japanese investment and the addition of the "invasion of the salarymen"—transferred chuzai-in employees—went hand in hand (Sullivan 1992). However, the reproduction of a fully transnational and global social life for new Japanese migrants in Southern California was possible because of what Nikkei had built. Nikkei were seen as cultural brokers—useful for economic expansion, and not least—among the first Americans to buy Japanese products spurned by mainstream America (Befu 2008).

At an early stage of development, daily life in the new expatriate community depended heavily on ethnic resources provided by the Japanese American community. However, as the (new) Japanese population has continued to increase, new actors came into this active marketplace. (Machimura 2003: 147)

The marketplace expanded rapidly throughout Southern California. To support the kaisha structure, numerous Japan-based service- and consumer-related businesses such as banks, supermarkets, restaurants, beauty shops, travel agencies, and language schools catering to Japanese nationals spread throughout Southern California (Kameyama 2012). From the 1980s onward, Japanese correspondents from *Nippon Hōsō Kyōkai* (NHK; Japan Broadcasting Corporation), Tokyo Broadcasting System (TBS), and *Yomiuri Shimbun* (newspaper) were commonplace at local news and community events. In 1989, a Sansei recalled how he suddenly realized that looking Japanese didn't mean you were Nikkei. Visiting a video rental in Torrance, California, he perused the aisles but found the offerings were all in Japanese. There were no videos with English subtitles. Speaking in English, he asked the young clerk why. The clerk's response in Japanese was brief and curt, "*Subutaitoru arimasen*—we don't have subtitles."

Niches of Opportunity

In these expansions, shin Issei saw a transnational outpost as a place where there was the promise of jobs and where they might participate in a "real Japan"—albeit, they hoped, without the social baggage they had left behind. In California, however, many of the types of jobs young shin Issei were initially able to secure did not lead to imagined equality or substantial opportunities for career advancement but instead reinforced transplanted divisions of subservient, gendered labor. For young shin Issei, confining Japanese women's roles followed them as they incorporated into the periphery of Japanese corporate life on American soil. With few discernible skills and hampered by a lack of English that may have increased their marketability outside the transnational community, they continued to be exploited and marginalized in the United States.

Shin Issei women in this study have found opportunities working and living around the edges of kaisha, but they were never equally participatory in the chuzai-in community, in a number of significant ways. Separated by Japanese constructions of class, education, and status as unmarried women, they existed outside a supportive corporate and government structure that sanctioned company benefits for male employees, and tangentially wives and children. Japanese kaisha men have been privileged as the epitome of the corporate presence (E. Hasegawa 2007). They were the norm, and their masculinity, the default (Ortner 1996). Overseas kaisha support included transfer visas, corporate salaries, year-end bonuses, medical care, children's education, housing stipends—in short, everything material life in a new country required. As followers of this gendered hierarchy, accompanying wives participated in the social capital accrued by their husbands. Wives' roles were seen as naturalized, unmarked, and subordinate to husbands. This peripherality among shin Issei women who are not a married part of a corporate structure is common among other chuzai-in communities, such as those seen in Singapore.

> They are also estranged from the wives of these Japanese businessmen who tend to be organized in rather homogeneous and tight-knit circles. (Ben-Ari and Fong 2000: 82)

Shin Issei also inhabited unmarked, precarious work in employment, subordinate in roles that were not exceptional but the norm (Neilson and Rossiter 2008). Nonetheless, their marginality allowed them to fill needed and valuable roles in an expanding transnational local economy. Jobs were plentiful in the 1980s; young shin Issei found their labor in demand in myriad businesses servicing overseas Japanese. Speaking fluent English was neither required nor sought and employers did not ask for proof of valid work permits. During this time, many shin Issei did not have green cards. At Japanese grocery stores and clothing shops they waited on customers and rang up sales. At import-export offices they answered phones. At some Japanese language schools they were teachers' aides distributing class materials. At Japanese restaurants they waited tables.

A much-favored job for shin Issei in their twenties was waitressing and hostessing. Dozens of bars and private clubs in Little Tokyo and Southern California signaled the appearance of transnational capital. Shin Issei found employment where they were euphemistically called bar hostesses and where chuzai-in men paid for overpriced drinks and friendly "company." These clubs are commonplace in urban Japan where sarariman go to drink and cement social ties after work. Similarly, during the inflation of the Bubble, hostess bars and clubs proliferated in Southern California in the 1980s. The expectation was that hostesses attended men, chatting and pouring liquor from bottles bearing the patron's personal name.

Hostess clubs are highly gendered and hierarchically specific—they are men's spaces. Women serve to make this male realm possible (Allison 1994). Little Tokyo and the South Bay were sites of countless small clubs and bars where transnational chuzai-in entertained other male business clients, including American men. In addition to an attractive appearance, shin Issei employees were single. "Pairing up" between hostesses and patrons was frowned upon by club owners because it detracted from a hostess's availability to other clients, thus making less money for the club. There was also an implicit warning that pairing up could lead to sex on the job. Aside from being illegal if there was payment, it could also mean less profits if other patrons had knowledge about an employee's relationship with another customer. At least three shin Issei in this study did meet boyfriends and husbands through their work as hostesses. They said they did not engage in a more intimate relationship until they quit working.

Before coming to the United States, none of the shin Issei women was employed at a hostess club in Japan. For middle-class Japanese families engaged in finding eligible husbands for their daughters, club work was not considered suitable. Working as a hostess in Southern California carried less stigma because there were no close friends or family present who knew where these young women were employed. If asked directly, women would most often say they worked at restaurants. Despite this euphemistic explanation, their work hours late into the night were self-explanatory of the hostess job description. During the day, some of the women were students, but later after classes, they worked night shifts dressed in kimono or cocktail wear.

Women were not especially uncomfortable talking about their experiences; it was just another job. Encounters with some of the white American male customers who frequented the bars, however, sometimes left them laughing nervously. About the attentive hostess services performed, one shin Issei woman commented, "Oh, those hakujins like it very much, good for business if they come back." In addition to being highly aware of Japanese men's expectations, shin Issei were also conscious of American stereotypes about Japanese women. In Japan, shin Issei women are members of the racial majority. This rendered them part of an unmarked, taken-for-granted category though they did not escape classifications of subordinate gender. This is no longer the case in the United States. A new degree of marginality accompanies these women, who are (in)visible not only as women but racially as Asian, foreign, and nonwhite exotica (Y. Fujita 2009). Shin Issei also experienced racism beyond exotica. Growing up in Japan had not prepared them for acts of aggression, and the encounters left them speechless and unable to respond.

> One time I was waiting for a bus, and somebody drove by and said "Jap." That was the most open. I was shocked and didn't say anything. I never had that happen to me before, and I was taken [aback].

Mediated American discourse has historically fueled simplistic, inaccurate, and one-dimensional images of Japan and Japanese. During the 1980s, while kaisha men were seen as threatening, images of Japanese women projected docility and subservience as both a naturalized and racialized femininity (Gee 1988; Nemoto 2006; R. Tajima 1989). Lotus blossoms, China dolls, and geisha girls form long-standing imaginings for many American men who desire supposed obedient and noncompetitive partners among Asian and Japanese women (Chen and Takeuchi 2011). The trope of the exotic Asian woman has long preoccupied Hollywood (Gee 1988). At a time when many shin Issei were migrating to the United States, this image was widely reproduced in the early 1980s through American television series such as *Shogun*, which aired on NBC. Its familiar theme of a British (white) sea navigator's romance with a doomed, Japanese female translator—"we cannot take our eyes off her"—registered blockbuster ratings (IMDb Reviews 2005).

Shin Issei hostesses honed acts of performativity—submissive attentiveness and ingratiating appreciativeness—all in keeping with others' objectifications. They assumed normative gendered roles as "a practice of improvisation within a sense of constraint" (Butler 2004).

> One does not "do" one's gender alone. One is always "doing" with or for another . . . the terms that make up one's own gender are, from the start, outside oneself . . . [it] has no single author (Butler 2004: 1)

One shin Issei hostess remarked that initially she was unable to speak conversational English to American customers, but it mattered little. "My boss said if I couldn't talk to them, then listen. Just make sure their glasses were full!" Years later, even at a dinner meeting with another woman in a small West Los Angeles Japanese restaurant, she hurried to fill the other's empty beer glass.

For her, the pay and the tips from hostessing were lucrative. Her earnings, along with a student visa, allowed her to attend classes at a junior college during the day, though she said she did not appear on a regular basis. At her club, she met an American who became her boyfriend. He took her out to dinner and talked about "getting together." They argued often about her working as a hostess although that was how they met. They never married. Her boss, a shin Issei woman in her late fifties, was hiring younger women in their early to midtwenties to train as hostesses. Soon, these younger women around her were garnering more customers. "My tips weren't good." She continued to work as a hostess until she was in her early thirties, saving enough money to open a small ramen shop. Because she had no green card, her invested savings and ownership were not in her name. A few years after quitting the bar, she married a white American man four years her senior who had been a fellow student in junior college.

She had no regrets working as a hostess since it allowed her to save money. Providing professional companionship was simply a requisite of the job. Practicing social norms such as those expected of hostesses signals the normalizing function of power. Norms "bind individuals together, but they can also create resistance" (Butler 2004). For bar hostesses in 1980s Southern California, that resistance was not only acknowledgment of the requirements of hostessing but also an agentive path toward achieving a degree of independence in preparation for their next step in life.

Chisa's first job in California came very soon after her arrival on a student visa. She found a position working at a small gift shop in Little Tokyo. Like other shin Issei, she managed her class schedule to prioritize work. She could be at the shop in the afternoons and early evenings, when Little Tokyo was busy with tourists and dinner patrons who frequented the area. Shin Issei most often worked full-time despite student visa stipulations about employment off campus. One shin Issei woman said her work schedule changed so frequently that she'd be late to class or wouldn't make it at all. The law for those with full-time student visas requires class attendance. However, as long as her tuition was paid and she studied enough for a passing grade, no one at the school monitored her attendance. In more recent years, U.S. immigration and education officials have been more proactive in investigating and prosecuting "pay-to-stay" facilities (Department of Justice 2017).

The jobs where shin Issei found work would not qualify as a career, but women still gained valuable experience in learning about life in a new country. Equally significant, since shin Issei arrived knowing virtually no one in the United States, early jobs provided links in establishing a network of contacts. Shin Issei say Nikkei provided needed early support.

> I had a roommate, she's Japanese American—her mom actually helped me a lot—I didn't really know anybody and didn't have family here—just me. She helped me get a job at a Japanese restaurant. So I was a waitress.

When shin Issei ventured outside Japanese and Nikkei circles, work life presented different challenges. Kyoko's last return to Japan did not last long. The shin Issei friend she'd met on one of her trips to California had not returned to Japan, and in letters home, she urged Kyoko to come back to California. "She told me, oh, you can find any job here." Though her parents objected to her leaving Japan again, Kyoko told them not to worry. She said she would stay for just a few months on yet another tourist visa. Within a week after returning to California, she was working two jobs waitressing. Kyoko got her daytime job after another waitress put in a word with the manager of a small restaurant in the Mar Vista area of Los Angeles. The café served a mixed clientele of Angelenos—Nikkei, Latino(a)s, and whites. Kyoko quickly found that with her limited English, the learning curve was steep.

I practiced my English. But it was hard, I didn't know there were so many kinds of breads—you know, whole wheat, white bread....

I had to ask [customers] different things. How about your eggs? Over hard, poached, I didn't know. In Japan, if you order toast, you get white bread, only one kind; you can't change it. I had no experience.

And American people are *picky*! Even coffee, decaffeinated or caffeine—you know you go to Japan—at least there, you go to a coffee shop, coffee is coffee! So I learned.

At night, Kyoko was on more familiar ground at her second job—a small restaurant and bar in Little Tokyo catering mostly to Japanese businessmen. She took the bus to downtown Los Angeles, even though she was often worried and afraid for her personal safety in getting to work. Within the year, she'd saved enough money to buy a used car. A friend taught her how to drive. It took her two tries, but she got a driver's license and stopped taking the bus to work.

Motherhood and Emerging Politicized Identities

After her marriage and eventual possession of a green card, Tomoko worked part-time at a preschool for shin Nisei children until she became a mother. Her story illustrates how shin Issei encounter new inequalities when they migrate, especially if they partner with white Americans or other non-Japanese. Although more inclusive narratives of multiculturalism in the United States may accompany racially mixed relationships, these narratives "may also obscure white patriarchy while at the same time, maintaining gendered discourses about family" (Nemoto 2009: 58). Tomoko's story also shows the ways in which shin Issei resist inequalities to forge new productive lives.

When shin Issei marry and have children, their social relationships with non-Japanese partners and multiracial children are additional layers of precarity that must be seen not only through a gendered lens but through a racial and class-based one as well. It is a subject needing further research.

> It seems that intermarriage, while revealing the declining social distance between the majority and certain minority groups, can also entail a complex co-mingling of economic and social integration and marginalisation. (Song 2009: 343)

Furthermore, it has been argued that there should not be an assumption of integration and assimilation. Rather, this "is problematic if only because of actual and perceived inequalities in a society that privileges Euro-Americans and Euro-American culture—a structural dynamic that destabilizes and will continue to create countercurrents and conflicts" (Chow 2000: 25).

Rieko was looking forward to a career as a registered dietitian. She was a recent California state college graduate, newly married, and her supervisor was encouraging her to apply for a management position at the community hospital. She was also pregnant. After her first auburn-haired son was born, her American husband said it would be better for her to stop working and stay at home. With no family on whom she could rely for childcare and with a partner who was absent throughout most of the day, Rieko reluctantly quit her job. The adjustment to stay-at-home parent was difficult.

> [I was] going through different stages, first liking it, then not liking it, and then finally seeing both sides. There's no perfect place.

As with many shin Issei mothers, Rieko's initial lack of a supportive network left her adrift. It reminded her of mothers in Japan who became ryosei kenbo, despite whatever aspirations they may have had or qualifications they possessed. It was something she had hoped to avoid in her own life.

> I find my brain thinking more negatively. At the end of the day, I don't feel good. [*Patting her chest over her heart.*] *Chotto* [a little bit]. I see that part [good wife, good mother] in Japan, too. So when I see that, that's not what I want.
>
> My good friends are like me, those who've been here a long time, who have husbands who are American, so we can understand each other.

For shin Issei women, this "crisis of migration" results in isolation, inability to converse with husbands and others in wider society, and oftentimes depression (Adler 1977). Seeking self-esteem and self-actualization doesn't end overnight; instead, it is a longitudinal process among shin Issei that is mitigated by what is familiar, such as associating with others like themselves. It is both comforting and self-affirming.

Tomoko's sense of vulnerability became a catalyst for adopting a more direct approach to dealing with her precarity. In this agentive move, "rich, textured understandings of oneself as a person linked to . . . particular histories (can) explain in personally meaningful ways why and how one must act politically in order to live a meaningful life" (Brodkin 2007: 8). Tomoko realized that for most shin Issei women like herself who were not part of a chuzai-in network, there were no social resources. It was one thing for shin Issei to work within the growing network of Japanese overseas businesses but quite another to participate in sanctioned kaisha social structures. She knew that without proper corporate affiliation, she would not be permitted to attend chuzai-in events for mothers and children. In her isolation, she began to think that there was no reason why she might not organize something for mothers like herself—with a common goal in mind—taking care of young children. After her son was born, Tomoko sought out other new shin Issei mothers, most of whom were also married to American citizens. At a local day-care center in West Los Angeles, a few shin Issei brought their children to playdates while they congregated among themselves, chatting in Japanese. Tomoko approached some of them and invited them to her home. At first, she was met with suspicion, but word soon spread. Her small home in the suburb of Mar Vista became a regular meeting place for shin Issei mothers whose lives spread over a wide area of the western neighborhoods of Los Angeles. Once every week or so, women showed up bringing snacks like homemade cookies and fruit drinks—kids in tow. Attendance was fluid, with no requirement for membership. Mothers and children came and went over a period of an hour or two.[2]

Soon, these casual get-togethers became more regular, but the ad hoc nature of their activities remained evident. Comparable social patterns are similar among shin Issei women married to non-Japanese in other large cities in the world. So-called meetups are largely unplanned social networks built among migrants through specific special interests and commonalities such as children (Nagatomo 2011). Among Tomoko's acquaintances, the mothers all had similar backgrounds as single women in Japan. Not particularly highly educated, they had been part-time workers or OLs who had still lived at home prior to emigration. Moving to the United States, they arrived alone without benefit of connections or family in the United States. Using various temporary visas with repeated extensions, they flaunted immigration laws by working full-time. Many eventually became overstayers. The precarious status of those who continued to be unauthorized was never mentioned, although it was common knowledge. If asked by an outsider, shin Issei would simply shrug, saying, "*Shiranai*" (I don't know).

One or two chuzai-in mothers came to a few meetings at Tomoko's, but they attended only once or twice, politely saying they were too busy. One of them told some of the other mothers her husband's company had formalized family activities—a day-care center and a women's group where she could bring her children and spend time with other company wives. Though none of the women in Tomoko's circle said anything, on both sides there was clearly a level of discomfort with disparate social positions. The conversation was more formal; only last names ending in a more honorific *san* were used. One mother in Tomoko's circle later said she had been asked twice by one of the chuzai-in wives whether her American-born husband ate Japanese food. The query was masked with utmost politeness, but the unspoken intent and barely concealed social disapproval called attention to differences of belonging. When asked if the question and veiled disapproval were because her husband was white or because he did not work for a multinational corporation, this shin Issei mother inclined her head slightly and did not answer. Given the ubiquity of Japanese food in the twenty-first century, as well as growing numbers of interracial relationships in the United States, perhaps this question now gets asked less often, but for shin Issei women and their chuzai-in female counterparts, clearly, social class parameters had not disappeared but were instead reified across national borders.

On a Thursday afternoon at Tomoko's home, shoes were stacked by the front door. Arranged next to the shoes was a pile of soft-sided backpacks, and sandwiched between were a half-dozen *randoseru*, the boxy, hard-sided packs Japanese children carry to school. For an hour or more before heading home to cook dinner, the women talked about immigration problems (Tomoko was the only naturalized citizen, and several other mothers had green cards), communication issues with husbands, the locations of the best public schools, volunteer work at the nearby Japanese language school, or the items on sale at Mitsuwa grocery store.

In the backyard, children splashed in the plastic wading pool or dug in the sandbox. The mothers were delighted to meet other Japanese migrants with whom they could talk more openly about everyday life. The number one subject was their children. At times, the clatter of dishwashing in the kitchen and mothers' chatter and admonishments of *"Abunai!"* (Watch out!) to children playing outside made for a cacophony of contented interaction. For the mothers, it was a time of respite they enjoyed.

> We were watching the kids out of the corners of our eyes. We chatted; the kids played. They were all having a fun time, and sometimes, we'd teach them something like singing songs.

Spread out on Tomoko's small kitchen table were photo albums of the children and their mothers. Birthdays, Christmas, Japanese *o-shogatsu* (New Year), preschool graduations, and classroom awards were all commemorated. Inside an album was a dog-eared, typed registration list of attendees—about fifteen names, addresses, phone numbers, children's birth dates. Tomoko grins when she looks at it.

> This is just the original list—it got bigger, expanded more and more as people found out. Maybe expanded to twice as big—thirty mothers, because people asked other people to come. At one time it was a pretty big group.
>
> It was important to talk with other Japanese moms. We don't do much gossip or anything. Definitely it was important to share information.
>
> Somebody talked about pre-care [preschool]. Otherwise we'd have no idea, or about a free program that was state funded—how do people know about this stuff? We focused on the kids and how to develop them.

Like Tomoko, a few of the mothers began to reach out to contacts in local schools and churches for guides and tips on education they could share with others. One Saturday, a mother was handing out flyers, written in Japanese, about how to get children into UCLA and the University of Southern California. She was inviting everyone interested to a talk at a nearby Sawtelle community center.

Tomoko also spent a few hours each week on a phone tree, alerting mothers about events and other neighborhood happenings in the West Los Angeles area. The group became known informally as Aki-chan's House (a shortening of her son's name, Akio, with *chan* added as a common Japanese term of endearment). Akio has an anglicized first name that students and teachers used at his Los Angeles elementary school. However, his mother's circle of friends was more comfortable with Aki.

Aki-chan's House fulfilled an important role for mothers and children at a critical time in their lives. Young mothers with limited social networks found common ground among others like themselves. Like contemporary Chinese migrants who also created ad hoc neighborhood groups, they forged new connections through their children and became part of a community of mutual interests whose work was literally achieved in backyards (Toyota 2010). For Tomoko it was an awakening to the politicized realities of community work—a politics that "does not delimit a pre-given set of institutions, relations, or actions, as much as describe a variable field of social practices . . . imbued with power" (Gregory 1998).

> This is the way I felt. Me and Akio, it's just two people; you need more people; you need to socialize. It [was] like the first time everybody knew somebody outside the family—friends making friends.

> Yes, some of the mothers are still connected; sure it was important for them. I used to wait for this day [to meet]. It [was] a good opportunity for Aki to hear Japanese.

Tomoko realized that this early shin Issei activism is a memory children carried with them as they grew into young adults.

> All the kids are preteens and are still bilingual. My husband and I can't make Japanese conversation, so it's important that Aki hear those words.
> Now, some of the kids I haven't seen for ten years, but I still recognize them. And the kids remember everything. When they go past our house, they say, "Oh, this is Aki-chan's house"! They remember.

In the years that have passed since the first meetups, both mothers and children have grown older. Children who are in high school have busy lives filled with school activities and sports. In reminiscing about these Aki-chan House sessions, women say they looked forward to them and say they were grateful there was someplace to share similar life experiences. It was a reaffirmation of identity—who they were as Japanese women married to non-Japanese and, at its core, how this was manifested in the raising of their children who are mixed race.

Tomoko's organizing around home and children resulted in a repositioning of self among this small cohort of new migrant women. Equally important, it was a way to mitigate marginalization, to seek out others with similar interests, and to achieve a sense of purpose and belonging. In no small measure, these women had constructed an emancipatory politics that was liberating, "thereby permitting a transformative attitude towards the future . . . and increasing social control over their life circumstances" (Giddens 1991). In a few years, Tomoko's initial activism would continue into other community-based work among shin Issei women. Although Tomoko would never call herself a leader, she fulfilled that role in network formation and consciousness shaping and as such was a key actor—a center woman (Brodkin Sacks 1988).

Aki-chan's House was women's space, yet in critical ways, this space was also defined as Japanese. It was not wholly integrative of their interracial marriages or the mixed racial backgrounds the children possessed, even if this was difficult to ignore while looking at youngsters with blond, brown, curly or wavy hair playing outside. Working husbands were physically absent at Aki-chan's House, though there was frequent discussion about them. Women said they rarely discussed details of their meetings when they returned home; some of the husbands were not even aware of these sessions, and it did not enter any conversation. Several shin Issei mothers never told their husbands about the meetings beyond describing them as playdates. "I don't talk to him about this" was heard often. Nor did it seem that husbands were overly interested in their wives' daytime activities.

On Becoming More Japanese

As intermarriage numbers have increased, so has the growing presence of bi- and multiracial children. However, among shin Issei women who have very high rates of exogamy, issues surrounding identity create tension for both mothers and children. Japanese call biracial individuals *hafu*, and Nikkei often use *hapa* to describe bi- and multiracial persons.[3] Since the 2000 U.S. Census, statistics on multiracial individuals have been collected with the addition of the question "What is this person's race?"—the designation of which is supposedly to jettison outmoded racial taxonomies (U.S. Census Bureau 2012).

> The census instruction, "mark one or more," is the early tremor of an earthquake in political and social life. What for 200 years had been a racial classification based on a handful of discrete groupings suddenly became 63 categories, and, when cross classified by Hispanic-Not Hispanic, 126 race-ethnic groups. (Prewitt 2002: 9)

The multiracial option was especially significant for Japanese and Japanese Americans. The growth and diversity of the American Japanese population in the United States (and its attendant parameters of definition), have been discussed for some time now (Omi, Nakano, and Yamashita 2019; Toyota 2012; Shichinohe-Suga 2006). The *decrease* in census counts of "Japanese only" may be partially attributable to the confining racial categories in the U.S. Census prior to 2000, when the number of Japanese declined 1.2 percent (U.S. Census Bureau 2012). However, with the addition of the more inclusive racial question, numbers of multiracial "Japanese in combination with one or more other races" soared by nearly 56 percent, from approximately 296,000 in 2000 to more than 460,000 in 2010 (U.S. Census Bureau 2012). Further, 2010 estimates showed that nearly 47 percent of these individuals were young, under five years to thirty-four years old, with nearly 25 percent under the age of seventeen years (U.S. Census Bureau 2010c). This last cohort of individuals under seventeen years old is where most of the shin Nisei children in this study were found.

The existence of hafu children brings into sharper focus not only how shin Issei mothers see their children but, by relation, how they see themselves. Multiracial children have emphasized shin Issei mothers' desires that their children not only understand and appreciate their Japanese heritage but that shin Nisei recognize that they *are* Japanese. Living in the United States complicates this project. Mothers at Aki-chan's House said it was even more important to emphasize Japanese cultural practices to their hafu children.

> It was a great place to meet other Japanese parents. We talked about everything, like taking our kids to Japanese school so they know Japanese. You start thinking more about teaching them Japanese culture.

A mother who has two biracial children said that in Japan, she never extensively questioned who she was as a Japanese woman. Living in the United States as a migrant, as a Japanese married to a hakujin, and as a mother with two daughters changed that.

> After I had my kids I started becoming more Japanese. They're [hafu], but my Japanese side comes out. The only childhood I know is Japan, and I started thinking that I want them to experience what I experienced.

Raising hafu children to understand their Japanese heritage becomes a full-time project for shin Issei.

> When you have kids you start thinking, what am I doing, what am I raising, what's my identity? When I came here, I thought everything was great, looked great; everything was new, fresh. But then I started seeing things I didn't like.

"What's my identity" is a small step to encompassing one's children as well. Shin Issei want their children to know Japan because it is a part of who they are. That involves exposing children to things Japanese, and for many shin Nisei children, it means travel to Japan. Shin Issei mothers who are permitted to travel with green cards make a point of taking children for yearly extended vacations after the American school year ends for the summer. Aki-chan House members who were able to travel returned to Japan each summer. The trips were partly vacation to visit grandparents, other family members, or perhaps Tokyo Disneyland. However, it was also important to enroll school-age children in Japanese public schools where schedules briefly overlap the school term in the Los Angeles area. Over the years, shin Nisei become bilingual and familiar with contemporary Japan, cementing strong cross-border ties with family and friends. Among these young twenty-first-century shin Nisei, their transnationality becomes a part of their daily lives.

Shin Issei mothers bear sole responsibility for teaching an awareness and value of being Japanese. American husbands do not participate in promoting "Japanese-ness" among their children, and mothers usually make the transpacific flight alone with their children.

> I'm the only source they have. My husband doesn't know anything about Japan. He's been there—but he's hakujin. [*Laughing.*] He's from Chicago and grew up in Lancaster [California].

She says there is no marital discord over her frequent trips to Japan as much as there is indifference and disinterest. Her comment is terse.

> I go back to Japan for one month during the summer and I take the kids. My husband stays here and works. My parents moved to Tokyo [to see them].

Some mothers do confront their own dissatisfaction with their roles as solo parent. Rieko says the longer she is married, the more keenly she feels dissimilarities between an envisioned life with an American husband and the reality of an inability to share ideas and feelings.

> The older I get, the more difference I feel with my husband. Raising kids, I feel the difference. In Japan, husband and wife don't talk much. A lot of things are understood, but here husband and wife are humans who have to communicate, which is a good thing. But I didn't learn that. I don't have that skill.

Likewise, explaining one's hafu children in Japan has not always been easy. A shin Issei mother who is married to an African American had worries about enrolling her oldest son in a public school in Japan. In the beginning, he was not accepted by some of his teachers and was ostracized and taunted by other students who called him *gaijin* (foreigner).

> They look different in Japan. But things have changed a lot, and nowadays, people are used to seeing foreigners, so it's nothing really different—no big deal.
> And the school he goes to [during summer] has an exchange program now. There are white Americans and half-black students. So, it's not too unusual.

No matter who their spouses are, among one another, shin Issei mothers are frank in appreciating opportunities to bond with other shin Issei and to talk about loneliness and depression.

There is no one who doesn't know the story of thirty-three-year-old Fumiko Kimura, who in 1985 walked into the surf at Santa Monica Beach in an attempt to drown herself and her two small children. She survived, but the children did not. Kimura's story is theirs: a shin Issei mother with neither friends nor family in the United States who wanted to become a pianist but quit when her children were born. She stayed at home, unable to drive, while her husband worked in a restaurant in the day and most evenings. Shortly before she decided on an *oyako-shinju* suicide, she discovered her husband was having an affair.[4] As will be further discussed, Kimura's arrest and legal case galvanized other shin Issei into an uncharacteristic show of public support.

Most shin Issei women say they spend the days alone with just children. Husbands are largely absent or don't come home until late. While this is often a similar work-family situation in Japan, mothers do have familiarity with social processes and connections with others that are absent in the United States. One mother used to take her daughter to a local park in West Los Angeles in hopes of meeting others but said she couldn't speak enough English or Spanish to converse with mothers and those taking care of young children. Because she has hafu children, she says some of the mothers at the park assumed she was a nanny.

> I was struggling. I cannot find people. I just stayed at home. I don't know anyone. I don't know where people are or where I should go. Sure, it worried me.
>
> I was isolated. I went to Santa Monica Library every week where they had a program, and I met this mom [another shin Issei]. When I asked, "What happens when you stay at home?"
>
> Nothing happens [*voice level barely registering*].

Another mother told her about Aki-chan's House. She found commonality among the other mothers and became a regular.

> I'm pretty sure there are lots of women who are isolated. But finally, I had a network, you call it that? Definitely. Hmm, I think about connections.

Constructing community networks among themselves was an important method by which shin Issei created belonging. In this process, they came to further understand their own experiences as Japanese women and, in relation, wanted their children to also understand their positionality as Japanese. This meant additional education in more formalized settings outside the home.

> I want them to know who I am, to understand me. So I find myself more and more, introducing Japanese books, Japanese music, and sending them to Japanese school.

In the context of both shin Issei and Nikkei community, "Japanese school" meant weekend language school. These types of supplemental education facilities, also known as Japanese heritage schools (JHS), meet for half days on Saturday (Douglas 2005). JHS are a long-standing institution begun in Nikkei communities in the United States (Asato 2006; Chinen and Tucker 2006). Issei migrants who founded JHS believed teaching language and cultural traditions were important for their American-born children. At the same time, Issei parents who did not speak fluent English often utilized Issei teachers as bridges between themselves and the public schools their Nisei children attended during the week. Some JHS are more than a century old and have been in continuous use except for the years around World War II when the schools were forced to cancel classes following the FBI arrests of the teachers (Morimoto 1997). By the 1980s, with the growing diversity of the Nikkei community, including the appearance of shin Nisei, JHS teaching goals were broadened because of the multicultural, multiracial makeup of students. Also reflective of the transformation among the student body, knowledge about the meanings of Japanese cultural processes and values, as well as the significance of Nikkei history, were included.

On a late Saturday morning, a small side street off Sawtelle Boulevard is lined with cars, some of them double-parked in front of a concrete playground and low-rise building. Shin Issei mothers are waiting for their mostly hafu shin Nisei children to finish classes at this small community center housing a JHS. This first JHS in West Los Angeles was founded in 1925 by Issei parents and still sits on its original property. It was one of at least eight other Japanese language schools opened in the early 1900s in Southern California to serve the growing Nisei generation during a period of intense anti-Japanese sentiment in California and the West (Asato 2006).

Through the years, the JHS functioned not just as a language school but as an important community center for Nikkei growing up in Sawtelle and West Los Angeles. However, in the 1980s and 1990s, it was limping along with dwindling numbers of students and would most likely have shut down had it not been for increasing numbers of shin Issei mothers who started enrolling their coming-of-age shin Nisei children. The presence of shin Nisei most likely saved the JHS. Within a few years, the JHS's several classrooms were overflowing. Students were taking classes in Japanese as a heritage language spoken at home, and nonnative speakers were learning JSL (Japanese as a second language).

Masami had a son a few years after marrying her hakujin American husband. As soon as the child started public school, she also enrolled the boy at the JHS for Saturday classes. By the time he was in fifth grade, he would argue with her about his continued attendance because it interfered with weekend soccer practice. Despite Masami's best intentions for her son, every Saturday became a battle.

> I do soul-searching every day, like what am I doing? Am I doing right or am I doing wrong? Do I send them to Japanese school? Is it too strict; what am a doing to their identity? He's half obviously, but he's in this very Japanese community [West Los Angeles area].

Like other shin Issei mothers, Teruko was caught in similar circumstances with her own eight-year-old son who would rather have played soccer.

> Am I torturing him? He goes to school all day Saturday. Am I doing him a favor? Japanese Americans tell me, "My parents sent me to Japanese school when I was little and I hated it, but when I grew up I wish that I'd continued it!" At the same time, I don't want him to miss out what his other American friends are doing on Saturdays.

On the surface, the toss-up between torture and favor appears to be simply a matter of language fluency. However, for shin Issei mothers, it resonates with deeper meanings that literally speak to *being* Japanese.

> For my kids, thinking about language and beyond, of course I want them to speak Japanese, but I don't want them to be caught in the middle, not knowing what they are. I want them to master one language so they can feel comfortable. I don't want them to be semilingual—neither [language] is perfect. I don't want them to get trapped in that.

"Language and beyond" has much more saliency for shin Issei mothers than simple proficiency as a Japanese speaker. Fluency implies racial homogeneity as Japanese (Yamashiro 2017). Speaking, reading, writing, and *thinking* in

Japanese is a primary marker of identity and belonging; it is a means by which Japanese have historically perceived themselves as Japanese, and it is how shin Issei choose to identify themselves. This cultural competence means you *are* Japanese despite the fact that shin Nisei are also American. As teachers tell parents and children, the continuing goals of the JHS reflect the relationship between culture and language in serving its multicultural community of students.

> In all classes, students practice listening, speaking, reading, and writing [Japanese]. Japanese culture is woven into the curriculum, as this is a key component to becoming fluent in the language and being able to master the Japanese communication style.

Mothers like Masami recognized the dualities of identity inevitable with bicultural children and, with this in mind, wanted to ensure they were exposed to what the JHS offered.

> So I realize that they are going to be American, they are going to grow up here. They will probably have some kind of identity crisis at some point, but I don't want them to feel they are any different than other American people. I realize that I can't force too much of Japan and they might not end up liking it.

A brief distinction needs to be made between what are considered community-managed JHS and other Saturday supplemental schools called *hoshuukoo*, administered for children of chuzai-in families (Douglas 2005). The children of transnational Japanese employees usually also attend American schools during the week, but on Saturdays, most are also enrolled in special Japanese *gakuen* schools.[5] Unlike local JHS, which earn most of their operating expenses from tuition and fundraising, these gakuen were established, financed, and overseen by Japanese businesses as more kaisha employees were sent abroad beginning in the late 1960s. The Japanese government was also highly proactive in recreating an approved, Japan-centric educational system for children of kaisha families. It is presumed these children will return to Japan when their fathers' transfers end. Students are "given large amounts of homework, in order to keep up with their grade level in Japan" (Gakuen, n.d.).

The goal of these gakuen, then, is not to acquaint students with Japanese language (since they are already native speakers) or Nikkei culture but to ensure that students do not lag in school subjects being taught in Japan. Falling behind a Japan-based curriculum while living in the United States might eventually harm children's chances of getting into a prestigious Japanese college or university when the families return to Japan. Not gaining admittance to the right university would ultimately cost them in the job market and mar their overall life chances.

Asahi Gakuen hoshuukoo opened its first school program in 1969 with a main office in Little Tokyo. As numbers of kaisha employees grew in Southern California, Asahi was soon renting overflow space in public school buildings around the Los Angeles and Orange County areas. By the mid-1980s, several thousand chuzai-in children were enrolled.

> Asahi Gakuen's main purpose is to teach the kids so they can go back to Japan and adapt themselves to the "Japanese system" which typically is a year or two ahead of American schools.
>
> The school's rigorous curriculum requires the Saturday students to cover in one day the mathematics, science, social studies and Japanese grammar their fellow students back in Japan have all week to learn. (Puig 1986)

The obligation to be fully participatory in kaisha life also extends to children's education (Minoura 1980). Hoshuukoo like Asahi provided insularity and a space for continuing immersion in Japanese educative processes while students are living abroad.

This chapter looked more closely at the presence of large numbers of Japanese foreign nationals in Southern California, which, initially, depended on both economic and social resources constructed by the first Issei migrants a century earlier. In turn, these resources were expanded by the transnational expatriate community from Japan and spread beyond the ethnic enclave to other urban and suburban communities in Southern California. At the same time, it was possible for newly arrived shin Issei women to piggyback on the presence of a global Japan locally in establishing themselves. However, it must be remembered that this shin Issei project was not all celebratory. Moreover, it would not have been possible without the strength of the Japanese economy nor the desires of local actors who mined its resources.

Young Japanese women found their lives in the United States a complex interplay in asymmetries of power, some of which, such as hostessing, recalled similar gendered schemes in Japan. For shin Issei, this precarity was encapsulated in the day-to-day negotiations of families that are also interracial. American and Japanese hybridity is a dynamic construct, ever present and observable in the lives shin Issei women have built for themselves in Southern California neighborhoods. It is a life that is often isolating, but in their isolation and self-doubt are the beginnings of deeper engagement.

5

Racial Talk

Shin Issei Palefaces and Dark Nikkei

We don't call ourselves shin Issei, just Japanese from Japan. There are so many of us here now.

As numbers of shin Issei increased in Southern California in the 1990s, leading to their heightened visibility in Nikkei communities, there came a point when their presence no longer went unnoticed. For Nikkei community leaders, the realization led to conversations about integration: how to incorporate both American-born Japanese and shin Issei migrants under a broader, more cohesive framework that would rework the parameters of Nikkei community. At its core, recasting began with acknowledging transformation. Despite conferences and meetings to discuss gaps in (mis)understandings, meaningful solutions on both sides were elusive (*Rafu Shimpo* 2018; Higuchi and Phillips 2017; Nikkei 2008). Embedded in these ideologies of belonging were attempts to identify important issues in each group as well as to work out racial and ethnic differences. Moreover, this dialogue assumed that there were reasons for better integrating these disparate groups—yet justifying the possibility of common purpose was itself an area of contestation. The dissimilarities are beliefs and values of what it means to be Japanese and Japanese American and originate in ontologies that are "historically grounded but not bound to the past, already and always emerging" (Goldberg-Hiller and Silva 2015: 2).

What Nikkei and shin Issei *did* agree on was a level of discomfort and uneasiness with one another. They saw themselves as very distinct groups, divergent and unlike each other on significant subjects such as citizenship, language, class, and historical memory. Put simply, "Nikkei have different cultural values than do Japanese . . . [creating] different social boundaries between Nikkei and Japanese" (Adachi 2010: 20).

This chapter investigates these social boundaries and intergroup differences and the ways they were manifested between shin Issei and Nikkei in Nikkei-settled neighborhoods like Sawtelle. Analyzed are how each group's cultural values and dissimilar histories morphed into a racial and ethnic distinctiveness further reinforcing social borders. For shin Issei, who often lived and worked near Nikkei, longer residence in Southern California did not imply integration within the Japanese American community, nor did shin Issei seek constituted membership with Nikkei. In fact, their continuing marginalizations hardened their identities as Japanese women. Similarly, among Nikkei the recent arrivals were not accepted as co-ethnics or co-racials but were seen as newcomers who did not understand their history or the tightly built cohesiveness among Americans of color regardless of generation or residential location (D. Nakano 2019; Fugita and O'Brien 1991). This is more specifically illustrated by Nikkei demands for recognition in a place they wanted to be known as Sawtelle Japantown. Conversely, shin Issei did not agree (or did not care) about this prioritization of community.

Here I make a distinction between shin Issei and wives of kaisha transnationals working for Japanese MNCs. Nikkei assessments are not directed at chuzai-in. This study did not focus on women married to MNC male employees; the women and their family members are largely viewed by Nikkei as temporary foreign nationals. Chuzai-in wives do not occupy similar unskilled jobs as bar hostesses or restaurant waitstaff, and their children attend different supplemental schools. Chuzai-in returns to Japan are predicated on specific contractual requirements—commitments shin Issei obviously do not have. Transnational kaisha *have* taken up residence in longtime Nikkei areas such as the South Bay because of corporate employment, but on the whole, they have far less close contact with either Nikkei or shin Issei.

It is notable that both groups acknowledge so-called different cultural values and that these boundaries, erected to distance and disidentify, have been infused with racial meanings along with class and gender (Hayano 1981). Shin Issei perceptions based on color differentials in Japan act as signifiers, against which Nikkei react on the basis of their divergent American sensitivities.

Symbolisms beyond Skin Color

Shin Issei characterize intergroup skin color not only as a real phenotypic group difference—an observable marker—but also as a carrier of additional, socially constructed symbolic importance. Perceived color difference acts to reinforce group inclusion and exclusion and, at the same time, illustrates the embeddedness of other social categories (Hedegard 2013).

Upon their arrival in the United States, shin Issei noticed almost immediately how differently Nikkei looked and acted.

> When I first went to [the United States], there were so many Japanese Americans. You do look different—much darker. Also, so many gestures you make. We don't open our mouths so wide. Japanese people are always hiding something.

Shin Issei who want to reinforce their own differences with Nikkei verbalize "much darker" as a negative descriptor. White skin and very pale faces have defined socially acceptable and desired body standards for both Japanese women and men since the eighth-century Heian era. Skin color denoted cultural and social capital and therefore class differences: "Her skin was very white and delicate . . . how exciting it must be to have such a girl for one's daughter!" (Murasaki 1960: 48). The enactment of these values through makeup and avoidance of the sun were status distinctions conceived by the upper class and those who aspired to be so included (Miller 2006). The inability to achieve pale skin tones inferred outdoor work such as farm labor, or worse—foreigners, untouchables, and others living beyond the periphery.

Among Japanese, "skin color has been related to a whole complex of attractive or objectionable social traits" (Wagatsuma 1967: 407). However, it is important to note that Japanese notions of whiteness should not be explained using a default ideology encompassing Western classifications. Paleness of skin must be analyzed within a Japanese framework in which "white faces serve as an item of vocabulary in a symbolic language, which communicates gender relations" (Ashikari 2003: 4). Pale skin still refers to traditional Japanese female coloring to which others are compared, but among Japanese, to say someone is white does not necessarily mean they are Caucasian (Ashikari 2005).

In addition, comments about skin color representing rac*ist* attitudes resulting in rac*ism* between Nikkei and shin Issei is somewhat misleading. Instead, it is a perceived rac*ial* signifier denying racial sameness and carries different valuations of class and gender that must be analyzed in historical context. The intent here, however, is not to subsume race to ethnicity nor to ignore the politics involved in the creation of ethnonational differences (Winant 2015). The acknowledgment that there *are* dissimilarities in color are, nonetheless, processes "in which economic, political, social, and ideological levels are partially structured by the placement of actors in racial categories" (Bonilla-Silva 1997: 469). Therefore, viewed as complex forms of unequal racialized multiplicities that may result in structures of domination, these placements can create new forms of racism (Trinh Võ and Torres 2004; Omi and Winant 1994).

For both shin Issei and Nikkei, categorizing physical manifestations also communicates larger issues of race in America. Within the United States' broader historical context of racial cultural production, both groups are positioned as the racialized Other. Nikkei have come to understand sociopolitical concepts of a "racial ideology that glues a particular racial order" (Bonilla-Silva 2018: 180). The "glue" is an acknowledgment of the influence of broader social beliefs constructed around race. This wider discourse sees race and ethnicity as naturalized and absolute, whereas in fact they are transformatively elastic. What is deemed a natural and fixed hierarchy is, instead, continually transforming—produced and reproduced socially in tandem and in tension with ongoing social struggles for inclusion (Grosfoguel 2004). Both race and ethnicity "depend far more on the claims people make about one another or themselves than on any physical or genealogical differences" (Cornell and Hartmann 2007: 32). This process of racialization—specific cultural meanings ideologically categorized as phenotypic variables that are aimed at intergroup distancing—float just below the surface in conversations among shin Issei and Nikkei (Tsuda 2016). It is a conflation of a politics of difference between race and culture—what has been labeled *racenicity*.

> [Racenicity] ... the process through which the sociohistorical and ideological construction of race ... has had a significant impact on defining national identity, ethnicity, and the perception of ethnic differences in the United States. (Leistyna 2001: 424)

Anachronistic Nikkei

Shin Issei apprehend, to a degree, the 150-year-long time warp that has bound Nikkei cultural values and ideological processes dating from the arrival of the first Issei migrants in Meiji-era Japan and the subsequent experiences of mass incarceration in the United States. However, Nikkei say most lack a more nuanced understanding about the tenacity of historical roots or the racial locations Nikkei still occupy as Americans of color.

> They've never experienced racism because they haven't lived here! I mean when you grow up in a country that's all one kind of people [Japan]. . . . You have to reeducate them.

This leaves shin Issei with the perception that much of Nikkei thinking and behavior is anachronistic—old fashioned and out of touch.

> One young Japanese American told me [a] produce position in the supermarket is a very good position for Japanese Americans. And he was completely serious!
>
> It really blew me away at the time, because you are in the United States and have so many opportunities and you can basically be what you want to be.

At best, shin Issei view American-born Japanese as somewhat odd.

> Who's Nikkei? I used to think, why can't Japanese Americans speak Japanese? How come? What's wrong? Can't you speak both?

For most shin Issei, who have few acquaintances among Nikkei, Nikkei are a topic of curious discussion.

> I remember having a conversation about this among other friends about some of the prejudices Japanese Americans have about themselves.

This shin Issei woman was sitting in a restaurant in West Los Angeles, overhearing a small group of Nisei women talking about how they and their Issei parents survived the Incarceration. She caught part of an overheard phrase, *yamato damashii*, in reference to how Issei and their Nisei children were able to endure imprisonment.[1] While yamato damashii is no longer often used in contemporary conversation (*ganbatte*—do your best, persevere with determination and spirit—is more commonly heard), Nikkei are familiar with the term. Shin Issei are acquainted with the phrase as well, but it is a historical relic that is part of neither everyday contemporary lexicon nor their life experience. Hearing the phrase still in use was surprising.

> I was shocked at some of their philosophy that they subscribe to. They were like, so *old* [thinking]. Like yamato damashii. *Nobody* in *my* generation believes that anymore. It's like prewar mentality.
>
> If you grow up in Japan, everybody knows what yamato damashii is, but they don't try to ingrain it anymore! It doesn't apply to us.

Shin Issei say that "old" thinking is self-confining and needlessly limits American-born Japanese. Growing up in postwar Japan has afforded shin Issei with manifestly different life experiences from Japanese Americans who survived camp incarceration and postwar discrimination.

Our generation has been brought up very spoiled. We had more options; we didn't lack for food, lodging, material goods, and if we had anything to complain about, it was we had to do too much studying!

I think what yamato damashii conjures up in my mind—if you were under a lot of adversities and you still persevered despite it all, that's what it means. That philosophy is connected in my head with war, during the war and that time you didn't have access to a lot.

In Sawtelle, neighborhood home to four generations of Japanese Americans founded by working-class Issei laborers, Nikkei interpret Japanese comments about darker skin color and old-fashioned views as markers of long-held ideas of class difference. These fraught relations between the two groups are based on historic social divisions that were exacerbated by Japan's emigration policies beginning in the late 1800s. Those selected for migration to the United States (as well as other areas of Asia and Latin and South America) were part of a larger plan by Japan to modernize the nation (Young 1998). Exportation of labor served to diffuse growing social unrest, supplement the national economy through remittances, and extend Japan's influence as a new nation-state (Azuma 2006; Takaki 1989). The majority of male migrant recruits were largely not well educated (though also not entirely illiterate), were lacking in abilities other than rural farming skills, and were a mostly young, exportable labor resource who found themselves commodified at the bottom of a restructuring Japanese economy (Dresner 2006). It was not an enviable social position.

When the 1932 Summer Olympic Games were staged in Los Angeles, many in the transpacific Issei community who had migrated to work and live in Southern California found that their enthusiastic support and pride in the athletes from Japan was one-sided and, even worse, often ridiculed and rebuffed.

> Japanese athletes and other visitors from Japan often expressed scorn for the Japanese [Nikkei] as "immigrants and their children." Such prejudices were common in prewar Japan because of the stereotype that, as government policy, it was impoverished farmers from the countryside who left Japan as *kimin* [discarded people].
>
> Japanese swimming coach Nomura Norio boasted at a hotel party that his team would not need any help from immigrants. (E. Yamamoto 2000)

After more than a century, social ostracism of discarded people remains steeped in discursive Japanese symbolisms of the poor, rural immigrant, culturally inferior and unrepresentative of modernity (Azuma 2003). Among Nikkei, it is embodied in the term *inaka*, a moniker meaning country bumpkins and peasants. Nikkei are highly cognizant of how skin color is employed to mark ancestral class differences between themselves and contemporary shin Issei.

> Oh, they look down on us [Nikkei], we are inaka.

In preindustrial Japan, peasant farmers worked in the fields daily, with constant exposure to the sun and other weather elements, which darkened skin. Possessing darker skin is indicative of pre-Meiji, rural Japan and is co-constitutive of class. It is code for a specific time in Japanese history that is still respected in contemporary Nikkei belonging and identity. Sansei who claim family origins from the late nineteenth and early twentieth centuries have proudly appropriated their farm labor and working-class ancestries in rural Japan.

> We take great pride in our culture, which is Japanese Meiji culture, not Japanese culture today. Shin Issei will never have that.

The connection and belonging to a historic, albeit idealized, Meiji Japan remain keenly felt across the generations. Still valorized within a rubric of a performative Nikkei identity are the same values and principles practiced by Meiji Issei migrants. The tenets taught by Issei persist and are still common and easily understood signposts among Sansei.

> [They're] the ones we all know—like the *gaman*, the *shikataganai*. These are values that undergird our community. We all have them; we aren't aware of them, but when you mention the words, the light bulb turns on. It's in our DNA. It helps define who we are and how we can build upon that. To me that's exciting.[2]

Furthermore, saying "we are Meiji" also delineates the truncated temporal demographics of Nikkei. After 1924, the United States barred all migration from Japan until 1952 (Maki, Kitano, and Berthold 1999). The result was that the Nikkei community became a cultural and racial isolate in which Nikkei describe themselves by specific generational identifications. Despite the sustained strength of this temporal model in describing Nikkei belonging, however, it should also be noted that generational labels have never been neatly formulaic or entirely homogeneous.

> By uncritically adhering to this framework, the existing literature on Japanese Americans tends to overlook other historical periods, other

subsequent waves of Japanese immigrants in the postwar era, and other ways of narrating and conceptually framing the Japanese American experience. (Omi, Nakano, and Yamashita 2019: 2)

A Sansei who worked closely with Japanese kaisha during the 1980s remembers that the time warp of Nikkei migration was a curiosity to Japanese businessmen.

> These Japanese always used to call us the true Japanese because our culture is fossilized in time. It's the Meiji culture which we still have, which is different from Japan today: the loyalty, the obligation—all these things you hold in high esteem. It's our parents personified.

Nikkei attribute the lack of significant migration until after the war as further evidence of difference with shin Issei.

> This whole period of time there's no growth [in Nikkei community]. That's another reason for the disconnect. We think one thing and they think something else.

That disconnect was felt among Sansei who were active and who participated in Nikkei activities in Southern California during the 1990s. Despite ongoing contacts and social relationships, the divide and inherent bias was most sharply felt in conversation with local representatives of the Japanese government.

> The [Japanese Consulate] say[s] the right things, but we're not seen as equals—by far. In the context of the U.S., they don't get it relative to being a person of color. If you are a person of color in the U.S., you have to find your own bearings. And that's what many of them don't get.
>
> They don't understand racism, the subtle forms of racism. They understand being called "Jap" or not being served, but they don't understand the more subtle forms and how you have to develop a strong sense of self in order to deal with it.

A Nikkei born and raised in Sawtelle talks about feelings of camaraderie and solidarity—not with shin Issei but with Nikkei and other Americans of color.

> If you talk to a Nikkei, even if you don't know each other, there's an affinity. Even with other minorities—I sit on a board with one black guy—we're the only two colored people, and we get along really well.

We have the same experiences, the same affinities. I don't feel that way with shin Issei.

Over bowls of noodles at a small *ramen-ya* (noodle restaurant) near Sawtelle, a few Nikkei women are talking about differences between themselves and shin Issei. The exact parameters for delineating the difference may be a bit vague, but once again, phenotypic characterizations enter the conversation. The women agree they can just look at someone and decide if they are native born or new migrants—not ethnically but because of skin color.

They're all palefaces! [*Everyone laughs.*]

Anybody [outside] looking at all of us would say, "You're all Japanese." Well, we're not! They look different.

No, we are not the same. Even when I go to Japan, I feel like a total outsider. They [Japanese] can tell immediately looking at me and just by the way I walk around. And I don't look like them. So you're an outsider there, you're an outsider here because of who we are [as Japanese Americans].

We always called them FOBS [fresh off the boat], but now they're FOPS—fresh off the plane, right?

Of the migrant women she sees in West Los Angeles, a Sansei woman comments, only half in jest, "They're always wearing hats" and "They wear gloves when they drive!" The hats and gloves are visible signs of an everyday shin Issei presence, not because of millinery fashion per se but because of what Nikkei interpretations of these symbols say about skin color differences. Another Sansei woman, though she refrained from articulating skin color variations, raised her arms above her head and formed an invisible circle with her extended fingers, shaping a halo imitating a large hat. "Palefaces" is as much a reaction to comments shin Issei make about Nikkei darkness.

What may be ethnically acquired cultural and ideological differences can morph into the perception of natural, biological differences. As a socially constructed category, flexible and malleable, racial discourse "allows strategic equivocation between nature and culture" where the boundaries between the two have often been blurred in practice (Wade 2002: 12). That is to say, what is occurring between shin Issei and Nikkei is a conflation of culturally acquired ideologies with racial appearances and characteristics. Sansei comment,

Maybe we all look Japanese, but we're different. They don't have the same beliefs, the same values as we do.

OK, you know how Japanese feel about us, anyway. And they're cold.

Classism is part of it. You know the car you drive, how you dress, where you live, what school you went to. All that. "Oh, your parents are from Hiroshima?" Oh, you're knocked down a notch or two. It's very Japanese, and it's still there.[3]

Parsing conversations about class reveals an added complexity regarding differentiated identities: class distinctions embedded in gender. When Nikkei talk about shin Issei attitudes, their comments are directed primarily to Japanese women, who are the majority of the new migrant population and therefore the most visible. Shin Issei have asserted membership in Japan's middle class; it may be assumed that this family status in Japan may have afforded them more opportunities. However, as has been shown, their class standing did not offer them additional social capital; instead, Japanese women were products of gendered structures that constrained their life chances. Moreover, their lack of an educative skill set in Japan followed them when they emigrated. In 1990s Sawtelle, Nikkei saw migrant women's positions reflected in service-related areas, such as restaurants, noodle shops, and beauty parlors, or in lower-skilled jobs, as sales and office assistants. At most, only on-the-job training was required, and fluency in English was not. A number of shin Issei did graduate from junior colleges with AA degrees, but only a handful attended four-year colleges in the United States. Conversely, many Nikkei women and men who appear in these pages possess four-year university degrees as well as postgraduate or professional training. Regardless of these intergroup disparities, the weight of original family ancestries still carries deep significance and meaning among Nikkei and shin Issei. Shin Issei do not consider themselves rural but, rather, see themselves as young, urbanite members from some of the most global cities in the world.

These differences in positionality produce tensions for those who have attempted to establish links. A shin Issei woman who migrated as a student in the 1980s remembers feeling slighted among Nikkei.

I found they tend to stick together, in their own clique. They aren't very friendly. I didn't have too many Japanese American girls around me in [junior] college.

She married an American, had two shin Nisei children, and subsequently divorced. She moved into the Sawtelle area so her young hafu children might have others with whom to play, but as a divorced mother, she was also seeking new connections for herself. Initially, she thought it would be easy to make friends among the Nikkei.

> When my children were four or five, I was thinking I need to expose them to some kind of religion because my ex is not religious. So I started taking them to [the local Buddhist] Temple and then to Sunday schools.
>
> Even after months and months I felt like nobody would talk to me, nobody was friendly. Everybody was related to everybody. The wife of the abbot was from Japan, and she told me it was so nice to see somebody from Japan bring their kids.
>
> There was one older lady who was friendly, but other than that I felt, my God, I never felt like I belonged. I understand that part of it may be they're shy, but at some point if you see the same face over and over . . . but their defenses were pretty high.

Desperate to make new friends for herself and children, she gave up on neighborhood Nikkei groups and instead asked another shin Issei mother for help. That woman mentioned Aki-chan's House as a place where she met with other shin Issei. A few weeks later, this shin Issei divorcée was introduced to Tomoko and became another regular visitor.

> I went to [her] house many times. She was very generous, and she opened up her home and yard and little kids played there. I was part of the group. We all went on playdates with our kids.
>
> You know [Tomoko was] a common mom . . . pretty soon you meet others. It's amazing, and we're all Japanese, so we know the Japanese Saturday schools and tutoring places . . . it's like a whole network.
>
> Women like to talk, the kids get together, they play, and we're talking the whole time, that's what we do. She said, "You can bring anybody you know." We brought our own food, watched the kids play. She was very generous. This is our life here.

This was clearly not Nikkei space. For shin Issei and Nikkei alike, the Other was unknowable. Nowhere did this dissimilarity lead to more social tensions than in established Nikkei communities like Sawtelle. In the 1990s, Nikkei still maintained residences in the neighborhood, and there was no small amount of nonacceptance and resentment for the transformations created by the presence of shin Issei.

> They walk around West LA like they own the place. Before, when we were [growing up] in Sawtelle—you know Issei and their *enryo* syndrome. My mother would say we couldn't walk around.[4]

> The Issei who came here had such a hard time in every dimension. These people who are coming now just don't have those fundamental rights problems. We really grew up with that enryo syndrome but now—absolutely they don't have that enryo!

Sawtelle Is Our Home

The Sawtelle Japantown naming project was important to Nikkei because it recognized the nearly century-old symbolization of Sawtelle as Nikkei space. This claiming points out that "these people"—shin Issei—don't belong and cannot assume ownership because they did not experience "a hard time" in the community's birth and maturation.

Japanese Americans were, of course, not the first settlers in this area of western Los Angeles. For several thousand years, the original inhabitants, Tongva American Indians, had made much of the Los Angeles basin their home, including Kurvunga village, on the grounds of what today is University High School, just blocks from Sawtelle (Villa, n.d.). In 1899, Sawtelle was named after W. E. Sawtelle, the manager of the Pacific Land Company, which had begun selling lots in the area. Two thousand people, primarily white, soon called the area home, and in 1906, Sawtelle incorporated. Shops, churches, fraternal lodges, a bank, a school, and a chapter of the Women's Christian Temperance Union added to the growing social structure (Ingersoll 1908).

At the same time, Issei migrants began moving into the neighborhood they called *So-te-ru* (CJACLC, n.d.). By then, Los Angeles' fast-moving urban center was already spreading its tentacles west from the downtown core (Wilkinson 2013). The Pacific Electric Car Company found it strategic to build a new Sawtelle depot station linking downtown Los Angeles to Santa Monica, fifteen miles to the west (Tanemori 2017). In 1922, Sawtelle was consolidated into the City of Los Angeles. The Westside of Los Angeles became a regionalized suburb, part of a wider "urban spatial causality [that] starts with the recognition that urban space . . . is *socially produced*" (Soja 2014: 249). Though suburbanizing, Sawtelle was still open land, much of it agricultural. The main boulevards from downtown Los Angeles were mostly unpaved dirt track, and south of Sawtelle were cultivated plots of beans, celery, and other vegetables that required cheap labor, regardless of color. The area was judged an agricultural paradise.

> Broad and fertile fields lie around it in all directions . . . invigorating ocean breezes tempered by a sweep over the land give it an irreproachable all year climate. Underlying strata at a depth of about 70 feet furnish an almost inexhaustible supply of pure soft water. (Ingersoll 1908: 347)

The crowded conditions of the oldest enclave, Little Tokyo, where jobs were increasingly scarce and where housing was at a premium, competed with this pastoral scene and its opportunities. Sawtelle was illustrative of a place where Issei entrepreneurial efforts might bear fruit. Migrant-owned businesses sprang up; among them were boarding houses. Tenant Issei families had their everyday living needs fulfilled, from meals to laundry, banking, and career advice. It wasn't only a place to live but an indispensable social hub. As Aki-chan's House became a place of belonging for shin Issei women seven decades later, Issei boarding houses functioned as common space where new migrants were able to gather and discuss similar life situations and to work out with others like themselves the challenges they faced in new homes.

One of the first boarding houses in Sawtelle—the well-known Kobayakawa house—was begun by owner Riichi Ishioka, who migrated from Hiroshima prefecture to San Francisco in 1910. Like many Issei, he initially worked on the railroads as a dynamiter with the Union Pacific Railroad in Wyoming before his second migration to Southern California and Sawtelle. Skirting alien land laws, Ishioka used proxy buyers to purchase land around Sawtelle, where he built his first boarding house in 1926 (Fujimoto 2007). Ishioka and his wife, Wakano, worked round the clock to meet the daily needs of their tenants. Equally important, Ishioka's boarding house also became a training ground for young Issei who were looking beyond farm labor to newer and more lucrative economic prospects. One of those prospects was a foundational business model built because of racialized segregation—residential gardening, including grounds maintenance and lawn care. In a rapidly expanding metro Los Angeles, the Hollywood movie industry moved west into new neighborhoods in the 1920s. Movie stars, producers, and other moneyed Angelenos built mansions in the Westside hills (Los Angeles Conservancy, n.d.). With mansions came the need for gardeners and groundskeepers.

Stories about how boarding-house owners like Ishioka were instrumental in creating a niche economy around gardening are still remembered by Sansei growing up in Sawtelle.

Everybody wanted to [move] into Sawtelle because of all the gardening jobs in Bel-Air, Brentwood, West LA. [Ishioka] would say, this is how you do gardening; this is how you take care of this plant. This is how you mow the lawn, and this is how you write memorandums for your expenses.

So he ran that boarding house, and he also taught these people. That boarding house trained so many people.

Contract gardening in Sawtelle was a racial and ethnic-specific trade by the 1930s—a space carved out by migrants who, in the face of exclusion and discrimination, saw opportunities in suburban economic growth in Los Angeles and were able to capitalize on them (Tsukashima 1995/1996; Jiobu 1988). Issei women, too, took advantage of new openings among the affluent. With Nisei children in school during the day, mothers hired out as domestic housekeepers, cooks, or seamstresses. The numerous help-wanted ads in local newspapers document the desires of white homeowners to hire Japanese day workers (*Outlook* 1925). Moreover, for the first time, Issei men and women found themselves working in different social enclaves, among wealthy white Americans.

My father was a gardener—his employers were all hakujin, so he had to learn to speak English. Everything had to be what we do in America.

Although Issei and Nisei worked north of Sawtelle in affluent Bel-Air, Brentwood, Beverly Hills, and Westwood, by dusk, everyone returned to Sawtelle. "That was all white man territory. You were a persona non grata to the white man" (Groves 2015). Redlining property was still enforced by real estate agents and banks making sure home purchase agreements contained restrictive covenants prohibiting home sales to nonwhites in white areas (Fair Housing Center of Greater Boston, n.d.; Madrigal 2014; Bruce 1977). Nikkei were well aware of the implicit boundaries and unofficial curfew that existed outside Sawtelle.

None of us could live in those areas because they were all redlined. Even though the white people said, "Oh, we don't have discrimination."

But you knew darn well the white real estate people weren't going to show you around, so we all got compartmentalized into this [Sawtelle] area here.

Before the war, we couldn't live east of Sepulveda [Blvd.], north of Wilshire [Blvd.], south of Pico [Blvd.], west of Bundy [Dr.]. We couldn't even *rent* beyond Sepulveda!

I asked my mom, "Why did you buy here and not over there?" She just said it's because they wouldn't let you buy.

By the late 1930s, white flight had already produced a highly segregated Japanese American community in Sawtelle. Like those living in Little Tokyo, Nikkei remember well both the sense of identity and self-reliance Sawtelle afforded, as "a cohesive community in a hostile environment" (I. Murase 1983: 9). Nisei who went to the local elementary school realized there were no other students in the school except Nikkei like themselves. Class and race were unthinking parameters of commonality and acceptance that were not challenged until students grew older and left the enclave for further education.

I never saw white kids. Then we went to junior high, and all of a sudden we saw all these white kids. And then we went to high school, and we saw all these Jewish kids.

You always asked yourself the same question, "Do I belong at the same table with these people?" Initial impression is *no*! Their vocabularies are so big, and they know so many things.

Thus, while economic opportunities grew in adjacent, more wealthy environs, so did a parallel racial enclave blossom to support workers and families. Dozens of Nikkei-owned stores, other small businesses, and community organizations catering to Nikkei workers and growing families were established around prewar Sawtelle (Shiraki 2008; Toyama 1926). The many men's and women's social organizations planned fetes where jiu jitsu matches and traditional Japanese dance were performed. There were community holidays around New Year celebrations, and in summer, *o-bon* festivities honored family ancestors. The Sawtelle and West Los Angeles communities were tied to a wider network of hundreds of Nikkei social organizations across the United States. A 1938 New Year's survey of Nikkei clubs is especially revealing, with its breadth of group listings and memberships. Along with listed Sawtelle area organizations, more than three hundred women's and men's clubs around the United States are cataloged from readers' surveys, many of them sponsored by Christian or Buddhist churches, the YMCA and YWCA, and local universities (*Rafu Shimpo* 1938). Emulating mainstream, segregated American organizations, these social groups provided a means by which Nikkei were able to practice a strengthening of community ties and a communality of identity and belonging that were uniquely American (V. Matsumoto 2014a).

Despite its distance from the downtown Los Angeles core, Sawtelle was still tied to the putative center of Nikkei life in Southern California—Little

Tokyo. By the 1930s, the Little Tokyo area was home to as many as 35,000 people crowded within a three-mile radius, and on weekends it was a beehive of activity, with people shopping, eating, or going to see Japanese movies. "Every weekend people from the 'inaka' came" (V. Matsumoto 2014b: 317). By contrast, tranquil, prewar Sawtelle was home to less than 1,500 individuals (Warren 1986–1987). Whether Little Tokyo or Sawtelle, however, each community's existential borders were similarly constructed by "an historically marginalized minority group weathering the consequences of radical shifts in its relationship to the American body politic and the geopolitical status of the ancestral nation with which it was associated" (Jenks 2008: 242).

Sawtelle was a racialized space where a strong Nikkei identity was constructed through common experiences. It was a flourishing Japanese American community whose founding Issei saw the neighborhood as a means to survive economically and support each other. Nikkei envisioned Sawtelle as an imagined and necessary embodiment of their inaka ancestries.

Three Nisei friends are sitting in the small living room of a bungalow a few blocks from Sawtelle Boulevard, talking, jumping in to finish one another's sentences, and reminiscing about their childhoods growing up in Sawtelle.

> I remember going shopping at [the corner store]. There weren't so many stores, just older stores. It wasn't young and hip like it is now.

> Before that it was like a countryside village, very provincial, quiet, slow . . . nothing was new. You didn't see beautiful people, young hip population like now. But in a good way, like inaka—it's sort of like your heart goes back.

The other side of this seemingly cheerful social picture, however, was a community built—and rebuilt—in response to racism and intolerance. The three women all retain memories of Sawtelle as an insular, supportive community begun by their Issei parents, migrants who built businesses and settled here to raise their American-born children and grandchildren. It was a racial and ethnic community where hybrid identities were born and practiced in the everyday experiences of a sequestered American life.

The women's families returned after incarceration to resettle in Sawtelle though it was a slow, often anxious, process for the prewar community. At the end of 1943, the *Los Angeles Times* had more than eleven thousand responses to its "Jap Questionnaire," with nearly ten thousand readers answering yes to the question "Would you permanently exclude all Japanese from the Pacific Coast states including California?" (*Los Angeles Times* 1943). Only one Nikkei had returned to Sawtelle by April 1946 (WRA 1945). Eventually, West Los Angeles, including the Sawtelle area, was among the top neighborhoods for resettlement, with as many as six thousand Nikkei residents (Fujimoto 2007; War Agency Liquidation Unit 1975; Nishi and Kim 1964). South American Nikkei released from U.S. prison camps after their forcible removals from their homes in Peru and other Latin and Southern American countries also moved to Sawtelle (Miyake 2008; Adachi 2007; L. Hirabayashi and Kikumura-Yano 2006; Masterson 2004; Ueunten 2002). The racialized space of World War II and the race-based trauma of mass incarceration marked all Nikkei as outsiders and added further signification in cementing an American identity (Nagata, Kim, and Wu 2019; Alexander et al. 2004). "If we are ever going to prove our Americanism, this is the time" (Kikuchi 1973: 42).

"One Hundred Ten Percent Loyal Americans!"

Further differences between shin Issei and Nikkei involve the dialectics of a hard-fought identity project that for Nikkei centered around what they were not—not Japanese and not foreign enemies (Fugita and O'Brien 1991). The embodiment of the Nikkei experience in the late twentieth century—a politics of a racialized American identity—is still central in the fight for inclusion and against injustice (J. Hirabayashi and Hirabayashi 2013). Despite shifts in the United States to a celebration of multiculturalism, Nikkei still do not have the option of jettisoning their racialized bodies; their marginalization is the elision of racial and cultural distinctions (ethnic differences) (Tuan 2001). Nikkei are still perceived as Japanese because they look Japanese (Masuda, Matsumoto, and Meredith 1970).

> Once Japanese Americans are categorized according to their ethnic origins, they are also culturally essentialized by racial appearance. . . .
> Because of the tendency to conflate race and culture, those of Japanese phenotype/descent are seen as inherently connected to their Japanese cultural heritage, even if they were born in the United States. (Tsuda 2015: 608)

Against this conflation, the claiming of American citizenship has been a hard-fought requisite of belonging that is still privileged by Sansei.

> We had to give that up [being Japanese] during the war to prove our loyalty—that we were Americans.

After 1952, when it finally became legal for Issei to naturalize, these elderly migrants actively pursued American citizenship. Naturalization was a way to demonstrate participation in the American process and to cement ties among themselves, their children, and their grandchildren. Among Nisei and Sansei, this story of citizenship and community is fundamental to the Sawtelle Narrative.

> It was said and not said in different ways—being 110 percent loyal Americans. Whenever my grandparents, parents got together they always talked about living in America. [My grandparents said], "We wanted to come to America." They were really proud to be living in America—not the United States, or California, or Los Angeles, but *America.*
>
> In [my grandfather's] interview when he went into camp, he was sent to prison (he was a community leader). In that interview he said, "My sons are born in America. We are Americans. I do not support Japan. I support my life here."
>
> America represents the idea of the land of opportunity. My grandfather got his naturalized citizenship in his eighty-fourth year. He died in his eighty-fifth year in 1954. He was bound and determined to get his citizenship.

> My grandfather died in 1955. In 1954 he got his [citizenship], and I recall at this time he was almost blind, very poor health, and he persevered through all those things to get citizenship before he died. Because that was important to him.

Citizenship and loyalty are co-constitutive of being American. Nikkei believe that being undocumented, maintaining a green card, and resisting naturalization are evidence of a temporality and an unwillingness to fully participate and embrace living in the United States.

> Take loyalty. If you asked everybody to hold up the [American flag], how many of them would do it? Even the ones who are naturalized American citizens? I'll bet you not very many.

American citizenship binds Nikkei with a sense of belonging and investment in practicing the rites of nationality and responsibility. It is not visible as a social category, but citizenship is, nonetheless, another key symbol of difference. It is a bellwether that sets them apart from Japanese foreign nationals.

> Insofar as the institution of U.S. citizenship is commonly presumed to differentiate subjects in relation to the power of the nation-state, differences, divisions, and inequalities are elaborated in terms of "citizenship" and "immigration."
>
> Who is a U.S. citizen? Who is a "foreigner," or an "alien"? Who is eligible for citizenship? Who is deportable? And moreover, who is a "real American"? (de Genova and Ramos-Zayas 2003: 19)

The assertion of American citizenship remains deeply ingrained in the definition of belonging among Nikkei, irrespective of generation. Sansei, especially, speak quite bluntly about those who aren't citizens.

> We don't like illegal immigration.
>
> I completely understand how Niseis feel [about loyalty, being American], and I completely respect them, what they went through, and I understand it. It's just a fact.
>
> That's part of our history [American citizenship]. That's the way it is. It's been so intense, the camps . . . we're like our own group. We've got the tie to Japan, but it's on a different kind of level.
>
> You know the Japanese view us as Americans. But I actually don't really care. I live here, and this is America—and you don't live here!
>
> Japanese from Japan and Japanese Americans have never homogenized as a group—*never!* So, what's the difference now and then? It's because of the Japanese *American* experience. We don't have that connection to Japan. It is what it is.
>
> The only way we'll homogenize is through the generations. But for the newer immigrants, there's just a different way to think about things. You can't talk about politics; you can't talk about anything because there's different reference points.
>
> *It's the way you grew up—it's the context!* We're left in the Meiji era! In college, I don't *ever* remember Japanese students and Japanese Americans hanging out together.
>
> What we consider Japanese American is never going to change. I don't care what they say. We will always be Sansei or Yonsei. They're another

group. I take great pride in what our families have done. It's something you can go to your grave and be really proud.

Whose Japantown?

In the practice of everyday life in Sawtelle from the 1900s into the 1980s, the built environment was symbolic—indeed critical—in the ways Nikkei generated common memories and beliefs within the constraints of urban public space (Low 2000). Beginning in the early 1980s, as had already happened in Little Tokyo, Sawtelle underwent rapid transformation. Sawtelle Nikkei who still worked, lived, and used public spaces felt increasing social strain and conflict over the changing neighborhood ecology, which they felt was no longer representative of what it meant to be Nikkei. The "whole Westside is exploding" with neighborhood Nikkei lamenting, "It's already ruined" (Stambler 1985). The manifestations of Nikkei community became progressively buried under an avalanche of urban gentrification. Builders and developers targeted homes and small businesses for demolition. The prices of homes (and the land on which they sat) soared. In 2016, a remodeled home a few blocks from Sawtelle Boulevard was on the market for $3.5 million (*Los Angeles Times* 2016). Multiunit apartments and condos replaced older single-family homes. Daily gridlocked traffic grew, as did a lack of parking on quiet side streets west of Sawtelle Boulevard.

Equally exasperating for local Nikkei, in numerous media accounts Sawtelle was recipient to a more global sounding moniker tied to foreign capital—Little Osaka.

> Visit Japan in California: Discover the eateries, tea shops, boutiques, and galleries of West Los Angeles' Little Osaka. (Hontz 2007)

> The latest I've heard for Sawtelle in West L.A. is "Little Osaka." Considering that Little Tokyo already exists, the name makes sense. (Sonksen 2012)

Sawtelle Nikkei were less sanguine about the new name.

> I went to [a restaurant] to get a hamburger, and they had a drink—the "Osaka Sour." Can you believe it?

Sawtelle became a foodie's paradise. There were new mini malls with stores whose headquarters were based in Japan; other businesses were often owned by Asian overseas investors. Patrons of these new businesses, including shin Issei who found work, were more multiracially and multiculturally diverse.

The attraction of large investments bringing redevelopment and policies favorable to capital interests is emblematic of the neoliberal urban experience in both consumption and cultural form. As evidenced by previous history in Little Tokyo, the "rights to the city" by those who have lived there are often forfeit (Harvey 2008: 23). For many Sawtelle Nikkei like George, the closing of the Yamaguchi variety store, a neighborhood touchstone since the 1950s, was the final chapter.

> The signature store of Sawtelle Boulevard was the Yamaguchi store, so the day that got sold, it's like my neighborhood was sort of gone, and now it's a totally different kind of culture and background. That happened just like that! [*Snapping his fingers.*] Really fast! I don't recognize it.

The Yamaguchi store quickly converted into a retail apartment complex. In 2009, rents there started at $2,800.00 per month (Broverman 2010). Each disappearing physical manifestation of a once-thriving Nikkei community meant a diminishment in a cultural process of ideological communal ownership and belonging. Grocery and hardware stores, mom-and-pop restaurants, pharmacies, barbershops, boarding houses, and most of the plant nurseries were gone by the first decades of the new century. Satsuma Imports, with its postage-stamp Japanese garden in the back, was a fixture in Sawtelle since the 1960s. Its original owners had bought land on the boulevard in the late 1930s. Satsuma offered sundry goods and was one of the few places you could buy Japanese-brand cosmetics. It closed in 2015, but like other shuttered Nikkei businesses along the boulevard, its physical place may be absent, but its imagined space is not. It remains real for other Nikkei who still work there.

> The history of their location will always exist. . . . As a retailer on the block, it's great to be part of the area that they helped create. I hope I can hold my end for a bit longer. (E. Nakamura 2015)

In the mid-1970s, the Nikkei demographics of Sawtelle had also begun to change. As many as half of those who lived in postwar Sawtelle had either passed away or sold family homes as the area was redeveloped. Many Nikkei residents moved to where housing was cheaper. Populations of Nikkei in Sawtelle had declined to 3,200 in the 1970s and to 2,700 by 1980, although clusters of Nikkei remained, living in the dozen blocks west of Sawtelle Boulevard between Pico and Santa Monica Boulevards, where Nikkei numbers were as high as 39 percent (Warren 1986–1987). In the 1990s, those who self-identified as Japanese or Japanese in other racial combinations were still the largest Asian category in and around Sawtelle, though overall numbers had dropped to about 2,500 (U.S. Census Bureau 2010b). For the first time, in the early 2000s, numbers of Taiwanese and Chinese residents, many of them recent migrants, topped Nikkei numbers in West Los Angeles (U.S. Census Bureau 2010b).[5] In the late 1990s, however, there was evidence that some Sansei were moving back into Sawtelle, reclaiming older family homes rather than selling to developers interested in constructions of multiple units (Dr. Jack Fujimoto, pers. comm., February 7, 2009). Nonetheless, by 2020, total housing units in Sawtelle had increased by 19 percent (U.S. Census Bureau 2020).

In terms of *who* lived in the Sawtelle area, it must be remembered that undercounts in the U.S. Census are a continuing problem, particularly among those who avoid government scrutiny, such as undocumented individuals. For shin Issei arriving in Los Angeles in the decade between 1980 and 1990, increasingly higher rents in gentrifying Sawtelle and West Los Angeles drove them out of the neighborhood despite their living arrangements with multiple roommates sharing costs. They were faced with record rent increases of 31 percent (Graviet Knapp 2016). Shin Issei lived in adjacent areas of Mar Vista, Culver City, and areas around downtown Los Angeles. They perused social media and community bulletin boards for multiple roommates, borrowed sofas and futons. If they could not afford to live in the neighborhood, their presence was still visible because they worked there. Japanese language newspaper and magazines were in abundance outside businesses. Want ads in throwaway Japanese magazines constituted spatial networks advertising numerous jobs for young women in both kaisha and Nikkei communities like Sawtelle (Japan Up! 2018).

Despite fewer Nikkei living around Sawtelle, there was no diminishment in its identifying significance. Similar to Little Tokyo, which had transformed from a residential community to a district with businesses, numerous Nikkei community centers, and other gathering hubs for community events, Sawtelle had morphed into a "paradox of dispersal . . . as the ethnic population becomes spatially less concentrated, these historic centers gain in value as sites for the maintenance of ethnic identity and a sense of ethnic community" (Toji and Umemoto 2003: 25).

It was a cool, early evening in March 2014. About twenty Nisei and Sansei who'd grown up in the neighborhood had come to a meeting at the West Los Angeles United Methodist Church. The church is still a common meeting ground for Nikkei activities, as are other churches, temples, and schools in

Sawtelle. Even among those Nikkei who moved away, these well-used venues endure as touchstones for those who claim ownership. Japanese *o-cha* (tea), coffee, and cookies were on offer, but this wasn't a happy social gathering. Throughout Sawtelle, at community gatherings and small group chats, informal discussions had been going on for some time over what many see as the dilution of Nikkei history. With dilution comes forgetting. "Something needs to be done" is a common refrain and signals the notion of home space based on both geography and a specific historical experiential (Nakaoka 2012). The March meeting was the beginning of that "something."

Sheets of blank paper were passed around, with attendees tasked with writing a list of what they thought was most important about preserving the Sawtelle Nikkei community. Some thought it was too late to do anything. Nonetheless, a brief list emerged: (1) creating a Sawtelle community organization as a way to improve life in Sawtelle; (2) preserving the legacy, history, people, and stories of Sawtelle; (3) increasing influence to control and shape community growth, including the onslaught of new development; (4) dealing with traffic gridlock on Sawtelle Boulevard as well as surrounding residential streets. Thus, that night's group claimed the privilege to both participate in the management of urban change and assert rights to a specific cultural citizenship (Harvey 2008; Gregory 1996; Rosaldo 1994). The evening church meeting was emblematic of a way to reappropriate and reclaim Sawtelle urban space, to resist and contest not only its fading physical boundaries but the stories Nikkei told about themselves in these spaces (de Certeau 1984). The feeling of a lost historical legacy was uppermost in peoples' minds, as was the outspoken ownership of place apart from shin Issei.

> I want a place to call home! It is important to say Japanese American—*not* Japanese. It was the Issei and Nisei that built this community. They say we don't care, we aren't interested—well, we do!

At the end of the evening, these few Sawtelle civic actors formed an ad hoc group called the Sawtelle Japantown Association (SJA).

> The meanings of a place inhere in the stories a community tells itself about its history and valued assets, and other shared knowledges about their place, its characteristics, shared values, boundaries, members, and their relationships.
>
> More significant, it is possible, and possibly universal, for relatively small groups to change or add to the meaning of particular places and spaces within the city. (Sorensen 2009: 209)

The SJA was an activist group in a community of fewer and fewer resident Nikkei, and the goal of "reclaiming" Nikkei Sawtelle seemed an impossible task. For this mix of Nisei and Sansei women and men, however, there were significant factors working in SJA's favor despite their numbers. All had previous grassroots organizing experience through churches, the JHS, the PTA, special events and other volunteer activities in Sawtelle, as well as other Nikkei venues in Los Angeles and Southern California. Much of this social structure was still active in the neighborhood and worked as a base of networked support. There were also deeper roots than even their own generational engagements. SJA members all benefited from knowledge gained through examples of family histories: their parents' and grandparents' civic participation and activism. These past stories of familial involvement and politicized activism remained crucial among SJA membership as powerful ways of confronting dominant ideologies creatively and resourcefully (Brodkin 2007).

For the next few months at various community locations around Sawtelle, Nikkei discussed ways to focus on the preservation of community. Almost immediately, they put their myriad experiences to work making critical inroads into wider community political organizations. They went to neighborhood gatherings to learn about current issues; they listened and got others involved. Two months after the first meeting, SJA sponsored four Sawtelle-area Nikkei candidates to run for positions on the West Los Angeles Neighborhood Council (WLANC).[6] One SJA member said the targeting of the WLANC was a deliberate choice.

> Neighborhood councils don't have much authority, but what they do is get more participation from community into government services that are available to all of us. If you don't participate, it's very difficult for us to say we want services.
>
> So, let's turn it around, so government . . . can provide service to us! The more we participate in what *we* need, come up with different ideas and feed them to different individuals, then we have a better and stronger community. For me, Sawtelle needs a vision—a community that has a vision. We have to have our voice in there, too!

All four SJA-backed candidates won seats in an election marking the emergence of a Nikkei voting/stakeholder bloc (West Los Angeles Neighborhood Council 2014). A few months later, WLANC officially revised its bylaws and changed its name to West Los Angeles Sawtelle Neighborhood Council.

In less than a year, SJA's most ambitious project—an official Los Angeles city designation of Sawtelle as Sawtelle Japantown—was accomplished in the astonishingly short time of a few months. Neighborhood street naming is a fraught political process, usually tense with community angst that can take months and years to accomplish (Woo 2015). There was some dissent about the naming at early SJA meetings, particularly from non-Nikkei individuals who lived in the neighborhood and felt marginalized. However, the speed and the organizing power with which the gathering of necessary signatures and petitions was accomplished by a strong SJA leadership base preempted and muted potential opposition. Utilizing the broad umbrella of long-established neighborhood organizations that sponsored activities and events where Nikkei gathered in the Sawtelle area, volunteers signed up supporters for the name designation and then buttonholed unanimous backing from local elected officials.

Eleventh District Los Angeles city council member Mike Bonin addressed the full LA City Council in February 2015.

> It is a multigenerational neighborhood. There are folks who've been there for years. It is a community that over the years has suffered persecution through restrictions on where they could live, through internment. . . . a very strong and vital neighborhood. (Rafu staff 2015)

In the audience was a small group of Sawtelle residents backing the council's motion. With alacrity, the city council voted fourteen to zero to "getting the signs made and installing them" (Rafu staff 2015). Less than two months later, blue metal signage bearing the name Sawtelle Japantown and the Los Angeles city logo was erected at both the south and north ends of Sawtelle Boulevard.

> "Welcome to Sawtelle Japantown!" 11th District Councilmember Mike Bonin declared to the applause and cheers of more than 100 who had gathered on Sunday. . . .
> "Today is a very, very special day. History has taken place in this town that we love and live in . . . Sawtelle Japantown." (Muranaka 2015b)

SJA members see it as a moment of vindication for Nikkei.

> It's a branding issue. Identifying Sawtelle as Japantown is very important because it ties that particular community to the Japanese [Americans], the Issei, Nisei, Sansei, and so on.

The Japantown street sign is a commemoration of the legacy of emigration from Japan that pays homage to a historical biculturalism where a "fluidity and contingency of identity within the ethnic community" is revealed (L. Kurashige 2002: 43). At the same time, *Sawtelle* Japantown became emblematic of that recaptured identity that is wholly Nikkei. An SJA member said,

> People were concerned because the area was being called Little Osaka . . . and the name Sawtelle was being somewhat forgotten. . . . We wanted to get this place named properly with a sign, so that people don't forget that this was a very strong Japanese American community with a lot of Japanese businesses, cultural events, Japanese churches and lots of citizens. (Nakayama 2015)

The power to create social memory and belonging among stakeholders transcends the mere presence of a metal sign. For Sawtelle Nikkei, the new designation evokes a historical archiving of remembrance that also reflects a dynamic, more contemporary process of participation tied to particular culturally relevant issues (Quayson 2010). The sign is literally that—a symbolic political statement that marks space and identity for all to see (Azaryahu 1986). It is an example of the socially constructed and contested process of commemoration and, as such, is "an important vehicle for bringing the past into the present, helping weave history into the geographic fabric of everyday life" (Alderman 2002). Furthermore, as an example of interpretive symbolism, the Sawtelle Japantown street sign is evocative of the "webs of significance" it represents to Nikkei (Geertz 1973). The successful campaign was widely covered by news media in both Southern California and Japan (Okazaki 2017; Groves 2015).

Little Osaka Is Better

Elided in the discourse about home and those who belong is the incursion of shin Issei who worked in the Sawtelle/West Los Angeles area and also frequented its spaces. Shin Issei were aware of the well-publicized naming campaign, but for them, it was much ado about very little. Shin Issei think Little Osaka is a much more appropriate name and still use it in their conversations. A shin Issei who worked at several restaurants for nearly a decade around Sawtelle said that from her perspective, the name Sawtelle has neither meaning nor context. She shrugged her shoulders.

> People don't know Sawtelle; they know Little Tokyo—do you remember they called it J-town? People say I go to J-town—it's the same. That's why Little Osaka is better.

> Tokyo and Osaka are the two biggest cities in Japan. [Why another] J-town? It's too similar to downtown Little Tokyo. Nobody uses the name Sawtelle Japantown.

"Nobody" conveys membership outside Nikkei identity. "People say" are shin Issei. The claiming of place and space determines boundaries of exclusion but also hints at deeper social differences, most notably indicating that shin Issei do not have historic membership in the Nikkei narrative. A longtime Sawtelle Nikkei said shin Issei do not understand the historical roots of the community.

> Shin Issei now call this area Little Osaka, but I don't know who came up with that? They have no clue, so why did they end up picking this [name]?

Performing identity based on early community formation was, and continues to be, a powerful unifier for those who grew up in and around Sawtelle as Americans of Japanese ancestry. For Sansei, it is emphatically not shin Issei history.

> I think Japanese American history—*our* history—is Nisei and has to do with the camps. It makes us different. That really cut the cord as how far back we look. Of course, you can say I came from so-and-so prefecture [in Japan]—have relatives, but you don't have that same bond. *Our* bond really goes to the Issei, period.

Life in the United States has continued to be a transformative experience for shin Issei women. However, even to say *shin Issei* is lumping what has always been a highly diverse group and has become even more so in the last two or three decades. Shin Issei who migrated in the 1950s are not the shin Issei who arrived in the United States in the 1980s, and neither are they similar to shin Issei women who migrated after 2000. This multiplicity of younger migrant lives is another facet of the shin Issei community Nikkei are also beginning to recognize in Sawtelle.

> My nail person came in the 2000s. She goes to the Methodist Church and sends her kids to Montessori school. She's married to an African American. I'm sure she's not here legally.
>
> [It's] kind of an underground economy. And a lot of them are younger. Same with the woman who does my mom's hair; her boyfriend is African American, too. So the shin Issei community is also very diverse.

Terri is a Nisei who has lived in the western part of Los Angeles most of her life. She got married and raised her two children in the Sawtelle neighborhood. She also realizes shin Issei are generationally different but also agrees with other Nikkei that shin Issei cannot yet claim membership among other Americans of Japanese ancestry.

> I see shin Issei everywhere—but we have very little to do with them. We just never mix. For one thing, a lot of us don't speak Japanese. Now they may speak English, but not good enough!

In the late 1960s and early 1970s, Terri was running several small shops near Santa Monica's Clover Field Airport, then headquarters of Douglas Aircraft. Douglas was the city's largest employer, and Santa Monica had been a company town since before World War II. Small businesses like Terri's provided services not just for Douglas employees but for thousands of other workers supporting aerospace production.

> [Other than whites], most of my store customers were predominantly immigrant Mexican. My Spanish is better than my Japanese.

By the 1980s, Terri began to notice more changes in the neighborhood—young, migrant Japanese women. For her, shin Issei may be *in* Sawtelle, but they are not *part* of Sawtelle.

> It's like a totally different society. They have their own social life, they have their own churches, they go to where they speak Japanese. Nisei, Sansei, they're going to go to English-speaking churches only.
>
> In Sunday school, I taught for ten years, but it was all in English. I never saw any shin Issei there. It's like they're a totally different community.

Terri poses a rhetorical question, albeit somewhat hesitantly, to explain what it means to be Nikkei and whether shin Issei might, at some point, qualify. Her answer is still freighted with a belonging that goes beyond legal definitions of citizenship.

> What *is* Japanese American? Do you have to be born here to be Japanese American? Yup. [But] what about becoming a citizen later? Well . . . if they become naturalized, then maybe . . . they can become Japanese American.

Seina is part of a new generation of shin Issei who migrated to the United States after 2000. She does not call herself Japanese American or Nikkei but simply Japanese, even though her goal was to naturalize. In addition to her more recent arrival in the United States, she is unusual for other reasons that set her apart from shin Issei women who migrated primarily in the 1980s and 1990s. She was engaged and left Japan to marry an American citizen. She is also well educated. In Japan, she was the beneficiary of an undergraduate education at a private school, had graduated from a four-year college, and was accepted into a postgraduate program at one of Japan's top universities. With her impressive academic credentials, she did not fit the typical OL profile. Nonetheless, Seina also realized that her goals to achieve an independent career would be limited in Japan. Her own job experience as a young woman is familiar to shin Issei women who've been in the United States since the 1980s.

> One of my surprises when I started working [in Japan], the women took for granted their role as women . . . supporting men's jobs, and [they were] happy with that, and even though they might be highly educated, they don't question and why they're not hired as career staff.
>
> They're happy with supporting staff. Clear division of roles. I was surprised because I say and act as I want . . . compared to other women. Opportunities in Japan for women are still limited . . . still a lot of challenges, more burdens for women to pursue careers or have an equal partner.
>
> We have a specific term, it's very discriminatory—I don't like the term, *otsubone-san*—someone who is over thirty years old and especially if you're single. But this otsubone group has a lot of experience! She's doing this specific thing for a long time, so she has skills and she knows people. She can say things, but people don't want to hear it; they don't want to be criticized!

Rather than succumb as an otsubone, Seina opted for better opportunities at finding employment and decided to migrate to the United States. Unlike other shin Issei, she decided to apply immediately for permanent residency after marriage and eventually for citizenship as well. Neither the LPR application nor her decision to become naturalized were simple tasks.

> I had a hard time getting a green card. I started with a fiancé visa, which took one year. We had to go through all these huge documents. I had to [stay] in Japan, and I couldn't come here. Naturalization? I did everything myself.

Her path to citizenship took another five years. Similar to other shin Issei like Tomoko, her earlier experiences with migration law in the United States turned Seina into an activist promoting the interests and projects of other shin Issei women. She is now the mother of a school-age child and is a familiar face at shin Issei community events. In her work outside her home, she says her primary goal is to establish meaningful ways to address issues important to shin Issei, though she recognizes the difficulties in overcoming diversity within shin Issei.

> Even for Japanese-speaking there are so many sub- and microcommunities because the window of immigration is like sixty, seventy years since war. Lots of different types of people coming in, and they've formed their own networks.

These experiences among active shin Issei are familiar to Nikkei. Nikkei history has privileged efforts to maintain and promote specific interests of Americans of Japanese ancestry within a framework of American participatory democracy—the building of collective narratives that act as counterhegemonic politicized identities (Brodkin 2007). At the same time, civic engagement by Nikkei has often necessitated stitching together a patchwork of multiple voices and discrepant stories that do not subsume wider group goals (Nikkei for Civil Rights and Redress 2018). Deciding on larger objectives has always been a freighted process of negotiation over resources that "are not always utilized for concerted collective action, primarily because of the considerable diversity in values, interests, and ideologies" among Nikkei (Fugita and O'Brien 1991: 164).

It may be argued that a similar instrumental outline among shin Issei migrants is also slowly emerging, though with a different trajectory that does not always center American citizenship, nor does it necessarily include Nikkei. Shin Issei look to benefit the migrant community. However, at the same time, it can also be said that community participation involving Nikkei and shin Issei can be an advantage in building communal strength. Perhaps it is not a common agenda but one that is allied and connected in ways that differential belongings can be incorporated.

This chapter has looked at ways in which Nikkei and shin Issei see and construct one another as dissimilar and distinct groups. Though there may be aspects of shared racial descent, there are significant differences in the identifying and asserting rights to specific symbols and group histories. With increased social interaction between shin Issei and Nikkei, these manifestations of ethnicization have overlapped and been conflated with racial conversations.

This attention to physical differences and processes of racialization is about reifying borders of belonging. Supposed "natural" racial variances are reflective of power relations and differences in worth between the two groups and each's marginality in the United States. Nikkei worked in more public arenas to emphasize both a racial and ethnic identity as American citizens. Shin Issei worked primarily out of the spotlight within their own spheres of recent migrants, although newer evidence in the latter part of the twentieth century suggests otherwise.

6

Shin Issei and Nikkei Searching for Community

In America it's different, yeah! If you don't demand, or speak about things, you don't get a job! I'm used to living here. But some moms aren't like me. Language is a handicap, and they don't get out. It's important to get out.

My son won an award in a speech contest. It's so different from Japan, they don't stress oral expression ability. [Students in Japan] may be book smart, but they can't express themselves. It's not considered important, and I know this is lacking, and I didn't want that to happen to my kids.

Shin Issei who have been habituated to life in the United States for several decades and work with both Japanese migrants and Nikkei have realized how new ways of communicating can create changes. Shin Issei say that, as difficult as it may be, expressing oneself means speaking up in order to be heard.

> Oh yeah, I'm more Americanized now because now everything with me is more straight, no hiding. If I have something to complain about, I say it, even when I'm in Japan. It's [the reaction in Japan] like *wow*! [*Laughing.*] My parents can tell the difference.

> Some shin Issei still don't understand Japanese American thinking. I get so many complaints from shin Issei mothers. I told them, this is the American way, so you have to follow them. After meetings now, they call me . . . this is American way? Wah.

With new ways of communicating, women who are now in midlife have found that collective group action beyond their immediate families and friends can reap benefits on common concerns. Tomoko and other migrant mothers practiced a social activism centered on childcare that also exposed them to wider community influences and in the process lessened their own isolation. They created a politics of participation, "[one of] a variety of alterities prompted by globalization processes" in which new migrants challenged their marginalization as Other (Ribeiros 2006: 365; Sanjek 2002; Cheah 1998).

This chapter reveals some of the beginnings of shin Issei engagement outside their immediate families. Shin Issei actions cannot be described as wholly integrative of social justice or identity and recognition issues that have been the hallmark of Nikkei advocates, such as the claiming of space in Sawtelle. However, shin Issei have begun to more fully understand the social context of Nikkei in the United States and the reason they have a stake in that positionality as well. During the period of this ethnography, there were no specific shin Issei activist organizations in Southern California. Of necessity, the few shin Issei who did become involved in social activism took their cues from longtime Nikkei organizations. A few of them joined Nikkei groups or utilized engagement methods practiced by Nikkei. Explored from this perspective is a construction of community space and the ways in which newer shin Issei activism both paralleled and overlapped the larger existing Nikkei community. While the benefits of this somewhat tenuous partnership accrue to both groups, to a large extent, more full adaptations and inclusions continue to be worked out. Nikkei have understood the importance of shin Issei issues, but it has been primarily shin Issei who have learned ways of a local—and longer established—Nikkei activism, not the other way around. These Nikkei spaces are both imaginary and geographically specific—areas that have "literally and metaphorically been developed and 'invented' through their racialized interpretation" (Bonnett 1996: 875).

The probabilities of broadening community-based awareness among shin Issei and of it becoming a foundation for membership, activism, and civic participation in a coalitional politics of identity with Nikkei is the ultimate question. In the first decade of the twenty-first century, it can only be said that there are possibilities—and potential—for new constructions of a wider Nikkei America. There will most likely always be degrees of difference and social tension among Nikkei and shin Issei. The disparities, however, do not mean that a collectivity and possible building of ties and networking cannot occur. In limited instances, it is happening, if for no other reason than proximity—the space and place both groups simultaneously inhabit—a collectivity in which larger issues affect both native- and foreign-born Japanese.

> As a symbol and aspiration, the idea of community continues to resonate in public discourse. . . . The term suggests many appealing fea-

tures of human social relationships—a sense of familiarity and safety, mutual concern and support, continuous loyalties, even the possibility of being appreciated for one's full personality and contribution to group life rather than for narrower aspects of rank and achievement. (Brint 2001: 1)

The space and place of community depends, of course, on how "community" is perceived and for whom "community" exists.

Disparate Views of Community

The meanings of community and the ways of solving collective issues have evolved differently among shin Issei and Nikkei. Dense social relationships and affective ties have knit together Japanese society for hundreds of years, particularly among those living in specific localities, although community may not have been an operative term or concept. More recently, the geographically prescribed *chokai* has been widely understood in Japan as the established neighborhood association. Membership was virtually mandatory, engaging "nearly all households in urban neighborhoods, helping to build a sense of community identity, expanding trust among citizens, and serving as a resource in crises" (Le Blanc 2016: 319). When the word *community* was used, it was in reference to a corporate community in which company employees subsumed personal goals for the larger social group. The term was not commonly understood in the sense of a generalized "Japanese community" (Suehiro 1998). As Japan began to modernize at the end of the nineteenth century, neighborhood women's groups—*fujinkai*—were active in coalescing into broader associations with a major objective of educating women on changing roles in urbanizing Japan (Patessio 2011). In early twentieth-century California, new Issei women migrants organized themselves for reasons that included not just their own survival but the future existence of rural Nikkei farm communities, especially as class divisions between Issei landowners and laborers became more pronounced (Tsu 2009; Yasutake 2004).

From the 1980s onward, the use of both *community* and *community building* appeared more frequently in Japanese media and public discourse (A. Imamura 1987). Civic comments often lamented disappearing community ties in urban cities like Tokyo and the ensuing loss of intimacy for the "precarious, social world outside the door" (Le Blanc 2016: 341). The increasing lack of social ties, the higher mobility among urban dwellers, the decrease in fertility, and the rise in two-person nuclear families were seen as contributing factors in the decline of networks and instrumental ties of support. In the early 2000s, the Japanese government began opening up so-called drop-in play centers to create spaces where young mothers and their children might build social ties (Kawano, Roberts, and Long 2014). However, among urban women, usage of the word *community* was often not understood.

> Despite . . . constant use of the term "community" in its newsletters and its widely distributed plans to build community centers, less than half of those surveyed and few of the housewives . . . could indicate what their community might be. (A. Imamura 1987: 104)

Urban women often perceived of community as a study or hobby group or as only the immediate neighborhood where one lived. Seina brought this idea of bounded physical space with her when she migrated.

> In Asia, space is important. People who live in the [that] space think about community building.

Soon, however, Seina's idea of community underwent a sea change in definition.

In 2010, she was living in Los Angeles, a multicultural and multiracial environment she had never experienced. She wasn't thinking about community beyond the neighborhood where she lived. She saw Nikkei, but they were unknown curiosities. Even though she possessed an elite Japanese education, her schooling, like most Japanese curricula, offered very little knowledge of Japanese Americans or their history.

> I didn't know much about Los Angeles at the time. Embarrassingly enough, I didn't know about the camps. I didn't know about it until 2007.

On her own, she began to read about the Incarceration and eventually visited Manzanar during one of the yearly pilgrimages first organized by Nikkei activists in 1969. She was surprised not only that she saw so many Nikkei in attendance more than seven decades after the Incarceration but that experiencing the campsite in person lent a reality she couldn't fully appreciate just reading about it. In Tokyo, her graduate school interests had concentrated on poverty and development issues in Asia. However, not long after she visited Manzanar, a meeting with a Little Tokyo activist changed her focus.

> He convinced me, you don't need to go to Asian countries to find poverty. Poverty is here. I said, "Really?" I mean, to me, America was rich!

> I attended a board meeting and that was an awakening for me. About twenty to thirty people were there, and they were talking about what is the future of Nikkei.

As a shin Issei, Seina realized she needed to rethink not only how involved Nikkei envisioned their community but how this drove a political agenda. She had grown up around examples of women—both in her own family and among some of her teachers in Japan—who had undertaken tasks beyond family and neighborhood, so for her, these early experiences made women's work outside the home unexceptional, and it seemed natural to pursue her new awakenings to Nikkei and community further. As she became more immersed in activities in Little Tokyo, Seina gained a deeper awareness of broader notions of community not limited by geography (Toji and Umemoto 2003).

> One thing I was really shocked about and didn't understand was that all these people were all from outside Little Tokyo! They didn't live in Little Tokyo, and that was the first time I saw this type of community building.

She realized that Little Tokyo was emblematic of being Nikkei; its imagined nexus of social ties and symbolized extension of community was a given.

> [In] Little Tokyo, people don't live here; they're all dispersed. But they are all thinking about persisting, and I didn't understand that.
>
> It opened up my interest in this community because I [had] never seen this kind of community building before. The way of community building is completely different here. So I wanted to find out why and what are they doing.

She saw that Nikkei community participation was characterized by models of active and sustained engagement through broad webs of affiliations.

> There is constant, conscious action of Japanese Americans to preserve this space through associations. [To] continually create and connect dispersed constituents to this space.
>
> [Groups are] not just space organizations, [but] also highly network-based organizations. Anchoring all these networks there and throughout history, they balanced power [and] this network got stronger.

Dissimilar to shin Issei thinking about community in Japan, activist Nikkei approached ideas of community participation through a broad-based system of social ties and linkages as part of a demand for social justice and equality in the United States. More specific explanations of community were unnecessary; its meanings were assumed and deployed by Sansei in a wider social movement for change.

> I grew up at a time when you *had* to see yourself as Japanese American. You couldn't act like just an American . . . by how you were perceived and received. It was racial awareness, and I came of age during the midsixties during the civil rights movement.
>
> I was profoundly impacted by Stokely Carmichael—Kwame Ture—talking about Black Power and basically saying, "If you white people really want to make change and help black people, talk to your parents and organize in your own communities."
>
> As an Asian American activist and a Japanese American activist, you realize, I'm not in the Black Power or Brown Power paradigm! You know? [*Laughing.*] And I'm certainly *not* a white person!

Community organizing used radical methods aimed at attaining empowerment in the politics of everyday life (D. Fujino 2008; Louie and Omatsu 2001; G. Matsuda 1990). Moreover, achieving change spoke to a type of Nikkei activism with a highly public face (D. C. Fujino 2020; Nikkei for Civil Rights and Redress 2018; D. C. Fujino 2005; Maki, Kitano, and Berthold 1999; Takahashi 1997; Tachiki, Wong, and Odo 1971). This public performance of community was supported by various coordinated groups and structured organizations representing Nikkei issues and interests in a ground-up movement.

> As we got more engaged in community, [like] Serve the People programs, I began to see the value of community and the value in being Japanese American.
>
> It showed me—this is a little trite—but the power of community. The fact that we had a sense of community, that we were able to set aside differences and were able to connect with people throughout the nation around some common kinds of things.

Nikkei inhabited space through ideological constructs of collective memory and experience—social space as history in which socially relevant expressions of behavior are made culturally relevant (Low 1994; Lefebvre 1991). In Sawtelle, SJA Nikkei described the importance of the Japantown signs, explaining that space and community signify ownership first as a physical presence and second as a larger, abstract extension of space, and explored the implications of belonging.

> There has to be some sense of identity that is Sawtelle. People have got to come up with some kind of common identity for what that community is, and a vision for where you want to go with it.

In the new century, Nikkei activists maintained commitments to social justice but at the same time realized transformations and growing diversity in the community.

> We have to understand that JA identity doesn't begin and end with the camps, doesn't begin and end with 1880 when we came over here, with agriculture, and alien land laws, and all of that.
> That's an important lesson and theme to our experience here, but it's a diverse community we need to understand.
> The camps and all that is context. When you're talking fourth or fifth generation—Yonsei, Gosei, and shin Nisei—they acknowledge that it's an important lesson, but it doesn't define them.
> In the JA community most parents don't talk about values. Did your parents? No! I talk about values, about social justice. If you're really committed, you don't grow out of it; you figure out ways you hold true to this. If you believe in equality, social justice, et cetera, it's a part of your life.

The attempt at cohesion and cooperation—setting aside differences—is never without discord. Much of the rhetoric and social action surrounding community building and empowerment among Sansei activists (or for that matter, Issei and Nisei activists) were underpinned by the need to subsume differences and build a cohesive narrative to confront larger social structures of inequality. These differences do not necessarily presuppose stumbling blocks in communal efforts (Creed 2004). Early activists understood this building of movement and process (Omatsu 1990).

Two crises in Southern California directly affected shin Issei and demonstrated the nature of their activist process. Without a similar kind of extant Nikkei community structure, shin Issei relied on ad hoc organizing, but with some guidance from Nikkei. And while some Nikkei found migrant participation a bit unsettling, the results of shin Issei actions did have an impact in the Nikkei community and beyond.

"We Should Do Something"

In many ways, as their own stories have revealed in these pages, shin Issei were already politicized migrants in numerous everyday situations though they may not have seen themselves as such. Yet their narratives, interpretations, and engagements are the results of their own creative acts that have performative force when circumstances dictate (de Certeau 1984). They did become mobilized over issues that directly affected them, and they did rely on other models of activism to pursue specific ends "premised on accommodating difference" (Brodkin 2007: 95; Ramakrishnan 2001). As did their settlement in and around Nikkei communities, these accommodations of shin Issei activism often map onto sites of an already highly politicized Nikkei field. An example from the mid-1980s demonstrates this mapping, although this example of shin Issei community action was its own issue.

After Fumiko Kimura was arrested in 1985 on first-degree murder charges in the drowning deaths of her two children, some shin Issei women began to talk about how they might get involved in her legal case. As pointed out earlier, many shin Issei women saw themselves reflected in Kimura's isolated Los Angeles life. A few of them met together at the Little Tokyo Service Center (LTSC).[1] Staff social workers remembered adding their voices about the case.

> Some people came . . . saying we should do something for her. Our agency is to help people . . . so we had a meeting. People came who said they could identify with her . . . they were all women. (Nakatomi 1991: 60)

LTSC staffers remember the concern shin Issei felt for Kimura but also noted that Nikkei did not share the same feelings about the charges against her (Nakatomi 1991). Some Nikkei wanted to distance themselves from the "cultural" aspects of Kimura's crime.

> We talk a lot about preserving our cultural heritage, but the question is this: must we try to preserve everything which is deemed to be part of Japanese culture? What about those elements of Japanese culture that are in direct conflict with our American sensibilities and values? (Okamura 1985: 5)

Nonetheless, shin Issei made two decisions that brought increased visibility to the case. First, they formed the Fumiko Kimura Fair Trial Committee to solicit money for Kimura's criminal defense. Eventually, they raised more than

$7,000 (Nakatomi 1991). Second, and arguably just as important, the fair trial members decided on a public campaign to increase awareness of the case. They gathered more than twenty-five thousand signatures, in Japan and the United States, asking leniency for Kimura. However, the majority of petition signers were not kaisha employees or their wives but shin Issei women living in the United States (Nakatomi 1991). In a move that received widespread news coverage, the committee presented the petitions to the judge, who took special note of their actions. In addition, numerous committee members were in daily attendance at the trial (Associated Press 1986; K. Hayashi 1985; Stewart 1985).

When Kimura was sentenced to probation and psychiatric treatment, shin Issei women in the courtroom applauded and wept (K. Hayashi 1985). Reporters covering the trial saw that shin Issei acquired valuable knowledge in understanding the public face of politics in the United States.

> I think they gained some skills as far as participating in the political process, as far as knowing how to mobilize people . . . I think they learned a lot of skills from the whole case. (Nakatomi 1991:67)

In that sense, Kimura's "win" was also theirs. Looking back at what they had accomplished, shin Issei believed these kinds of learning experiences were vital in getting women involved in more confrontational methods of community involvement.

> If they're not engaged in community and they aren't organized in a timely manner and don't [speak] out, then their voices aren't heard.

The Fair Trial Committee was ad hoc, but several women subsequently took advantage of their experiences to jump-start other, more formal organizations to assist shin Issei women. Among these was a group to provide family counseling. Within a few years, the Association of Japanese International Marriages USA had a hotline, a newsletter, and clients in forty states (Nakatomi 1991). Other outreach efforts begun by shin Issei initially involved in the Kimura case included a bilingual Nikkei Help Line and a shin Issei column in a local newspaper (Nakatomi 1991). Shortly after the trial, Kimura began volunteering at a Nikkei community center in Los Angeles (Associated Press 1986).

Three decades after the Kimura trial, the sale of Keiro Senior Healthcare in Southern California once again propelled shin Issei to activism. With two nursing homes, an intermediate care facility, and a retirement home, Keiro was the original idea of a group of young, forward-thinking Nisei men in 1961 who were concerned that aging Nikkei would need eldercare that was culturally sensitive and responsive (Keiro 2021). This health-care concept included in-language assistance, specific types of foods, and senior activities geared toward Nikkei experiences. By the late 1970s, Keiro facilities began to serve not just aging Issei and Nisei but also a growing population of shin Issei. At the time of the sale in 2016, more than half of Keiro residents spoke Japanese as their primary language (Nakaji Monnier 2016). Rumors about the continued economic viability of the Keiro facilities had been circulating for some time, but in 2014, the board's decision to sell everything to an outside developer created a firestorm of anger and backlash that reached Washington, DC with members of Congress weighing in against the sale (Sonksen 2015).

When she heard about the sale, Takako went to the first meeting of a newly formed group called the Ad Hoc Committee to Save Keiro.

> I saw just three men sitting there. I was the only woman, and I asked, "Is this where the Keiro meeting is?" So I became involved. It's so important for shin Issei women. I felt it was something I had to do. They cannot go back to Japan; where will they live here?

Takako is highly educated with a doctorate in clinical psychology. She is a naturalized shin Issei, though she doesn't use that label.

> I never heard the term *shin Issei* until 2015—we are Japanese, but Nikkei use the word. It was the hardest thing I had to do was to become naturalized—to give up my Japanese citizenship when I was twenty-one. It is an in-between—I am not Japanese, and I am not Japanese American, either.

For her, the Keiro sale was deeply personal.

> My mother . . . suffered a major stroke which nearly killed her. She was paralyzed, lost her speech, and could not digest food. She lost her English language comprehension completely and reverted back to basic Japanese language.

Takako was able to have her mother admitted to Keiro for extended nursing.

> The [Keiro] staff were very kind and attentive and provided her with services in Japanese, including Japanese food and speech therapy in

Japanese. Keiro was a life-saving facility for my mother, and she became well enough to be discharged.

I was very grateful to the Japanese and Japanese American staff who cared for her with compassion and professionalism.

The Ad Hoc Committee to Save Keiro had assistance in organizing from Sansei activists. It quickly mushroomed to dozens of Japanese migrants, many of them women, who demanded to meet with Keiro board members. Among these women, their anger gained traction after reported comments by one of Keiro's Nikkei board members.

> Keiro was founded for Issei and Nisei, not Shin-Issei, I'm sorry to say. They don't participate in our community. They have no right to say, "You can't do this, you can't do that." They have no right. (Nakaji Monnier and Nakanishi 2015)

Shin Issei did garner support among other Nikkei who found board remarks ill timed and insensitive.

> They have suddenly cast out the Shin-Issei from the Japanese American community—kind of like throwing your own relatives under the bus. It took might and courage for the Ad Hoc Committee to go against the naysayer tide of "too little too late." . . . I applaud them and the Shin-Issei community, which has come out in force to fight this sale. They are not strait-jacketed by model minority myths or the internal politics of Little Tokyo or the JA community. (Kao 2016)

When a community-wide meeting was finally arranged, hundreds of people filled a local gym to try to stop the sale. They confronted both Keiro's Nikkei administrators and the new, white owners, one of whom could not pronounce the name of the properties for sale (Nakaji Monnier and Nakanishi 2015). Protestors spoke in Japanese and English, with Japanese speakers getting the most positive reception from the audience. However, in either language, the meeting did not go well.

> Last Thursday night was unlike any I have experienced in the JA community. Thick storm clouds gathered, the microphone hissed and crackled, and a community that has so much to celebrate, gathered together and, for one evening, threatened to split apart.

"*Kikitakunai*! (I don't want to listen) No! No!" shouted a Japanese man.... The sense that Keiro was speaking *at*, not *with* the community only served to inflame tension that finally devolved into angry outbursts. (Muranaka 2015)

Once again, issues of what community is and who belongs were stark. Shin Issei and Nikkei were equally vehement in their positions. Keiro was not shin Issei space; shin Issei felt marginalized and abandoned by those who didn't understand changing demographics. When Keiro opened its doors in the 1960s, Nikkei were still the bulk of Japanese Americans in Southern California. Fifty-plus years later, that was no longer the case. Despite vocal and sustained negative reactions from both Japanese and Japanese Americans, as well as attempts by local politicians, the Keiro sale could not be stopped, and escrow closed in 2016 (Nakayama 2016). Shin Issei active in trying to save Keiro still felt it was a valuable lesson for shin Issei women who had come together and spoken out.

> You know, [with] the Keiro thing, some fear works. I think the shin Issei population learned from that experience. They started to organize after the sale was announced, but it was too late. Probably first time on a big scale [organizing].

Takako found the whole experience disheartening. Until then, she hadn't fully realized the differences in political styles and motivations.

> I was so disappointed that Nikkei didn't get involved. They didn't help at all. They told us, "You don't understand." [They said] "We have to fight; we have to have demonstrations."
>
> But shin Issei didn't see it that way. This was a specific problem with the sale, and that [was], where are these people going to go for care? When Keiro was sold, it was devastating and we all cried. Such a loss. What were we going to do?

What Takako did not do was give up. In 2018, she helped put together a questionnaire asking about health-care needs. More than 1,500 people—shin Issei and Nikkei between seventeen and one hundred years old from across the United States answered, and nearly two-thirds were women (Miyawaki et al. 2020). It would appear from their responses that shin Issei women did not plan to return to Japan but instead expected to remain in the United States to retire or live with assistance in culturally sensitive Nikkei facilities. "[The] Shin Issei population in the U.S. is a major presence that cannot be ignored when we discuss the needs of the Japanese" (Miyawaki et al. 2020: 5). Of note, the study addressed a shortcoming in the research and offered a caution about isolated shin Issei.

> This population segment is not part of any study simply because Japanese people do not openly speak of their situation. This is not a culturally sensitive issue, but rather an entire community issue that will continually need to be addressed or too many will suffer. (Miyawaki et al. 2020: 25)

Although Takako realized there were major differences with Nikkei, she and other shin Issei started thinking about larger goals. Part of that was being more comfortable using newer terms to define one another.

> We now have a task force to rebuild the Nikkei senior facility. Ten people—six Sansei, four shin Issei, and half are women—both Sansei and shin Issei. We want to build a hundred-bed facility.

In 2019, the task force of Nikkei and shin Issei began a public campaign to move forward with a ten-year, $22 million business plan to develop a new Nikkei senior care facility (Endo 2019). Takako knows how much work lies ahead, but she is familiar with challenges. She recalled a period earlier in her life when she went back to Japan to try to get a job.

> I was told I had to make tea for the men. I told my boss I cannot make tea—so I sat there while the other young women did it. Then after tea, they collected all the cups of the men and washed them out.
> I was told that this was how they did things and I had to think about it or it would jeopardize my position. I didn't make tea.

Other models of intergroup collaboration in more intimate but still important circumstances are bridging differences.

Seeking Limited Commonalities

In Sawtelle, the idea of a community inclusive of shin Issei and longtime Nikkei residents is being worked out at the JHS in ways that allow each group to learn from the other. The JHS has been a part of Sansei Shelley's life ever since she, herself, was a reluctant student. She grew up in Sawtelle and remembers being pressured (and resisting) by both her parents and grandparents to attend Saturday supplemental classes. Despite her initial foot-dragging, years later she registered her own Yonsei children, who were equally unwilling and indifferent to JHS pedagogical aims. Yonsei, however, were no longer the majority of students. By the 1990s, the JHS overflowed with shin Nisei students, and school administrators appealed to established Nisei building owners nearby for extra class space.

After her children graduated, Shelley remained involved in JHS activities, though she no longer lived in the neighborhood. Her commitment to community involvement in Sawtelle comes from her father. She says she is carrying on because of him, a local Sawtelle businessman who saw his role as more than a small grocer and his grocery store as more than a place where Nikkei could buy tofu.

> My dad would pick up fresh doughnuts and bring it to the store just for the day. He'd go to the produce market four times a week. The fish market, he took us to San Pedro for fish.
>
> We delivered, things of that sort; Dad was very social, so he made friends. With the Filipinos, he delivered food to their camps; he delivered groceries to the Japanese boardinghouses close by. He gave [people] rides home.
>
> New people who came from Japan would find out about us. My dad took a class in citizenship and taught citizenship to many Issei and helped graduate them, helped do translations [for] people who wanted to get licenses.

Like other Sansei whose families played significant roles in Sawtelle's Nikkei history, Shelley bears a sense of duty and obligation—an "ethical imperative . . . to preserve social relationships"—that began with founding Sawtelle Issei and continue to be maintained (Fugita and O'Brien 1991: 28). She speaks with deliberation in describing this responsibility.

> It comes from being such an integral part of the community. I was raised in Sawtelle . . . and almost all of our neighbors were Nikkei—Nisei, most of them having been to camp. I was born after camp, but we *all* had this similar history.
>
> My father was just an important part of the community. He felt obliged to stay open late every night because most of the people were gardeners and they had one car, and you wanted to be open so they

could come and cash their checks because they couldn't make it to the bank in time. So he was almost like the bank. He felt this duty.

Shelley became a board member at the JHS. In the 1990s, shin Issei filled the teaching staff, but the board was a mix of both Nikkei residents and shin Issei who held positions in school administration. Shelley remembers that it was tough going at board meetings. Everyone sat on tiny student chairs in one of the classrooms, trying to curb frustrations. "Oh, no, it wasn't easy in the beginning!" Cooperation and consensus between the two groups on school activities, fundraising efforts, or community celebrations were difficult to achieve. At some meetings, the shin Issei chair would look around the room, ask, "*Ii des*'?" (Is it OK?) and then say, "*Sugoi des*'" (great), with little comment from others. Shelley saw that shin Issei mothers were active in the JHS but only insofar as their children remained students. Outside of JHS work, shin Issei and Nikkei did not interact.

In the early 2000s, however, Shelley was surprised to notice that social relations were changing—that time and the exigencies of daily life had shifted.

> It was really weird, I was at a Sawtelle restaurant about a month ago, and I saw this table of women. They're all from Japan; I knew them. They are all shin Issei. And they were telling me how they go for their walks, then they get together and have lunch, and how's my family? They were doing yoga, and they're looking for places [to work out].
>
> All these, quote, "American things" they're doing. When they were raising their children, it was *only* their children. They're in their fifties now, been here for twenty years or more.

Shelley hoped that shin Issei women would become active in the Sawtelle Nikkei community and that maybe it was time to take advantage of altered circumstances in their lives as older shin Issei women whose growing children no longer needed round-the-clock attention.

> I have to say I was really shocked, really shocked that they talked to me! To actually say, "What are you doing?" You know, having this conversation about interests and stuff! I thought wow!
>
> Maybe I can invite them to have a class or whatever and slowly introduce them [to community]. They still live in the area.
>
> Japanese people doing yoga? My focus is to start with these people who used to be involved [at JHS], went away, and then to get them back because they are still all around here. A lot of them. Really come back to Sawtelle, so to speak.

Terri also thinks shin Issei ought to be included in Japanese American community: "They're still part of our heritage." She realizes many Nikkei are reluctant to make the first move and attributes it to reserve.

> The JAs are the quiet Americans—they still are, even my kids are . . . [Laughing.] Afraid of being embarrassed. Comes from old Japanese tradition of not being embarrassed in public . . . one of my parents used to say to me, "Yakamashii [too noisy]—shut up and be quiet, don't make no waves, and don't embarrass us!"

She believes getting shin Issei involved in community issues is important and is frank in challenging Nikkei who think otherwise.

> Why don't we embrace shin Issei? We should. I don't see why not. [Their] English maybe isn't perfect or their ideas won't be affirmed. For me, I don't care. I don't have any misgivings. Should we make first move? Yeah, I think it is our responsibility to reach out.

Terri says promoting intergroup ties is important in addressing critical issues among new migrants, especially because shin Issei lack established network groups where they might find assistance. She recalls one local Nikkei group that began getting calls from troubled shin Issei, including some who were contemplating suicide but didn't know where to go or what to do. By working through its Nikkei membership and connections with others active in West Los Angeles, the group set up meetings and began bilingual help sessions.

> We have lots of community infrastructure. Community activism is, to me, volunteering for various activities within the civic structure. That would be political structure, city council, neighborhood council.

In 2012, Nikkei and shin Issei worked together at the JHS to broaden knowledge about the Incarceration—a learning experience quite literally, instructive for both groups.

One warm, summer morning, a small Nisei woman stood on the sidewalk in front of the JHS. She was watching shin Nisei students and some of their shin Issei mothers getting on a bus. They were going to Manzanar. She was struck by parallels from her own life seventy years earlier. As a thirteen-year-old girl, she stood in line at this same spot, waiting with her family to board a bus that would take them to an unknown destination. Observing the children, old memories resurfaced. She shared her personal story with the students.

> Oh my, they couldn't believe it—that was the place we all met to leave for Manzanar. Things came back to me about what a frantic morning it was for all of us. A frightening morning.
>
> I was scared; we didn't know where we were going. We get on the bus, and they tell us to pull the shades down, so we have no idea. There were stories that there were scorpions like this [*lifting her index fingers about five inches apart*], and to this day, I don't even know if the bus made a stop.
>
> We left early in the morning, and the bus got there at sundown. The minute we got off the bus, we got typhoid shots! And it was so cold, and they took us to the mess hall and gave us this army tin dish and food. We go to our barracks, and it's bare, with straw mattresses and iron beds.

The commonality of the forced removal and subsequent incarcerative experience is an intergenerational Nikkei reality. In the twenty-first century, however, circumstances are vastly different for the shin Nisei boarding the bus. For them, the day journey to the Owens Valley desert to visit what is now the Manzanar National Historic Site promises to be an enjoyable field trip. Nevertheless, though it may be a pleasant break from the classroom, the reality is that they are native-born Americans and Manzanar is part of their history.

A few months before the JHS field trip, Sawtelle Nikkei met with the shin Issei teachers and administrators, including Risa, who is a key member of the staff. She made her first trip to the United States in the late 1980s as a tourist and returned a few years later on a student visa to attend junior college. Eventually she got a teaching job at the JHS and moved to a small apartment near Sawtelle.

> I came to Sawtelle to eat and shop, like at Nijiya market. The area was totally different then. It was like an old Japantown. My impressions were different. I saw lots of Japanese people—they looked *chotto* [little bit] Japanese, [*tilting her head to one side*] but they didn't speak Japanese!

Years later, with the influx of Japanese women migrants in Sawtelle, and subsequently of their enrolled children at the JHS, the neighborhood no longer seems strange.

> Now I can speak Japanese here and I feel comfortable. There is no inconvenience. There's Japanese television, Japanese newspapers, Japanese magazines.

Risa still returns to Japan at least once a year for several weeks and keeps in close contact with family via internet phone and email. She is now divorced with one child and speaks of Japan as a "very traditional" place where "there are no opportunities for women." She still has a green card, and like many shin Issei women, she feels "both American and *Nihonjin* [Japanese]," but at the same time, she has no plans to naturalize. Though she will tell you she is Japanese, she also deliberately uses *shin Issei* when speaking to Nikkei because it is the term with which Nikkei are familiar. Although she would never call herself an activist or characterize her work at the JHS as political, her story demonstrates how shin Issei women begin to assume leadership roles.

Initially, it was Risa's idea to take the students to Manzanar, but the idea was not universally well received by either several Nikkei with whom she spoke or some of the teachers.

> Most of the teachers here said Manzanar is not Disneyland! They don't want to discuss it. Nobody wants to talk about it.
> But the Sansei, the Yonsei, the shin Nisei have to know the history of the camps and about Japanese Americans during the war and how difficult [it was]. Yes, it was very racist. Racism still exists, I think so.

Bridging knowledge about Nikkei history between shin Issei mothers and their shin Nisei children was critical in furthering understanding race in the United States, something that ethnoracial Japanese from Japan did not experience. Furthermore, Risa said the Manzanar trip was a way to balance history by offering oppositional viewpoints in narratives about World War II.

> That's important because we were educated in Japan. Always, it was the U.S. that attacked Japan, but here kids are educated that Japan attacked Pearl Harbor, and that's why the U.S. dropped the atomic bomb on Hiroshima.

To further student dialogue, Risa rented videos of the Incarceration to show in class.

> We saw [a] movie about Manzanar . . . a documentary about Toyo Miyatake history and his *shashin* [photographs]. I saw that, and the high

school students watched it, too, and wow, this is American history! Some of the students said, "Oh, my grandma was there," and we discussed in class how difficult it was and if you have time, do you want to go visit?[2]

Students elected to visit Manzanar, but not without some apprehension about what they would experience. A shin Issei teacher remembered the long trip and the lasting impressions the site made on everyone.

> Nobody was really happy after [seeing the movie]. We felt so bad, you know. It was a long bus ride, but everybody was so quiet, very quiet on the bus. We showed movies on the bus and some cartoons, so they were watching that, but nobody talked. That day we went it was *so* hot.

The supervised tour of Manzanar elicited much interest.

> The children asked a lot of questions. Like where we were in the dining room, at the table, what kind of food did they cook? They didn't fight among the people? . . . We saw the beds. It was really terrible. I was really shocked. I really didn't want to see it actually.
>
> It was sad. They took us to a beautiful shrine . . . it is destroyed, but maybe one-tenth is still there, and you can see it. You know, even though they lost everything, they still [built] that kind of thing [she says this with wonder in her voice]. They are strong. If I am in their shoes, I don't think I would have that energy [but would be] unbelievably unhappy.

The Manzanar trip was the highlight of that year's JHS Holiday Show, presented to friends and family in the school's auditorium. Students shared photographs of their tour and gave speeches in English and Japanese about the Incarceration. In one memorable photo taken in the searing afternoon sun, nearly fifty students, parents, and staff are grouped around the Manzanar Cemetery Memorial.

After the presentations, everyone gathered at the back of the auditorium where long tables full of potluck and o-bento lunches had been set up. Some shin Issei parents in the audience expressed surprise about Manzanar, saying, "I didn't know anything about this in Japan." Another mother commented, "A lot of things are hush-hush in Japan. Nobody talks too much about it." And some mothers were angry.

> My husband, he's a Caucasian. He didn't know anything about it. They [the U.S. government] did a wrong thing. They were Americans! And they took them; that's wrong!

While some of the teachers had not been enthusiastic about visiting Manzanar, in the end they were grateful for the learning opportunity.

> Is this important for shin Issei and shin Nisei to find out about Japanese American history? I really think it was beneficial.
> It's history that shouldn't happen again. If the children don't know anything, then how can they defend what's important if something happens again in the future. Don't you think that history can repeat? I hope not.

For students, field trips always play an important part of childhood memories, of wider community beyond school grounds. Aside from the novelty of going somewhere, the larger goal for Risa and other JHS Nikkei was to ensure that students understood how a chapter in American history is also a vital element of their own heritage.

Two years after the Manzanar trip, Risa received more staff support in planning another bus trip, this one an enjoyable visit to Tanaka Farms, about fifty miles south of the JHS, in Irvine, California. In the early 1900s, an Issei migrant left Hiroshima prefecture for Central California, where he became a farmworker. Eventually he and his new family moved to Southern California and established a trade in shipping fresh produce. Tanaka Farms is now a fourth-generation Nikkei business and the only remaining family-owned farm in Irvine (Farms, n.d.). Each year, the Tanakas arrange for hundreds of schoolchildren to visit and to participate in educational programs about farming and Japanese American history. During the summer, the highlight of the visit is picking strawberries. After a guided tour and lecture on another hot summer day, students and their mothers are out in the fields, small baskets in hand, bent over rows of ripe red berries. Almost everyone is wearing a concealing sun hat, making it difficult to see how much is picked and how much is eaten.

Over a period of a few years, Risa emerged as a leader at the JHS, a center woman who facilitated and attempted to bring Nikkei and shin Issei together at school meetings to work on various community projects benefiting both the JHS and the wider Sawtelle neighborhood. She often attended local government hearings, planning with others about who would speak. Self-effacing, she rarely addressed officials publicly at these meetings but waited for others to voice opinions. She was willing to learn leadership skills from active Sawtelle Nikkei, yet she had strong opinions and her own style. Longtime Sawtelle Nikkei who learned how to work with shin Issei like Risa left little doubt that she was unique among both Nikkei and other shin Issei women. They marveled at her capacity to bring people together.

> I say she is such a strong leader. Does she have the same motivations as [Nikkei] in terms of [JHS] as a community center tying Sawtelle together? I would say not yet . . . [*speaking thoughtfully*] not to the extent that I have it. But I'm older; I've been here much longer than she has, but I think she is slowly getting more involved. I do.

Nikkei also learned that inherent differences in leadership and objectives could be subsumed.

> I don't even think about it anymore, just the common goal. I'm just really impressed that she's come this far, is expressing so much more, the need for this [JHS] community center, and her passion. I'm really blown away by it.
>
> Only because my image of a shin Issei Japanese woman from Japan—they're not supposed to be like that! However, more and more I am finding out that they *can* speak for themselves, speak their mind!

Risa was less upbeat about cooperative efforts over community work and leadership. She acknowledged that it's hard to gloss over dissimilarities between American-born Nikkei and shin Issei.

> Of course it's different! It's very stress[ful], very stress[ful]. I was growing up in Japan, so in traditional Japanese, [everything] is very soft. Do not say anything straight; talk around it; sometimes no means yes, yes means no.
>
> But this feeling . . . [*Shaking her head.*] I want to show the kids that growing up in the United States is *very* demanding. "I'd like to do this . . . and that and that!"

Risa was shocked when she was told that many Nikkei chide themselves for not being more outspoken and direct. "Oh really! Oh my God!"

> You know the shin Issei are always talking [that] even if Japanese American look like Japanese, their thinking is *totally* different! [*Laughing.*]

> Maybe looks like Japanese, but the mind is totally American! That's a big difference. I'm getting adjusted to that. [*Laughing.*]

She has been conscious of her role as a bridge and said of herself, "I'm kind of the middle person now." One of her biggest challenges was involving the migrant mothers in activities outside the school. They did not have the same understanding of the wider political implications Nikkei attach to the meaning of community.

> First several years they don't care; they just watched. But they realize now that it's important to be involved in community. They live here now, and they realize how important it is. It's good!

Risa expressed confidence that, although perhaps not imminent, shin Issei and Nikkei can be part of a broader alliance.

> Yes, of course! Even though it is *muzukashii* [difficult] but *dekiru* [able], we can do it! Shin Issei have to understand what Japanese American people are thinking. American style—shin Issei have to respect that way of doing.

Those with whom Risa has worked in Sawtelle assume her voluntarism was launched by the example of what she saw around her in the neighborhood—Nikkei working to preserve Sawtelle and Japanese American space. However, other influences earlier in life also lent impetus to her JHS work.

Reforming Good Wives and Wise Women

Active shin Issei women's own lives resonate with models of others who did not fully acquiesce to the role of ryosei kenbo. One of Risa's strongest influences was her own mother. She says simply, "My mom is *so* significant!"

> My dad forced her to stop [working]. It is the traditional Japanese way; you stay home and take care of the kids; that's your first priority.

Risa is the youngest in her family and credits her mother as an important historical and personal link in her own community work. Her mother had a fulfilling occupation in Japan's legal arena but gave it up when she got married. She satisfied the good wife, wise mother role, staying home to raise Risa and her siblings. Risa remembers that when she reached elementary school, her mother had more free time and decided she needed to go back to work.

> She doesn't want to stay at home; she wants to be more social, and she wants to give her knowledge to the community. Fighting in divorce cases, bankruptcies, everything for free. She didn't get anything.

Her mother also saw herself as a middleperson—someone who could be a liaison between the court system and those who couldn't pay for legal assistance.

> She became a volunteer. She did so much volunteer work in the court, like especially low-income people who cannot afford to hire an attorney, so she helped them. She saw this as a way to help community.
>
> She laughs when she talks about her father's "acceptance" of this pro bono community work. "At first, he disagreed, but you know, she is very strong woman, very strong."

By the time she was forty, her mother was twice honored with a *kunsho* award for her countless hours of volunteering.[3] Her father's continuing admonishments about proper women's roles were now directed at his daughter: "Don't be the top person; don't be like a snobbish leader; always take care of others." Observing her mother's work created an opening for Risa in Sawtelle. "I saw this as a way to help community." Her own involvement became a tactical project in informing her own life and her position and identity as a migrant woman in the United States, buttressed by a deeply meaningful personal history (V. Matsumoto 2014a; Brodkin 2007).

Risa characterized her mother as a modern Japanese woman who came of age during the 1960s, a time considered the peak of postwar civil turmoil in Japan, with urban rioting and citizen activism against the downsides of economic growth on issues like overdevelopment, rapid urbanization, and air pollution (Avenell 2010). A vocal women's movement gained traction in the 1970s with activist women working in the labor and environmental movement. At rallies and demonstrations, they fought for equal pay, representation, an end to the division of labor, and safety in consumer products (Gelb and Estevez-Abe 1998). In the streets, they carried placards saying "Housewives are unemployed!" (Takagi 1986: 50). The "new" take on women's assertiveness was described by some Japanese men: "Women and nylons have gotten stronger" (Sasaki-Uemura 2001: 112). Participatory demands by Japanese women in public spheres have a long history that belies more common Western and gendered stereotypes of acquiescence and deference within a paternalistic social system (Dalton 2015; Shibuhara 2014; Dales 2009; M. Murase 2006). Women as social actors in civil society—those spaces where sustained and organized social activity occurs outside of family and mediated state power—have been significant (Pharr 2003). Their actions provide an example to new generations of women, whether at home or farther afield. In Sawtelle's Nikkei neighborhood, Risa's activism is welcomed.

By the mid-2000s, Seina was putting to use her ideas about wider community building and voluntarism at the Little Tokyo Service Center. The LTSC had for some time prioritized the needs of clients beyond Little Tokyo in a broader, more dispersed Nikkei community. Its mission statement was revised to read, in part, to "contribute to community revitalization and cultural preservation in Little Tokyo and *among the broader Japanese community in the Southland*" (Little Tokyo Service Center, n.d.) (italics auth). In 2016, LTSC opened an office in Gardena with space on the second floor of the Gardena Valley Japanese Cultural Institute (GVJCI), another social service organization begun by Nikkei nearly half a century earlier. Speaking of its new location, LTSC staff recognized an adjustment in its work.

> For us, the growing Nisei and Shin-Issei senior populations are an emerging issue. These folks desire to live independently for as long as possible. So, LTSC felt it necessary to make sure that we were closer to where we can assist them. (Ikeda 2016)

For the LTSC and others active among Nikkei, being "closer" signifies an acknowledgment of demographic changes and redefinition of membership. It presupposes geographic location but also displays a willingness by Nikkei activists to embrace new visions of community where there might be shared space.

Racialized Geography in Nikkei Territory

The previous pages in this ethnography have revealed a diverse and wide-ranging geography of Southern California in which Nikkei and shin Issei occupy similar spaces, although unevenly and unequally. This is Nikkei geography, begun by nineteenth-century migrants, and goes beyond simply physical space. It also resides in an imaginary of hierarchized marginalizations imposed from without. Generations of Nikkei prioritized these spaces as foundational in a specific ethnic and racial identity created against dominant discourses of the alien Other. Here, racialized geography is a process in which "construction of space, place and scale overlaps with the construction of racial-ethnic and immigrant identities and with racism itself" (L. Liu 2000: 169). Although geographically dispersed, Nikkei spaces examined here—Little Tokyo, Sawtelle, and in this chapter, Gardena and South Bay—are the result of common racialized places of historic struggle and resistance. As Seina realized as she immersed herself in Nikkei activities, these racialized spaces are areas of imagined representation and collective identity in which geography is culturally imbued with social processes of meaning making that determine parameters of belonging (Silvey 2013; Y. Lee and Park 2008).

Like Little Tokyo and Sawtelle, Gardena has historically been a Nikkei place—familiar terrain for Nikkei and home to a longtime community prior to World War II. In the 1970s, it had the largest percentage of Nikkei outside of Hawai'i (L. Hirabayashi and Tanaka 1988). By the 1980s, the Nikkei population was decreasing from a high of more than 20 percent, dropping to just 11 percent by 2010. Nonetheless, Gardena remained a hub for Nikkei business and community activities and was an important proving ground for numerous Nikkei who jump-started business and political careers there (Higuchi and Phillips 2017; L. Hirabayashi 1993; Goodman 1989). Like Nikkei activists in Sawtelle who asserted ownership over an increasingly diverse area, Gardena Nikkei also claimed space and at the same time were active agents in maintaining cultural and community affinities in positioning themselves as Americans of Japanese ancestry.

In the early 1980s, when Japanese transnational capital discovered more affordable and available land on which to build MNC subsidiaries in the region, Gardena Nikkei acted as brokers in attracting Japanese capital. Global corporations like Toyota established a hundred-acre headquarters in Torrance in 1982, followed by Honda, Nissan, and other Japanese MNCs eventually making their headquarters in the area. Kaisha were followed by myriad ancillary Japanese businesses, including restaurants, grocery stores, travel agencies, tutoring services, and mental health counseling specializing in women in "cross-cultural marriages" (Wyzant 2015; *Psychology Today* 2015). Japanese language media based in the South Bay were quick to tout the benefits of living there (*Japan Up!* 2019). Thousands of chuzai-in employees and their families became temporary residents, as did more permanent shin Issei women who found jobs in Japanese-owned businesses. Added to Japan's forty-seven prefectures, Torrance was labeled its forty-eighth (Blackmore 2009).

> [Nikkei] improved their social status and increased their own political and economic power within the suburb by drawing on transnational connections to Japan to drive the city's growth. They made themselves valued and valuable residents of the suburb, accessing the full benefits of first-class citizenship. (Jenks 2014: 20)

Soon, the area became known as the "Little Tokyo of the South Bay" (Jenks 2014: 14). The tie between Gardena (as well as the South Bay) and Little Tokyo extended beyond geographic boundaries and constructed an overarching vision of what Nikkei membership meant.

Adjacent to Gardena is its larger neighbor, Torrance, which was another site for prewar Nikkei settlement. Issei pioneers had farmed thousands of acres in the area and referred to Gardena, Torrance, Compton, Hawthorne, Inglewood, and other communities as far south as Palos Verdes as the Gardena Plains and the South Bay (L. Hirabayashi and Tanaka 1988). By 2010, the South Bay was a vibrant place of settlement layered upon historic Nikkei neighborhoods. More than fifteen thousand Japanese and Japanese Americans lived in the area, adding up to 12.7 percent of the city's population, the largest demographic among Asians and Asian Americans in the Torrance area (Torrance 2012).[4] The bulk of contemporary migrants in the South Bay were shin Issei women who were still Japanese nationals, many with green cards (Higuchi and Phillips 2017). It should again be pointed out that Japanese nationality does not necessarily indicate an unwillingness to become naturalized. Newer women migrants may not have been residents long enough to apply for citizenship in the United States. In addition, Japanese nationals who registered with Japan's consular offices did so on a voluntary basis. Any reported numbers most likely did not include individuals who were undocumented.

In 2017, Nikkei again asserted themselves in defining the area, but they were not alone. In what can be labeled as a joint project, shin Issei were adding their voices and working with longtime Nikkei organizations. The LTSC initiated a large study incorporating focus groups in both Japanese and English languages to measure South Bay community needs and issues upon which common ground for solutions might be forged between Nikkei and shin Issei. Shin Issei working at LTSC were principal organizers in documenting the first-ever survey, which paid homage to Nikkei but also called attention to substantial gaps between the two groups.

> There is significant potential to strengthen and build upon the large Nikkei community in the South Bay. The most significant challenge is to bridge the social and cultural gaps between the more established second, third, and fourth-generation Japanese Americans and the large postwar Japanese immigrants, or Shin-Issei, in the South Bay. (Higuchi and Phillips 2017: 17)

The LTSC "South Bay Japanese American Community Needs Assessment" identified critical issues between Nikkei and shin Issei, including bilingual senior health care, immigration and Japanese law, permanent resident rights, Japanese American history, and workshops for children with limited English facility. Moreover, study results found that it was vital to begin thinking about ways to energize participation and engagement: "Many of the community organizations and programs started by earlier generations of Japanese Americans could be revitalized and strengthened by the participation of more recent Japanese immigrants" (Higuchi and Phillips 2017: 18).

A first-time public workshop at GVJCI to discuss findings was attended by a large percentage of Japanese-speaking shin Issei women. On the registration desk were piles of headphones for language interpretation; at the back of the room sat a row of Japanese and English volunteer translators. Panel discussants were shin Issei and Nikkei educators as well as businesspeople who addressed the audience in both Japanese and English. The event was eye opening for many Nikkei, not to mention thought provoking in regard to future collaboration. One South Bay Sansei who attended said,

> I really enjoyed it. One thing just on logistics, having the translators—*wow*! That made just a huge difference. I don't understand Japanese. I've never seen [immediate translations] before, so I was thinking that's a really good idea.

Beyond language, however, misunderstandings were almost immediately apparent. A shin Issei businessman panelist said that he didn't know why he was there and that he didn't see the need for shin Issei and Nikkei to collaborate. His attitude disappointed some Nikkei.

> Does he not understand why he's been invited? Or maybe he's been invited because he has a counter opinion. If I didn't have those headphones, I would never have known he said that! I could see how other people didn't get much out of it.

Another major issue among shin Issei that affects much of their daily lives is the problem of migration status. Neither a representative from the Consulate General of Japan who was in attendance nor LTSC staff addressed the subject of undocumented shin Issei, noting only that "the South Bay is home for a significant number of undocumented Japanese" and that further study is warranted (Higuchi and Phillips 2017: 6). Shin Issei organizers discussed only those migrants who were in the United States legally.

> All these green card holders, permanent residents, the number is growing, and their kids are American born and they live here twenty to

thirty years, so their life is already like an American; they just don't have that right to vote. I want to educate them that they are not a guest here.

They do have rights—for example, when they get older, they can apply for some social services, or senior services, and they can still be involved in the political process or civic[ly] engag[ed].

On becoming citizens, a shin Issei volunteer added,

If they want to get naturalized, we can support that. A lot of people don't know how to get naturalized. I want to let them know they can engage more in the local community because there's a lot going on here.

We get a lot of phone calls since Trump got elected. "Should I be naturalized?" They're worried. Even green card holders are worried. The political environment is changing, and there are a lot of uncertainties.

So it's a good time to think about being a Nikkei and ways to help each other and share resources. [For Nikkei], the other key thing is that every organization needs to think about hiring bilingual staff.

Community—a term frequently characterized as harmonious and cooperative, as a collection of communal narratives and subsequent building of social ties and actions in concert with others—can be problematic (L. Hirabayashi 1995). This chapter has explored commonalities between Nikkei and shin Issei with the possibility of forging new relationships and bringing both groups together in an evolving and broader vision of Nikkei community. Examples of how shin Issei women's activism in Southern California maps onto sites of an older Nikkei activism rooted in imaginaries beyond physical boundaries were discussed, as were some of the inherent differences between the groups.

The geographical imagination, however, needs not only to project a possible future, but also to understand how imaginations of the past have brought us to the present, how race has been inscribed on bodies, in boundaries and landscapes, and how that racialized legacy continues to work its way into every material thing. (A. Kobayashi 2013: 67)

For those wanting to claim a shared membership, it is critical to understand an overarching sense of participant activism in social struggle and to acknowledge that each group has its own common ties of affect, history, life events, and experiences that link its members together. The previous pages have shown that integration is still a possible future. Shin Issei and Nikkei individuals possess a wide and unique range of life experiences *within* each group, although a mutuality of relations is not always amicable. Taken separately, *a* Nikkei or *a* shin Issei community with a singular, overarching narrative where harmony and cooperation exist is never a neutral project. In the construction of a wider Nikkei identity in the United States, heterogeneity, conflict, and no small amount of social tension have been the rule and not the exception (Toji and Umemoto 2003; Maki, Kitano, and Berthold 1999; Okihiro 1973).

As this chapter pointed out, culturally defined notions of community, not to mention history, differ between Nikkei and shin Issei. Subsequently, drawing the outlines of union and establishing *intergroup* social solidarity is a task where outcomes may also be inherently divergent but where oppositions can be acknowledged and accepted as constitutive of coalition building in community work (Creed 2004). A critical part of constructing new political projects is to realize that conflict and social tension are not always avoidable, nor should they be.

Perhaps partnerships may be configured not as a traditional community organization but as a loosely connected aggregation of individuals in which place, networks, and activities have neither permanent leadership nor hierarchy, but exist with social bonds that are relatively fluid (Brint 2001). "This image of community does not demand consensus or homogeneity" but can draw on other shared histories of racial reception and social inequality (Creed 2004: 56). The future of collaboration may conceivably be "more sporadic ad hoc connections in place of long-term memberships" and "increasing *porousness* of social institutions" (Wuthnow 1998: 5).

Examples of shin Issei activism related in this book indicate the often ad hoc nature of community work. This is similar to active shin Issei living in other transnationalized areas of the world. For example, memberships among shin Issei in Australia have been fluid, not highly organized, and aimed at fairly immediate results (Nagatomo 2017). Porosity aside, however, there is still a need for directed and purposeful cooperation. Embodied geographies of belonging make for key differences in life experientials between migrants and those native born. However, at its base is the knowledge that physical and emotional presence is required (Marcu 2014).

> We all need to gain control over the conditions under which we struggle with the challenges of life—but for most of us such control can be gained only collectively. It can only be (and it needs to be) a community woven together from sharing and mutual care; a community of concern and responsibility for the equal right to be human and the equal ability to act on that right. (Bauman 2001: 149)

Both Nikkei and shin Issei have utilized former and existing social institutions and individuals to build less structured, though still cooperative, community work. In many instances, this supportive activism has been organized on the basis of specific group needs. Having said this, "informal ties are not as loose as they seem because they run through organizations that have long played a stabilizing role in their communities" (Wuthnow 1998: 208).

For Nikkei, social justice and the pursuit of equality have been long-term historic narratives. These goals are not dissimilar to those of activist shin Issei women, who begin to understand this more fully the longer they are in the neighborhood. Shin Issei women say they look to Nikkei individuals and organizations as examples of leadership for what has been accomplished in the past. In this process, shin Issei are redefining themselves with new forms of expression and behavior and learning new roles that challenge norms and expectations (Pharr 1981). Nikkei believe there is a basis for a collective agenda of social action in the future.

> I try to find a common challenge or objective and through that educate these people. I [tell them about] their rights, their abilities. They're not aware of what they can do.
>
> Once they're outreached, they listen and they start to engage. Once they can relate themselves to issues, or faces of politicians, or language, they can engage more.
>
> They feel challenges, they need help from community, they need to be part of something, and they want someone to think about their futures.

No one—neither Nikkei nor shin Issei—believes the way forward is effortless, but most think it necessary, especially as contemporary Japanese migrants living in the United States incorporate more fully and begin to understand not only how Japanese American history has been constructed (and still is) but how it affects their lives as well. They are realizing the value of embracing Nikkei community, but equally vital to shin Issei is not losing sight of who they are and what is important to them.

> Shin Issei must understand and recognize that Issei and Nisei efforts to combat racial discrimination and prejudice have made possible the basis for a life in the U.S. for all Nikkei.
>
> Nikkei communities can continue to survive and flourish by meeting the linguistic and cultural needs and interests of Shin-Issei. At the same time, Shin-Issei can also learn from the experience of other Nik-

kei... [Shin Issei children] will go on living in the U.S. as Japanese Americans. (Tsukuda 2004)

In Sawtelle, shin Issei and Nikkei have come to know each other over the years. Common goals of preserving the neighborhood, educating shin Nisei children (and their shin Issei mothers as well), and making a place in the larger Southern California community are forging new alliances, though the learning curve is still steep for shin Issei women.

I'm the foreigner, and I can't speak English. I didn't know about racism in this country before I came.

For nonresidents, noncitizens, [our] lifestyle is already American. We have kids, even grandkids here, so [we're] really living an American life.

The learning curve is also tenuous for Nikkei, who say it's time for building coalitions.

We need to make the connections to Japanese who've come here after World War II. Basically, I'd like them to start stepping up!
A lot of gaps exist. Both sides feel the communities are disconnected. Both sides feel that there is a lot at stake. What [does] it mean [to shin Issei] to be Nikkei? What can we do together to have a comfortable life here?

For Nikkei and shin Issei, tension surrounding the recognition of differences and possibilities of collaborative agendas should not be minimized. At the same time, it is also important to acknowledge that these projects of inclusion and justice are still mediated by larger institutional forces, both domestic and international. Both groups make themselves, but they also continue to be made and subjectified racially and culturally by larger social structures (Ong 1996).

Epilogue

Oh, I know, if we go back to Japan, we cannot do anything. We have to be just old ladies! We cannot find jobs. Of course, you know the economy is very bad. Even young people cannot find jobs; even *guys* cannot find jobs—it is very bad.

I know when I go back to Japan—no job. But now, too many Japanese here [Southern California] looking for work, too. Many Japanese companies are gone. I sometimes help my husband here at his office, but he thinks it's no good because I'm his wife.

Despite a booming Japanese economy in the 1980s, young women in this book were constrained in seeking remunerative and meaningful work. After the Bubble collapse, Japanese companies downsized and sought flexibility in reorganizing workforces that put Japan in "the slow lane" (Iida and Morris 2008: 1072). A gendered reorganization of women's work continued on a path of flexible employment (Shire 2000). In the early 2000s, full-time employment among women fell, and just 15 percent had what may be termed as management jobs (Oishi 2007). By 2007, nearly 90 percent of all part-time workers were women (Asao 2010). At the same time, with concomitant economic conditions of downsizing and employment restructuring, as well as a more restrictive immigration climate in the United States, the incentives driving shin Issei migration from Japan have lessened.

The more noticeable aspects of a "global Japan" lost visibility in the United States during the first years of the new century. The three most conspicuous of those global features had been tourists, students, and corporate workers. First, Japanese were the largest group of overseas tourists visiting the United States into the 1990s. Their numbers swelled to nearly five million yearly, far outpacing the next largest group, from the United Kingdom (Service 1999: 1072). Japanese women traveling overseas still outnumbered men by almost two to one in the 1990s (Communications 1997). However, in the early 2000s, the total numbers of Japanese traveling abroad began to decrease, and by 2010, more than four million Japanese did not renew their passports, with growing economic concerns in Japan cited as major reasons for stagnant tourism (Isogai 2010). By 2018, numbers of Japanese tourists had dropped by nearly 40 percent (Security 2018b). Although their numbers have decreased, the estimates of gender imbalance of women to men continued into 2018 at the same two-to-one ratio (U.S. Census Bureau 2018). Second, Japan was the top sending country for students in the late 1990s, but by 2018, numbers had fallen below those of China, Canada, Mexico, India, and South Korea (Security 2018b; Service 1999). Third, more than 280,000 chuzai-in were still working temporarily in the United States in the mid-1990s, but by 2018, fully one-third of those employees had disappeared (Security 2018b; Security 2015). Despite dwindling figures, nearly one-third of all legally resident Japanese outside Japan live in the United States, making it the top country for permanent or long-term Japanese nationals (K. Matsumoto and Britain 2022).

So how have shin Issei's lives evolved since their arrivals in the United States? These contemporary migrants who appeared in the last quarter of the twentieth century and utilized all three circumstances of a global Japan to establish new lives initiated another Issei generation. They came as tourists and students and found jobs as supplementary labor in the then-burgeoning kaisha community. And what of those doors shin Issei women used to gain new lives? Among undocumented Japanese nationals living in the United States—individuals who arrived with legal visas but never left—exponential growth of 133 percent was recorded in just one decade between 1990 and 2000 (Office of Policy and Planning 2001). However, it must be remembered that these figures are estimates. In just one year—2017–2018—rates were significantly less but still showed a 19 percent growth in numbers of Japanese who were admitted legally but remained in the United States without documentation (Security 2018a). The smaller numbers of undocumented Japanese mirror the total decrease in the numbers of *all* overstayers in the United States—a decrease that has been labeled "stunning": between 2000 and 2009, the overall drop was estimated at 73 percent (Wasem 2014: 8).

No one would disagree that the methods of counting those who overstay visas or violate the visa law, such as by becoming employed, don't need improvement (Delfico 1995). On the one hand, efforts by the United States to curb illegal migration are certainly not new but gained impetus in the 1990s with laws such as IIRIRA. Since the 1990s, for example, enhancements in biometric screening have been used in place of reliance on airline and sea passenger manifests to track overseas arrivals (State, n.d.). On the other hand, once individuals are in the United States, achieving an accurate account of those who remain without proper documentation is almost impossible. Among shin Issei, the nature of "overstaying" was highly fluid, as was demonstrated by women who arrived with various visas, got renewals or extensions—or didn't—and subsequently never left.

> The phenomenon of foreign nationals who enter legally on a temporary basis and continue to stay after their visas expire is a fundamental problem of immigration control. . . .
> The failure of DHS [Department of Homeland Security] to consistently update the alien's record—for example, if the authorized period of admission is extended, if deferred departure is granted, or if the immigration status changes—is a major factor that prevents DHS from calculating reliable estimates of overstays. (Wasem 2014: 13)

At the beginning of the twenty-first century, young Japanese women who are weighing their options of staying or leaving Japan for life elsewhere face a dilemma. They still value the link between travel and migration to the United States. For young women, there remain fewer opportunities for them in Japan, unlike young Japanese men (Huong and Wilkins 2016). Moreover, they also know that a tightening economy and increased inability to find supplemental work among shrinking kaisha communities makes migration to the United States far less desirous than in the 1980s.

It is also useful to remember that while young shin Issei who choose to migrate in the twenty-first century constitute yet another new generation of migrants from Japan, they are not the women in this book—shin Issei who chose that route in the twentieth century. The shin Issei migrants of the 1980s are now—or will be shortly—senior citizens contemplating matters of old age. They have spent more years living in the United States than in Japan. The Japan they left four decades ago is now largely unknown to them, even for those who manage to return once or twice yearly. They are strangers in their homeland and often strangers as well among their own Japanese families and other key social relationships.

One of the most important issues for aging world migrants is the desire to (re)unite with families left in the homeland, especially children and grandchildren who may be counted on for eldercare (Percival 2013). For shin Issei, however, their immediate families are in the United States, and the challenges of transnational caregiving may not be a primary issue (Baldassar 2007). In the United States, shin Nisei children will soon be adults with independent lives and families of their own. Coresident, multigenerational living arrangements are no longer an assumed norm or an option among Nikkei families in the United States. This also applies in Japan's fast-aging society, where institutional eldercare facilities, staffed by migrant caregivers from other Asian and Pacific countries, are an increasingly common feature of the social landscape (Kolpashnikova and Kan 2021). Aging Japanese are finding that it is no longer a matter of moving in with one's children regardless of where they are but a legal business contract that requires advance planning.

Although beyond the scope of this study, the looming issue is whether shin Issei decide to age in place—stay in the United States or return to Japan. Married or single, on what kinds of support systems can shin Issei rely? Perhaps this explains, in part, why shin Issei appear to keep their options open by not naturalizing. Even among Japanese migrants who are here legally and have been in the United States for some time, those issued LPRs declined steadily in the decade 2000–2010. Taking into consideration that some applicants may have been denied LPRs, the rate of those receiving green cards had fallen by 35 percent (Security 2015). Furthermore, those shin Issei desiring naturalization continue to maintain low levels, hovering around a few hundred a year since 2000. This is despite the fact that thousands of shin Issei have most likely lived in the United States long enough to qualify for citizenship (Security 2018b).

There are other factors that may govern women who keep their options fluid. No matter how many years shin Issei have lived in the United States, and while there may be a plurality of home and identity, clearly there is still a continuing sense of being Japanese (George and Fitzgerald 2012). Shin Issei say these feelings intensify as they age.

> It's becoming more obvious that Japan is important to me. I'm using more Japanese; I have more Japanese friends than before. After thirty [years old] my body started to want more Japanese food. I started watching more Japanese dramas on TV. I find myself going backward as I get older. Back to my roots.

Among all migrants in the United States, Japanese nationals have found it most difficult to give up their Japanese citizenship. Their reluctance is based on the strong links between blood and membership for ethnic nationals, for whom one of the primary markers of being Japanese is speaking and reading Japanese. Fluency in English appears to be an ongoing issue. Of all those with Japanese ancestry in the United States, nearly one-third do not speak English, and another 13.5 percent speak English less than "very well" (U.S. Census Bureau 2018). Whether this will change among shin Issei women in a few years remains a question. Even as shin Issei become more involved in Nikkei activities or further integrate into mainstream communities, learning English "very well" is often contingent on the necessity of its frequent use. For the majority of shin Issei whose lives are illustrated here, use of English is not a daily necessity.

Other options for keeping Japanese citizenship are financial. Japan still has a social safety net with government benefits allowing for a survivable retirement life at a level not available in the United States. Foremost is that healthcare costs in Japan are more affordable, with the added benefit of culturally competent health services. As Takako experienced with her severely ill mother, aging shin Issei want health care that is sensitive to specific cultural needs such as language and food. However, despite facilities in the United States that may provide these advantages, newer forms of more costly privatized assisted living and eldercare for aging Japanese are leading to unequal access to these services (Laratta 2010).

In Los Angeles and elsewhere, shin Issei have attempted to alleviate this situation by becoming more active in creating alternative forms of senior citizen housing and care by building their own facilities that would allow them to age in place (Izuhara and Shibata 2001). This "bricolage of care" utilizing existing services in the host country while tailoring it to specific group needs is most often initiated by migrants with more politicized community experiences and financial resources (Hall, Ono, and Kohno 2021). Issues around aging and health-care options among undocumented shin Issei warrant further study.

Life Course(s)

As part of the conversation on the feminization of migration, this book has made several points about the construction of shin Issei lives through the examples of young Japanese women who move to the United States, not as wives or mothers following male migrants, but on their own, as economic and labor migrants. Shin Issei left Japan because of unequal gendered stratifications in life and work that limited their ability to earn a living and seek a meaningful existence outside social norms. However, those shin Issei who initially envisioned their migration as enhancing opportunity have been largely disappointed. Arriving in the United States, they left one system of gendered inequality but, because of limited skills, found themselves enmeshed in other gendered discourse that was also paired with racialized images. They were frank to admit they faced continuing difficulties with isolation and marginalization in both work and personal lives. No matter what their migration status, liminality in everyday life did not end.

A migrant life move always carries both gains and losses, but they were not passive victims of circumstance (Zlotnik 1990). Although they had limited resources and social capital, their stories also demonstrate that they sought ways in which to minimize their precarity and be active agents of change. Over the years, their individual agency, reception, and incorporation have been constructed and conditioned through larger social and economic forces. Women have taken advantage of more modern forms of communication and connections abroad to create and transform their new lives and reconfigure their identities (S. J. Mahler 1995). This transnationality has shaped and reinforced themes of belonging and identity, as they remain Japanese women. At the same time, however, a transnational life is not at odds with the desire to incorporate into community life in the United States (Itzigsohn and Giorguli-Saucedo 2005). They have been met with varying levels of marginality and acceptance and consequently have learned to adjust in myriad ways, including integration among Nikkei. This book has enlarged on those socioeconomic circumstances both in historic and contemporary contexts, but it is their own stories and experiences of adaptation that have taken precedence.

Through their narratives, what has been shown is their nascent community involvements and beginning forays outside their multiracial, multicultural families and circles of both Nikkei and other shin Issei. These ventures have served to lessen their social isolation and also afforded them a means of self-affirmation. Again, social practices and the formation of new, complex identities remain largely Japanese, not Nikkei. However, it is also clear that essentializing *a* culture and cultural behaviors as only Japanese is misleading. In their new homes, shin Issei adaptations are hybrid and alternative (Pratsinakis 2018). In this sense, the addition of new migrants is transforming the parameters and definitions of a Nikkei identity and, by relation, participatory political agendas.

For Nikkei, who see themselves as stakeholders in symbolic struggles over defining who belongs to a larger, racialized American identity, a fluid syncretism of cultural values and experiences is occurring among those who say integration with contemporary Japanese migrants is warranted. Critical in this task is an acceptance of differences that will always exist between those who are native and foreign born. Despite growing diversity, Nikkei activists still feel a strongly held belief that, "first and foremost, there will be a Nikkei community in the 21st century. . . . We must nurture, support and preserve this network of ties that bind if our community is to thrive in the next century" (Little Tokyo Service Center 2018). Sansei activists say,

> [It's] partly language, partly cultural kinds of things. And we have to do things that don't define the camps about what it means to be JA. It's got to be something that's much broader.
>
> We are always going to be a community that changes and evolves. We're never going to be stagnant with just Meiji Japan values. We will

evolve, but we want to keep those things in place that are of value, about what our culture and our community are in the context of the U.S.

In a historical context, shin Issei women have followed a familiar life course pursued by nineteenth-century Issei migrants—marriage, family, and the birth of children. Future and continuing emigration from Japan will doubtless chart similar courses.

Another Nisei Generation

Like Issei migrants 150 years ago who built the foundations of the Nikkei community with their American-born Nisei children, shin Issei women are, once again, mothers to another first generation of American citizens—the shin Nisei cohort. Like Nisei, shin Nisei are bilingual and often multicultural. Most of them will be adults by the middle to late 2020s. How will multiracial and multicultural shin Nisei view their Japanese American-ness? Will it be a singular, unremarked upon part of self or one among many normative repertoires of identity and belonging?

In the late 1980s, Nisei activists who transformed a Nikkei community's social and political goals postwar were beginning to retire. Their children, the Sansei who grew up in the turbulent 1960s, advanced and enlarged that agenda. In the twenty-first century, it is the Sansei's turn to cede leadership. New leaders and activists are emerging who will be shin Nisei and other multiracial Americans who are of Japanese ancestry. Sansei say these new actors are what Nikkei America is becoming.

> I have much more hope for the shin Nisei—for the children who've grown up here.

Multiracial youth are already the fastest-growing group in the country (Saulny 2011). This echoes the state of Nikkei America as well. Both Nikkei women and shin Issei women are exogamous in high numbers, but this is particularly so for shin Issei, whose outmarriage figures are significantly higher than those of Nikkei women. In the past few decades, the "disappearance" of Nikkei has been much discussed, but in fact, allowing for the addition of the racial question on the U.S. Census since 2000, the number of multiracial individuals who count Japanese in their family trees has increased. By 2018, using this metric, those who say they are of Japanese ancestry have enlarged the total Nikkei population by nearly 34 percent (U.S. Census Bureau 2018). Whether they are hafu or hapa, almost 43 percent of Nikkei are no longer one race but multiple races (U.S. Census Bureau 2018). Nikkei activists are looking ahead.

> Shin Nisei are the future of Japanese America. I think they have sufficient American (experiences). They've grown up in the U.S., and they understand some issues regarding racism. They understand issues regarding community a little bit more, and they speak English.

Tomoko's shin Nisei son, Akio, is now in high school. He plays on the basketball team and is an avid watcher of NBA games. The family still lives in the small home in West Los Angeles everyone knows as Aki-chan's House. Though he is not totally bilingual, Akio fully understands his mother, who converses with him mostly in Japanese. His linguistic abilities get more practice during his summer trips to visit his mother's family in Japan. Certainly, he is more competent linguistically than his American father, who neither speaks nor understands Japanese. Akio's embrace of things Japanese is unremarkable; so too, is the performance of an American citizenship. All his life, Akio has watched Tomoko work late at night calling other mothers, typing up notes, thinking about how to bring people together. She wants Akio to know his Japanese heritage, but she has told him many times he is an American. He thinks he wants to go to law school.

Tomoko now works part-time before Akio gets home from school and says she's still organizing the other shin Issei mothers. Of late, she has also been talking to her husband about building an addition to their house so she will have more room for meetings. Tomoko's current work involves putting together information on university applications. She wants to share it with other shin Issei mothers who are focused on laying the groundwork for their children's college education. In conversations, she now more easily uses the term *shin Issei* to describe herself and friends.

> Everything is preparation. A shin Issei mother, her son just got into Columbia University. She gave me so much information. I did a lot of hard work. You need to prepare for three or four years in advance. I want to tell people how to take the first step [since] I was struggling.
>
> Many people don't know how to put their kids into quality schools. It's easy for shin Issei to say, "I don't know" . . . so I say, "If you don't know, why don't you find out?" Oh sure, it's so important to try to help. I'm thinking about how I can organize something. My husband doesn't care. I'm the boss.

Tomoko is, once again, buttonholing people she thinks may be able to help, including Nikkei, some of whom she now calls friends. Her outlook on community engagement has transformed over the years.

> Nowadays, I think the community is much more important. I never used to think that. We never thought about the outside. So we were narrow-minded, just focused on how to raise my kid. This is my responsibility, and that's it.
>
> For me, it's different now. I am trying to help the community. We are from Japan, and we have no knowledge of the education system here. I want to help shin Nisei to get a better education here because if Mom doesn't have any knowledge, you can't help your kid get into a better system here. I think I can help people in the community.

Shin Issei activities do not yet constitute a mature social project because they don't have the benefit of years of experience. Nikkei have strategized American selves within a politicized agenda for more than a century. However, shin Issei women are not an anomaly in this endeavor. Instead, their appearance as part of continuing migration from Japan makes their voices only the newest ones in a wider membership of Japanese and Nikkei.

As was the case in the late 1800s, then again in the late 1970s, socioeconomic changes in both Japan and the United States shaped Japanese migration. At the beginning of the twenty-first century, there are differing circumstances at work, but there may still be similar outcomes in migration patterns from Japan. After the Meiji Restoration, Issei left economic deterioration to take advantage of new job opportunities abroad. Subsequently, migration from Japan swelled, peaked, and declined (World War II notwithstanding). The same appears to be occurring now with contemporary Japanese migration patterns (Iida and Morris 2008). It is lessening though not ending. While transforming global circumstances most likely will not mean another truncated, isolated Nikkei generation, there are still generational changes occurring within contemporary Japanese migration—changes that will continue to pose both risk and reward to any broader Nikkei collective.

The idea of Nikkei belonging is not homogeneous—it never has been. Stitching together an agenda for social action and recognition is challenging, but as many Nikkei have learned since the first Issei migrated in the late nineteenth century, this is what it means to be active, engaged members of American society. Redefining Nikkei meanings in the twenty-first century will require—as it always has—compromise, accommodation, empathy, and necessity.

Notes

ACKNOWLEDGMENTS

1. The first usage of romanized Japanese words appears italicized. Subsequent uses do not.

2. Meiji refers to Emperor Meiji, whose succession to power was restored in 1868 after the disintegration of the Tokugawa Shogunate. The young emperor Meiji presided over the growth of an industrial economy, mass emigration, and a restructuring of Japanese society. In less than three and a half decades, Japan was transformed into a world power. See Norman 1940.

INTRODUCTION

1. In Japanese, *shin* means new and *Issei* is a generational designation referring to the first group of migrants who left Japan in the mid-1800s to live overseas. Thus, in the broadest terms, shin Issei is used for new immigrants from Japan who arrived post–World War II to distinguish them from the initial nineteenth-century diaspora. It should be noted that few contemporary Japanese migrants refer to themselves as shin Issei, simply calling themselves Japanese. The shin Issei appellation is used by native-born Americans of Japanese ancestry to delineate between themselves and the newly arrived foreign born.

2. American-born Japanese use derivatives of the Japanese language's numbering system to delineate generational cohort or belonging. The term *Issei* refers to first-generation immigrants from Japan in the nineteenth century; *Nisei*, children of Issei and second-generation native-born Americans; *Sansei*, children of Nisei and third-generation native-born; *Yonsei*, children of Sansei and fourth-generation native-born; *Gosei*, children of Yonsei and fifth-generation native-born Americans. See the following endnote for the definition of *Nikkei*.

3. *Nikkei* initially referred primarily to native-born U.S. citizens of Japanese ancestry. However, by the 1980s, the term Nikkei was expanded to reference any Japanese born or living outside of Japan. For example, this encompasses the descendants of nineteenth-century Japanese immigrants who settled elsewhere in North and South America. See L. Hirabayashi and Kikumura-Yano 2006; Kasamatsu 2005; Lesser 2007; Workpermit.com 2007; Yokota 2008.

4. As the term *shin Issei* refers to contemporary Japanese migrants in order to distinguish this group from the first generation Issei who migrated to the United States beginning in the late 19th century, shin Nisei are members of a contemporary cohort of American citizens who have shin Issei mothers. They are distinguished from second generation American born Nisei, the children of Issei.

5. Figures on the numbers of Japanese women who married American servicemen post–World War II, the majority of whom subsequently moved to the United States, varies widely. Until 1965 when major immigration reform was enacted, perhaps as many as 55,000 women emigrated to the United States, with the peak reached in 1957. Neither the U.S. military nor public discourse in Japan and the United States sanctioned these unions. No Japanese national married to an American was permitted entry until 1945, when the so-called War Brides Act was passed. See B.-L. Kim 1977; Williams 1991.

6. Tokugawa refers to the ruling military dynasty of Japan that began in the twelfth century. The entire country was unified under military rule shortly after 1600. This led to nearly three centuries of relative peace under the Shogun until power was restored to Emperor Meiji in 1868. See Dower 1975.

7. The United States defines lawful permanent residents (LPRs) as "persons who have been granted lawful permanent residence in the United States." They are also known as "green card" recipients.

8. Roughly speaking, Issei arrived from 1885 to 1908; Nisei (also Nisei *Kibei*—young Americans sent by their Issei parents to Japan for education) were born between 1915 and 1935; Sansei between 1945 and 1965; Yonsei between 1975 and 1995; and Gosei were born after 2005.

9. Given the transitory nature of contemporary migration generally, it is difficult to accurately count individuals who are "living abroad." The United States continues to be the premier destination for Japanese nationals. Since 1998, Japanese women migrants who have become legal, permanent residents have outpaced Japanese men. These figures do not include those who are undocumented. See Horiuchi, Hirai, and Matsuura 2023.

CHAPTER 1

1. Matsuda defines the use of *culture* in "the broader sense of relating to life of a people as a whole" (2007: 6). By example, the author further posits that American culture was practiced by the U.S. Occupation as a shared system of beliefs and customs achieved through a wide range of contacts and personal relations.

2. Though ryosei kenbo was promoted by the state as the preferred role for modern Japanese women, the concept did not achieve full adherence among women and elides the widespread, vibrant postwar activities of women in the public sphere. For a more complete analysis of ryosei kenbo as state policy—vestiges of which still remain—rather than everyday practice, see Uno 1993.

3. Women in their twenties were targeted with other terms of social rejection, as were young men. Those no longer looking for work were called *NEETS* (not in employment, education, or training). Freeters (*furita*) were those who were working in a series of temporary jobs. See Genda 2007.

4. While Japanese women's groups can take partial credit for the passage of the EEOL, the Japanese government was also sensitive to foreign influence. In 1980 it had signed off on the United Nations Decade for Women declaration ending all forms of discrimination against women. See Kawashima 1995. See also AMPO 1998.

CHAPTER 2

1. In the 1980s, a temporary, nonimmigrant work visa, which most multinational Japanese corporations used, was the L1 or the L2 (spouses and families). Generally, with renewals, L1 and L2 visas carry a seven-year limit. While it is illegal for temporary, nonimmigrant work visa holders (tourists or students) to seek most jobs, L1 and L2 holders are usually exempt. It is not uncommon for some L1 and L2 visa holders to apply for a U.S. green card (LPR—legal permanent residence) that permits both residence and employment, with a path to U.S. citizenship without losing their status. For further legal definitions of migrants, see Security 2017.

2. After Japan's economic collapse, the kaisha structure has changed as Japanese multinationals seek to reorganize their overseas operations. See Itoh 2006; Kurotani 2005; S. M. Lee and Edmonston 2005.

3. Most Japanese who are in the United States on work visas or green cards register with the Japanese consulates where they reside. This figure is most likely an undercount since individuals who are in the United States without authorization would not register.

4. In the 1980s, individuals on a tourist visa who wanted to take a short course of study that was defined as recreational (not for credit toward a degree) and that was less than eighteen hours per week were permitted to do so on a visitor visa. See Yializis, n.d.

5. Since 2009, the Electronic System for Travel Authorization (ESTA) program was instituted by the United States. Japanese citizens (as well as citizens of additional visa-waiver countries) must apply for an ESTA permit, which is a preauthorization to travel. The ESTA is not a visa but, in effect, a prescreening process done by the Department of Homeland Security, and it applies only to those countries with visa waivers. See Esta.U.S., n.d.

6. Usually foreign nationals who want to study for credit in the United States are given F1 visas. Study can be done at a college, university, private school, seminary, or other "academic institution." An M1 visa is issued for vocational, nonacademic study such as airline training, cosmetology, or specialized mechanical training. In both cases, international students must have prior acceptance at their educational facility before applying. They are allowed to stay in the United States or to obtain renewals while they complete coursework. Potential students list the end date of their program and then have sixty days in which to leave the United States before their study visa expires or they are approved for a change of status. See Travel.state.gov, n.d., Study and Exchange.

7. Nonnative English speakers who want to enroll in post–high school educational programs such as junior colleges in the United States are often required to take the Test of English as a Foreign Language (TOEFL). The standardized test measures a potential

student's ability to use and understand English. For Japanese, TOEFL testing is offered throughout the year at dozens of locations in Japan. Though virtual testing was not available in the early 1990s, the TOEFL is now offered online.

8. Although Japanese educational reforms in the 1980s prioritized "internationalization," including English language skills, Japanese students' success rates on the TOEFL remain among the lowest in Asia. See Cave 2014.

CHAPTER 3

1. Individuals visiting the United States as tourists on B2 visitor visas are not permitted to work. Moreover, it is not possible to exchange a visitor visa for a student visa. A separate application for an F1 must be made for students. See Travel.state.gov, n.d., Employment.

2. The rules on ability to work while on a student visa are complex. Generally, F1 holders may be allowed to work part-time on campus. Off campus, employment that may be related to one's intended course of study, such as an internship or other specialized training pertaining to study, may be permitted. Other kinds of work are not permitted. See Dashew Center UCLA, n.d.

3. There are two broad ways a migrant may qualify for an LPR, through family or through employment. Aside from these categories, there are specific other requirements that must be met. The woman in this example needed to have a sponsor make application. See Security, n.d., Green Card Categories.

4. One of the unintended consequences of this mid-twentieth-century immigration reform was that the demographics of the United States changed dramatically. Particularly well known is the exponential growth in Asian Pacific American communities—transformations due to post-1965 migration. See Võ 2008.

5. Hana's uncle might have sponsored his sister, Hana's mother, if she wanted to migrate to the United States. Once here and with her own green card, her mother could have then sponsored Hana under regulations governing unmarried daughters and sons.

6. Gifts of money/obligation called *koden* are remitted to help pay expenses for life passages such as funerals or other debts. Nikkei also observe this tradition in the United States. See Asakawa 2016.

7. The green card lottery was mandated by Congress and implemented in the early 1990s. Known as the Diversity Immigrant Visa Program, it allows for a random selection of qualified migrants who are from countries with low immigration, such as Japan, to receive permanent residence status (green cards). The first year of the lottery, millions of migrants from around the world applied, and 970 Japanese nationals won green cards. See Security, n.d., Green Card through the Diversity Immigrant Visa Program.

8. These numbers would eliminate the international marriages of postwar Japanese women and U.S. military personnel because postwar international brides in the 1990s likely would have been in their sixties or older.

9. One of the first steps toward naturalization is continuous residence in the United States as an LPR, usually for five years. See Sanchez and Batalova 2021.

10. Individuals born in the United States are guaranteed citizenship—*jus soli*—birth by location, whereas in Japan, *jus sanguinis* attributes citizenship only through blood parentage though not necessarily by descent. The politics of nationality in Japan make giving up one's Japanese citizenship difficult and even more so for individuals who wish to acquire

Japanese citizenship. As seen in the example of many Issei parents who registered their American born Nisei children as Japanese nationals prior to World War II, confusion and suspicion followed those with dual nationalities.

CHAPTER 4

1. United Television Broadcasting Systems (UTB) began airing in Los Angeles in 1971 to take advantage of the growing Japanese national population. It provided current news and various Japanese cultural programs. Because of declining viewership and a resulting decrease in advertising revenues, UTB signed off in April 2018. See Culross 2018.

2. For those shin Issei who were not married or had no children, this created other invisible marginalizations. Only two or three women were not married, and although everyone in Tomoko's circle knew one another, only those shin Issei with children came to her home. Women like unmarried Kyoko maintained a friendship with Tomoko, but Kyoko socialized among other shin Issei who were also single.

3. Both terms are in common usage but not without a degree of etymological tension. Originally, *hafu* was a derogatory term used in Japan for someone Japanese and Other. Postwar, it was used in connection with the U.S. Occupation, unwed mothers, and poverty. More recently, newer connotations tie *hafu* to internationalized and more glamorous images of mixed whiteness. See Yamashiro 2017: chap. 3. *Hapa* is a native Hawaiian word that initially referred to someone who was part native Hawaiian. A more contemporary definition has expanded *hapa* to someone who is any multiracial combination. Native Hawaiian sovereignty supporters argue that this is cultural appropriation and identity theft. See A. Johnson 2016.

4. The case of Fumiko Kimura was widely covered by media. Kimura attempted parent-child suicide—known in Japan as *oyako-shinju*—by walking into the ocean at Santa Monica Beach. She survived, but her two small children drowned. Japanese media labeled the case as "less than murder" while American media attempted to understand the "apparent cultural implications." The judge in the case received thousands of signatures from Japanese and Japanese Americans pleading for leniency. Kimura was placed on five years' probation and time served. See R. Goel 2004; T. Bryant 1990; R. Stewart 1985.

5. Facilities mandated by the Japanese government and Japan-based organizations more commonly use *gakuen*. The JHS that had its beginnings among local Issei in Sawtelle is also known as a *gakuin*. There are lexical differences between the terms gaku*en* and gaku*in*—the former related to a garden of learning and the latter to an institute or temple of learning. There may also be religious differences. Gakuin have roots among Japanese Christians, while gakuen may be more closely related to Buddhism. See Higashi 2016.

CHAPTER 5

1. The term in its simplest definition refers to the spirit of the Japanese. The phrase has been in usage since perhaps eighth-century Japan; its invocation implies resolve, valor. In the early twentieth century and during World War II, it was appropriated as a rallying cry for Japan's military as well as for ultranationalists. See Carr 1994.

2. *Gaman* means to persevere or endure. *Shikata-ga-nai* translates to "it can't be helped." Both terms imply hard work toward eventual success. For more on Meiji values and vocabulary, see Ogawa 1978; Takamori 2010.

3. Between 1868 and 1912, more than 60 percent of all Japanese male migrants to Hawai'i and the West Coast came from just two prefectures in Southern Japan—Hiroshima and Yamaguchi, both heavily agricultural. The Japanese government, which closely administered and monitored labor recruits, hoped to alleviate poverty in these areas created by the country's drive to industrialize. Fictive kinships cement contemporary relationships. Prefectural associations still proliferate, and it is not uncommon to hear Nikkei ask one another, "What ken (prefecture) are you (your family) from?" See Moriyama 1985.

4. *Enryo* is an often-used and familiar Meiji Japanese word among Nikkei, described as Nikkei reticence, self-effacement in "situations as diverse as their hesitancy to speak out at meetings . . . their refusal of a second helping; their acceptance of a less desired object when given a free choice, their lack of verbal participation." For further explanation, see Kitano 1969: 104.

5. These U.S. Census figures include residents in the 90025 zip code, which encompasses the Sawtelle neighborhood but also extends into adjacent areas of West Los Angeles. For a detailed zip code map, see U.S. Census Bureau 2010b.

6. Neighborhood councils were enacted by LA City in 1999 as elected advisory bodies to local government on numerous issues such as zoning, redevelopment, fire, and safety. Nearly one hundred councils cover the city, with budgets paid through tax dollars. Councils usually have a dozen or so board members and can be influential in local elections—for example, city council members. In turn, neighborhood councils can also be quite open to significant pressure from neighborhood stakeholders and other constituents. For further information, see Department of Neighborhood Empowerment, n.d.

CHAPTER 6

1. The LTSC is a well-known, broad-based Nikkei organization offering social services in Little Tokyo since 1979. Among its services is a staff of multilingual social workers. LTSC's commitment to community service remains, as does its headquarters in Little Tokyo. See Rafu Staff 2013.

2. *Toyo's Camera* is a ninety-eight-minute documentary directed by Junichi Suzuki in 2009 featuring well-known Issei photographer Toyo Miyatake's story about his incarceration in Manzanar and his experience smuggling into Manzanar a photo camera with which to record his experiences. See Densho Encyclopedia, n.d.

3. Kunsho are awards of outstanding national and international service and merit bestowed by the emperor of Japan. In the case of Nikkei living outside Japan, kunsho are awarded usually by the consuls general of Japan in a yearly ceremony. Fields of contribution are wide ranging—politics, academics, arts, literature, sports, science, the promotion of social good.

4. The South Bay growth rate is impressive despite the collapse of the Japanese economy beginning in the early 1990s, which fueled the demise of many Japanese corporations in California, most notably Toyota Motor Sales North America, then the largest employer in Torrance, in 2014. The company had been a fixture in Southern California since the 1950s and decided to move to Plano, Texas, giving its nearly four thousand employees the option of relocating. Local politicians saw the move as a blow to the community and the result of both the decline of the Japanese economy and the high cost of doing business in California. See Reid 2014.

References

Abu-Lughod, L. 1991. "Writing against Culture." In *Recapturing Anthropology: Working in the Present*, edited by R. G. Fox, 138–162. Santa Fe: School of American Research Press.
Adachi, N. 2006. *Japanese Diasporas: Unsung Pasts, Conflicting Presents, and Uncertain Futures*. London: Routledge.
———. 2007. "Racial Journeys: Justice, Internment and Japanese-Peruvians in Peru, the United States, and Japan." *Asia Pacific Journal: Japan Focus* 5 (9): 1–11.
———. 2010. "Reconsiderations of Race, Ethnicity, and Identity: Transnational Migrants in Post–World War II Global Society." In *Japanese and Nikkei at Home and Abroad: Negotiating Identities in a Global World*, edited by N. Adachi, 1–30. Amherst, NY: Cambria.
Addison, P. 1992. "Japan Inc.: The Juggernaut That Never Was." *Nikkei Weekly Japan*.
Adler, S. 1977. "Maslow's Need Hierarchy and the Adjustment of Immigrants." *International Migration Review* 11 (4): 444–451.
Agency (Economic Planning Agency). 1982. *Annual Report on National Life: Household Economy under Low Growth and Changing Regional Life*. Tokyo: Economic Planning Agency.
Alba, R., and V. Nee. 1997. "Rethinking Assimilation Theory for a New Era of Immigration." *International Migration Review* 31 (4): 826–874.
Alcala, Maria Jose. 2006. "State of the World's Population 2006: A Passage to Hope; Women and International Migration." United Nations Population Fund. New York: United Nations.
Alderman, D. 2002. "Street Names as Memorial Arenas: The Reputational Politics of Commemorating Martin Luther King Jr. in a Georgia County." *Historical Geography* 30:99–120.
Alexander, J. C., R. Eyerman, B. Geisen, N. J. Smelser, and P. Sztompka. 2004. *Cultural Trauma and Collective Identity*. Berkeley: University of California Press.

Allison, A. 1994. *Nightwork: Sexuality, Pleasure, and Corporate Masculinity in a Tokyo Hostess Club*. Chicago: University of Chicago Press.

———. 2012. "Ordinary Refugees: Social Precarity and Soul in 21st Century Japan." *Anthropological Quarterly* 85 (2): 345–370.

———. 2013. *Precarious Japan*. Durham, NC: Duke University Press.

———. 2015. "Discounted Life: Social Time in Relationless Japan." *Boundary 2* 42 (3): 129–141.

American Immigration Council. 2016. "The Three- and Ten-Year Bars: How New Rules Expand Eligibility for Waivers." Accessed November 22, 2019. Available at https://americanimmigrationcouncil.org/research/three-and-ten-year-bars.

Amit, V. 2014. "Inherited Multiple Citizenships: Opportunities, Happenstances and Improvisations among Mobile Young Adults." *Social Anthropology / Anthropologie Sociale* 22 (4): 396–409.

AMPO staff. 1998. "One Step Forward, Ten Steps Backward: Changes for Women in the Labor Standards Law." AMPO: *Japan Asia Quarterly Review* 28 (2): 4–10.

Anderson, B. 1991. *Imagined Communities: Reflections on the Origin and Spread of Nationalism*. London: Verso.

Andressen, C., and K. Kumagai. 1996. *Escape from Affluence: Japanese Students in Australia*. Brisbane: Centre for the Study of Australia-Asia Relations.

Apodaca, P. 1992. "L.A. Makes Its Last Car: End of the Road for GM's Van Nuys Plant." *Los Angeles Times*, August 28, 1992. Available at http://articles.latimes.com/1992-08-28/business/fi-6132_1_van-nuys.

Asahi Shinbun. 1956. Advertising and Lifestyles. *Asahi Shinbun Shukusatsuban* (Tokyo), 1: various.

Asakawa, G. 2016. "Funerals in the Japanese American Community." *Discover Nikkei*, June 2, 2016. JANM (Japanese American National Museum). Available at http://www.discovernikkei.org/en/journal/2016/6/2/funerals.

Asao, Y. 2010. "Overview of Non-regular Employment in Japan." Japan Institute for Labour Policy and Training. Accessed December 13, 2014. Available at https://www.jil.go.jp.

Asato, N. 2006. *Teaching Mikadoism: The Attack on Japanese Language Schools in Hawaii, California, and Washington, 1919–1927*. Honolulu: University of Hawai'i Press.

Ashikari, M. 2003. "Urban Middle-Class Japanese Women and Their White Faces: Gender, Ideology, and Representation." *Ethos* 31 (1): 3–37.

———. 2005. "Cultivating Japanese Whiteness: The 'Whitening' Cosmetics Boom and the Japanese Identity." *Journal of Material Culture* 10 (1): 73–91.

Associated Press. 1986. "Woman Whose Children Died in Suicide Attempt Living Quietly." *AP Wires*. April 6, 1986. Accessed March 20, 2019. Available at https://apnews.com/d2d8d50c37dd2ceb7cce311551f328e5.

Association (Nikkei Women Legacy Association). 2012. Newsletter.

Atoh, M. 2008. "Family Changes in the Context of Lowest-Low Fertility: The Case of Japan." *International Journal of Japanese Sociology* 17 (1): 14–29.

Avenarius, C. 2002. "Work and Social Network Composition among Immigrants from Taiwan to Southern California." *Anthropology of Work Review* 23 (3–4): 3–15.

Avenell, S. A. 2010. *Making Japanese Citizens: Civil Society and the Mythology of the Shimin in Postwar Japan*. Berkeley: University of California Press.

Azaryahu, M. 1986. "Street Names and Political Identity: The Case of East Berlin." *Journal of Contemporary History* 21 (4): 581–604.
Azuma, E. 2003. "The Politics of Transnational History Making: Japanese Immigrants on the Western 'Frontier,' 1927–1941." *Journal of American History* 89 (4): 1401–1430.
———. 2006. "A Transborder Japanese Community in U.S.-Mexican California: A Preliminary Study of Borderland Nikkei Experience." In *World of Transnational Asian Americans*, edited by D. Yui, 101–118. Tokyo: Center for Pacific and American Studies, University of Tokyo.
———. 2008. "'Pioneers of Overseas Japanese Development': Japanese American History and the Making of Expansionist Orthodoxy in Imperial Japan." *Journal of Asian Studies* 67 (4): 1187–1226.
Baldassar, L. 2007. "Transnational Families and Aged Care: The Mobility of Care and the Migrancy of Ageing." *Journal of Ethnic and Migration Studies* 33 (2): 275–297.
Bardsley, J. 2008. "Girl Royalty: The 1959 Coronation of Japan's First Miss Universe." *Asian Studies Association of Australia* 32 (2): 375–391.
Basch, L., N. Glick Schiller, and C. Blanc. 1994. *Nations Unbound: Transnational Projects, Postcolonial Predicaments, and Deterritorialized Nation-States*. Amsterdam: Gordon and Breach.
Batalova, J. 2011. "Asian Immigrants in the United States." *Journal of the Migration Policy Institute*. Accessed April 3, 2013. Available at https://www.migrationpolicy.org/article/asian-immigrants-united-states-0#14.
Baubock, R. 2003. "Towards a Political Theory of Migrant Transnationalism." *International Migration Review* 37 (3): 700–723.
Bauman, Z. 2001. *Community: Seeking Safety in an Insecure World*. Cambridge: Polity.
Befu, H. 1992. "Symbols of Nationalism and Nihonjinron." In *Ideology and Practice in Modern Japan*, edited by R. Goodman and K. Refsing. New York: Routledge.
———. 2001. *Hegemony of Homogeneity: An Anthropological Analysis of Nihonjinron*. Melbourne: Trans Pacific.
———. 2008. "The Japanese Diaspora: Dekasegi, Imperialism, and Transnational Trade." *Pan-Japan* 6 (1–2): 2–27.
Ben-Ari, E., and V. Y. Y. Fong. 2000. "Twice Marginalized: Single Japanese Female Expatriates in Singapore." In *Japan in Singapore: Cultural Occurrences and Cultural Flows*, edited by E. Ben-Ari and J. R. Clammer, 82–111. Richmond, Surrey: Curzon.
Berkofsky, A. 2010. "Japan's Post-war Constitution: Origins, Protagonists and Controversies." *Il Politico* 75 (2): 5–25.
Bibler Coutin, S. 2003. "Cultural Logics of Belonging and Movement: Transnationalism, Naturalization, and U.S. Immigration Politics." *American Ethnologist* 30 (4): 508–526.
Bishop, B. 2000. "The Diversification of Employment and Women's Work in Contemporary Japan." In *Globalization and Social Change in Contemporary Japan*, edited by J. S. Eades, T. Gill, and H. Befu, 93–109. Melbourne: Trans Pacific.
Blackmore, W. 2009. "Top 10: Japanese Noodles Shops in Torrance." *LA Weekly*, September 22, 2009. Available at http://www.laweekly.com/squidink/2009/09/22/top-10-japanese-noodles-shops-in-torrance?mode=print.
Bonilla-Silva, E. 1997. "Rethinking Racism: Toward a Structural Interpretation." *American Sociological Review* 62 (3): 465–480.

———. 2018. *Racism without Racists: Color-Blind Racism and the Persistence of Racial Equality in America*. Lanham, MD: Rowman and Littlefield.
Bonnett, A. 1996. "Constructions of 'Race,' Place and Discipline: Geographies of 'Racial' Identity and Racism." *Ethnic and Racial Studies* 19 (4): 864–883.
Bretell, C. 2007. "Adjustment of Status, Remittances, and Return: Some Observations on 21st Century Migration Processes." *City and Society* 19 (1): 47–59.
Brint, S. 2001. "Gemeinschaft Revisited: A Critique and Reconstruction of the Community Concept." *Sociological Theory* 19 (1): 1–23.
Brinton, M. C. 1993. *Women in the Japanese Economy after the Bubble*. Washington, DC: Woodrow Wilson International Center for Scholars.
Broder, J. 1986. "Arco, B of A Will Sell Twin Tower Complex in L.A." *Los Angeles Times*, August 5, 1986. Available at http://articles.latimes.com/1986-08-05/business/fi-1544_1_arco-plaza.
Brodkin, K. 2007. *Making Democracy Matter: Identity and Activism in Los Angeles*. New Brunswick, NJ: Rutgers University Press.
Brodkin Sacks, K. 1988. "Gender and Grassroots Leadership." In *Women and the Politics of Empowerment*, edited by A. Bookman and S. Morgen, 77–93. Philadelphia: Temple University Press.
Brody, B. T. 2002. *Opening the Door: Immigration, Ethnicity and Globalization in Japan*. New York: Routledge.
Broverman, N. 2010. "West LA's Yamaguchi Apartments Opening Soon." *Curbed LA*, March 1, 2010. Available at https://la.curbed.com/2010/3/1/10519968/west-las-retail-laden-yamaguchi#comments.
Bruce, N. C. 1977. "Real Estate Steering and the Fair Housing Act of 1968." *Tulsa Law Journal* 12 (4): 758–773.
Bryant, T. 1990. "*Oya-ko Shinju*: Death at the Center of the Heart." *Pacific Basin Law Journal* 8 (1): 1–31.
Buckley, J. M., and D. Graves. 2016. "Tangible Benefits from Intangible Resources: Using Social and Cultural History to Plan Neighborhood Futures." *Journal of the American Planning Association* 82 (2): 152–166.
Bureau (Public Information and Cultural Affairs Bureau). 1989. *Information Bulletin 1988–1989*. Tokyo: Japan Ministry of Foreign Affairs.
———. 1991. *Information Bulletin 1990–1991*. Tokyo: Japan Ministry of Foreign Affairs.
Burkett, P., and M. Hart-Landsberg. 2003. "The Economic Crisis in Japan: Mainstream Perspectives and an Alternate View." *Critical Asian Studies* 35 (3): 339–372.
Butler, J. 2004. *Undoing Gender*. New York: Routledge.
Butler, Y., and M. Iino. 2005. "Current Japanese Reforms in English Language Education: The 2003 'Action Plan.'" *Language Policy* 4:25–45.
Calisphere. n.d. "Japanese American Camp in Burbank." University of California. Accessed August 2019. Available at https://calisphere.org/search/?q=japanese%20american%20camp%20in%20burbank.
Campbell, B., and C. Laheij. 2021. "Introduction: Urban Precarity." *City and Society* 33 (2): 283–302.
Cargill, T. F., and T. Sakamoto. 2008. *Japan since 1980*. New York: Cambridge University Press.

Carr, M. 1994. "Yamato-Damashii: 'Japanese Spirit' Definitions." *International Journal of Lexicography* 7 (4): 279–306.

Cave, P. 2014. "Education in the Lost Decade: Stability or Stagnation?" In *Capturing Contemporary Japan: Differentiation and Uncertainty*, edited by S. Kawano, G. Roberts, and S. Orpett. Honolulu: University of Hawai'i Press.

Chavez, L. R. 2013. *Shadowed Lives: Undocumented Immigrants in American Society*. Belmont, CA: Wadsworth.

Cheah, P., and B. Robbins. 1998. *Cosmopolitics: Thinking and Feeling beyond the Nation*. Cultural Politics. Minneapolis: University of Minnesota Press.

Chen, J., and D. T. Takeuchi. 2011. "Intermarriage, Ethnic Identity, and Perceived Social Standing among Asian Women in the United States." *Journal of Marriage and Family* 73 (4): 876–888.

Chiavacci, D. 2005. "Changing Egalitarianism? Attitudes Regarding Income and Gender Equality in Contemporary Japan." *Japan Forum* 17 (1): 107–131.

Chinen, K., and G. R. Tucker. 2006. "Heritage Language Development: Understanding the Roles of Ethnic Identity, Schooling and Community." In *Heritage Language Development: Focus on East Asian Immigrants*, edited by K. Kondo-Brown, 89–126. Philadelphia: John Benjamins.

Chow, S. 2000. "The Significance of Race in the Private Sphere: Asian Americans and Spousal Preferences." *Sociological Inquiry* 70 (1): 1–29.

CJACLC (California Japanese American Community Leadership Council). n.d. "California Japantowns." Accessed August 2019. Available at http://www.californiajapantowns.org/sawtelle.html.

Clifford, B. 1994. "Pullback from U.S. Real Estate Swells: Japanese Investors Selling More, Buying Less." *Nikkei Weekly* (Tokyo). Available at http://www.lexisnexis.com/hottopics/lnacademic/?

Cogan, J., J. Torney-Purta, and D. Anderson. 1988. "Knowledge and Attitudes toward Global Issues: Students in Japan and the United States." *Comparative Education Review* 32 (3): 282–297.

Commerce (U.S. Department of Commerce). 1990. *The Foreign-Born Population in the United States Bureau of Census 1990 CP-3-1*. Washington, DC: U.S. Department of Commerce.

———. 2000. *Sex by Year of Entry by Citizenship Status for the Foreign-Born Population*. Washington, DC: U.S. Census Bureau. Accessed September 14, 2002. Available at http://www/census/gov/prod/cen2000/doc/sf4.pdf.

———. 2010. *American FactFinder: 1-Year Estimates*. Washington, DC: U.S. Census Bureau. Accessed April 20, 2012. Available at http://factfinder2.census.gov.

Communications (Japanese Ministry of Internal Affairs and Communications). 1997. "Survey on Time Use and Leisure Activities B. o. Statistics." Accessed March 3, 2018. Available at http://www.stat.go.jp/english/data/shakai/2.htm.

Constable, N. 1997. *Maid to Order in Hong Kong: Stories of Filipina Workers*. Ithaca, NY: Cornell University Press.

Cornell, S., and D. Hartmann. 2007. *Ethnicity and Race: Making Identities in a Changing World*. Thousand Oaks, CA: Pine Forge.

Creed, G. W. 2004. "Constituted through Conflict: Images of Community (and Nation) in Bulgarian Rural Ritual." *American Anthropologist* 106 (1): 56–70.

Creighton, M. 2017. "A Tree House in Tokyo: Reflections on Nikkei, Citizenship, Belonging, Architecture, and Art on the 75th Anniversary of Japanese American and Japanese Canadian Internment." *Contemporary Japan* 29 (2): 246–260.
Culross, M. 2018. "UTB Signing Off." *Rafu Shimpo* (Los Angeles), April 5, 2018, 1.
Daily Yomiuri. 1994. "Young Workers Flocking Abroad to Find More Challenging Jobs." *Yomiuri Shimbun* (Tokyo), April 19, 1994.
Dales, L. 2009. *Feminist Movements in Contemporary Japan*. New York: Routledge.
———. 2015. "Suitably Single? Representations of Singlehood in Contemporary Japan." In *Configurations of Family in Contemporary Japan*, edited by T. Aoyama, L. Dales, and R. Dasgupta, 21–32. London: Routledge.
Dalton, E. 2015. *Women and Politics in Contemporary Japan*. New York: Routledge.
Dasgupta, R. 2000. "Performing Masculinities? The Salaryman at Work and Play." *Japanese Studies* 20 (2): 189–200.
Dashew Center for International Students and Scholars UCLA. n.d. F1 Students. Available at https://internationalcenter.ucla.edu/f-1-students.
Davis, M. 1992. *City of Quartz: Excavating the Future in Los Angeles*. New York: Vintage.
de Carvalho, D. 2003. "Nikkei Communities in Japan." In *Global Japan: The Experience of Japan's New Immigrant and Overseas Communities*, edited by R. Goodman, C. Peach, A. Takenaka, and P. White, 195–208. New York: RoutledgeCurzon.
de Certeau, M. 1984. *The Practice of Everyday Life*. Berkeley: University of California Press.
de Genova, N., and A. Y. Ramos-Zayas. 2003. "Latino Rehearsals: Racialization and the Politics of Citizenship between Mexicans and Puerto Ricans in Chicago." *Journal of Latin American Anthropology* 8 (2): 18–57.
Dekker, R., G. Engbersen, and M. Faber. 2015. "The Use of Online Media in Migration Networks." *Population, Space and Place* 22:539–551.
Delfico, J. 1995. *Illegal Immigration INS Overstay Estimation Methods Need Improvement*. Washington, DC: United States General Accounting Office.
Densho Encyclopedia. n.d. *Toyo's Camera: Japanese American History During WWII*. Available at https://encyclopedia.densho.org/sources/en-toyoscamera-1/.
Department of Neighborhood Empowerment. n.d. "To Find Your Neighborhood Council." City of Los Angeles. Accessed September 26, 2014. Available at https://empowerla.org/councils/.
Dirlik, A. 1999. "Asians on the Rim: Transnational Capital and Local Community in the Making of Contemporary Asian America." In *Across the Pacific: Asian Americans and Globalization*, edited by E. Hu-DeHart, 29–60. Philadelphia: Temple University Press.
Division (United Nations Department of Economic and Social Affairs Population Division). 2013. "232 Million International Migrants Living Abroad Worldwide." Accessed July 18, 2014. Available at http://esa.un.org/unmigration/wallchart2013.htm.
Douglas, M. 2005. "Pedagogical Theories and Approaches to Teach Young Learners of Japanese as a Heritage Language." *Heritage Language Journal* 3 (1): 60–82.
Douglass, M., and G. Roberts, eds. 2000. *Japan and Global Migration: Foreign Workers and the Advent of a Multicultural Society*. New York: Routledge.
Dower, J. 1975. *Origins of the Modern Japanese State: Selected Writings of E. H. Norman*. New York: Pantheon Books.
Dresner, J. 2006. "Instructions to Emigrant Laborers 1885–1894: 'Return in Triumph' or 'Wander on the Verge of Starvation.'" In *Japanese Diasporas: Unsung Pasts, Con-

flicting Presents, and Uncertain Futures, edited by Nobuko Adachi, 52–64. London: Routledge.

———. 2008. "International Labour Migrants' Return to Meiji-Era Yamaguchi and Hiroshima: Economic and Social Effects." *International Migration Review* 46 (3): 65–94.

Dunn, K. 2009. "Embodied Transnationalism: Bodies in Transnational Spaces." *Population, Space and Place* 16:1–9.

Duthie, T. 2014. *Man'yoshu and the Imperial Imagination in Early Japan*. Leiden: Brill.

Economic Planning Agency, Ministry of Finance. 1977. *National Life: Towards New Affluence of Living*. Tokyo: Economic Planning Agency, Ministry of Finance.

———. 1981. *Annual Report on National Life: In Search of a Good Quality of Life*. Tokyo: Economic Planning Agency, Ministry of Finance.

———. 1986. *Annual Report on the National Life for Fiscal 1986*. Tokyo: Economic Planning Agency, Ministry of Finance.

Edgington, D. 2014. "Patterns and Organization of Japanese Tourism in Canada: 1960–2010." *Canadian Geographer / Le Géographe Canadien* 58 (3): 355–376.

Education (Japan Ministry of Education). 2015. "Overseas Study by Japanese Nationals." Accessed February 11, 2021. Available at http://mext.go.jpennewstopicsdetail1372 624.htm.pdf.

Endo, E. 2019. "Study: Need for Culturally Sensitive Care for Nikkei Growing." *Rafu Shimpo* (Los Angeles), September 12, 2019, 1.

Esta.U.S. n.d. U.S. Travel Authorization. Available at http://www.esta.us/japan.html.

Estévez-Abe, M., and T. Caponio 2022. "Badante or Bride? Patterns of Female Migration in Italy, Japan, Korea, and Spain." *International Migration Review* 56 (4): 1–28.

Fair Housing Center of Greater Boston. n.d. "Historical Shift from Explicit to Implicit Policies Affecting Housing Segregation in Eastern Massachusetts." Accessed October 22, 2018. Available at http://www.bostonfairhousing.org/timeline/1934-1968-FHA-Redlining.html.

Faist, T. 2000. "Transnationalizaton in International Migration: Implications for the Study of Citizenship and Culture." *Ethnic and Racial Studies* 23 (2): 189–222.

Farms (Tanaka Farms). n.d. "It All Started in Japan." Accessed July 3, 2020. Available at https://www.tanakafarms.com/our-history.

Fine, A. S. 2017. "Preserving a Place with Difficult History: Parker Center." *City Watch*. Accessed July 28, 2018. Available at https://citywatchla.com/index.php/los-angeles/12541-preserving-a-place-with-difficult-history-parker-center.

Fiset, L., and G. Nomura, eds. 2005. *Nikkei in the Pacific Northwest: Japanese and Japanese Canadians in the Twentieth Century*. Seattle: University of Washington Press.

Foner, N. 1997. "What's New about Transnationalism? New York Immigrants Today and at the Turn of the Century." *Diaspora* 6 (3): 355–372.

Fouron, G., and N. Glick Schiller. 2001. "All in the Family: Gender, Transnational Migration, and the Nation-State." *Identities: Global Studies in Culture and Power* 7 (4): 539–582.

Frey, W. H. 2018. *Diversity Explosion: How New Racial Demographics Are Remaking America*. Washington DC: Brookings Institution Press.

Fugita, S., and D. O'Brien. 1991. *Japanese American Ethnicity: The Persistence of Community*. Seattle: University of Washington Press.

Fujimoto, J. 2007. *Sawtelle: West Los Angeles's Japantown*. Chicago: Arcadia.

Fujimura-Fanselow, K., and A. Kameda. 1995. "College Women Today: Options and Dilemmas." In *Japanese Women: New Feminist Perspectives on the Past, Present, and Future*, edited by K. Fujimura-Fanselow and A. Kameda, 125–154. New York: Feminist Press, City University of New York.

Fujino, D. 2008. "Race, Place, Space, and Political Development: Japanese-American Radicalism in the 'Pre-movement' 1960s." *Social Justice* 35 (2): 57–79.

Fujino, D. C. 2005. *Heartbeat of Struggle: The Revolutionary Life of Yuri Kochiyama: Heartbeat of Struggle*. Minneapolis: University of Minnesota.

———. 2020. *Nisei Radicals: The Feminist Poetics and Transformative Ministry of Mitsuye Yamade and Michael Yasutake*. Seattle: University of Washington Press.

Fujita, K. 1988. "Women Workers, State, Policy, and the International Division of Labor: The Case of Silicon Island in Japan." *Bulletin of Concerned Asian Scholars* 20 (3): 42–53.

Fujita, K., and R. C. Hill. 2005. "Innovative Tokyo." World Bank Policy Research Working Paper 3507, World Bank, Washington, DC. Accessed July 2014. Available http://econ.worldbank.org.

Fujita, Y. 2009. *Cultural Migrants from Japan: Youth, Media, and Migration in New York and London*. Lanham, MD: Lexington Books.

Gakuen, Asahi. n.d. Available at https://www.asahigakuen.com/pdf/AsahiGakuen_brochure.pdf.

Gee, D., dir. 1988. *Slaying the Dragon: Asian Women in U.S. Television and Film*. San Francisco: Asian Women United of California. DVD.

Geertz, C. 1973. *The Interpretation of Cultures: Selected Essays*. New York: Basic Books.

Gelb, J., and M. Estevez-Abe. 1998. "Political Women in Japan: A Case Study of the Seikatshusha Network Movement." *Social Science Japan Journal* 1 (2): 263–279.

Genda, Y. 2005. *A Nagging Sense of Job Insecurity: The New Reality Facing Japanese Youth*. Tokyo: International House of Japan.

———. 2007. "Jobless Youth and the NEET Problem in Japan." *Social Science Japan Journal* 10 (1): 23–40.

George, M., and R. Fitzgerald. 2012. "Forty Years in Aotearoa New Zealand: White Identity, Home and Later Life in an Adopted Country." *Ageing and Society* 32 (2): 239–260.

Gerteis, C. 2009. *Gender Struggles: Wage-Earning Women and Male-Dominated Unions in Postwar Japan*. Cambridge, MA: Harvard University Asia Center.

Giddens, A. 1979. *Central Problems in Social Theory: Action, Structure, and Contradiction in Social Analysis*. Berkeley: University of California Press.

———. 1991. *Modernity and Self-Identity: Self and Society in the Late Modern Age*. Stanford, CA: Stanford University Press.

Glick Schiller, N., L. Basch, and C. S. Blanc. 1995. "From Immigrant to Transmigrant: Theorizing Transnational Migration." *Anthropological Quarterly* 68 (1): 48–63.

Glick Schiller, N., and A. Caglar. 2009. "Towards a Comparative Theory of Locality in Migration Studies: Migrant Incorporation and City Scale." *Journal of Ethnic and Migration Studies* 35 (2): 177–202.

Goel, R. 2004. "Can I Call Kimura Crazy? Ethical Tensions in Cultural Defense." *Seattle Journal of Social Justice* 3 (1): 443–464.

Gold, J. 2012. "Daily Dish: Tsukumen from a Different Kitchen." *Los Angeles Times*, July 25, 2012. Accessed July 1, 2013. Available at http://latimesblogs.latimes.com/dailydish/2012/07/tsukemen-from-a-different-kitchen.html.

———. 2013. "L.A. Now Has Oodles of Noodles." *Los Angeles Times*, February 2, 2013. Accessed July 1, 2013. Available at https://www.latimes.com/archives/la-xpm-2013-feb-02-la-fo-0202-gold-20130202-story.html.

Goldberg-Hiller, J., and N. K. Silva. 2015. "The Botany of Emergence: Kanaka Ontology and Biocolonialism in Hawai'i." *Native American and Indigenous Studies* 2 (2): 1–26.

Goodman, A. 1989. "Toward Equality: Exploring a World of Difference on the Street Where You Live: Gardena." *Los Angeles Times*, February 13, 1989. Accessed March 10, 2014. Available at https://www.latimes.com/archives/la-xpm-1989-02-13-ss-1609-story.html.

Gordon, A. 2007. "Consumption, Leisure and the Middle Class in Transwar Japan." *Social Science Japan Journal* 10 (1): 1–21.

Gottfried, H. 2009. "The Reproductive Bargain and the Making of Precarious Employment." In *Gender and the Contours of Precarious Employment*, edited by L. F. Vosko, M. MacDonald, and I. Cambell, 76–91. London: Routledge.

Graviet Knapp, Y. 2016. "How Has LA Rent Changed since 1980?" Inman Access. Accessed February 26, 2021. Available at https://www.inman.com/2016/07/14/how-has-la-rent-changed-since-1980/.

Gregory, S. 1996. "Race, Rubbish, and Resistance: Empowering Difference in Community Politics." In *Race*, edited by S. Gregory and R. Sanjek, 366–391. New Brunswick, NJ: Rutgers University Press.

———. 1998. *Black Corona: Race and the Politics of Place in an Urban Community*. Princeton, NJ: Princeton University Press.

———. 2007. *The Devil behind the Mirror: Globalization and Politics in the Dominican Republic*. Berkely: University of California Press.

Grosfoguel, R. 2004. "Race and Ethnicity or Racialized Ethnicities: Identities within Global Coloniality." *Ethnicities* 4 (3): 315–336.

Groves, M. 2015. "West L.A. Neighborhood to be Recognized as 'Sawtelle Japantown.'" *Los Angeles Times*, March 28, 2015. Accessed September 2, 2019. Available at https://www.latimes.com/local/lanow/la-me-ln-west-los-angeles-neighborhood-to-be-recognized-as-sawtelle-japantown-20150328-story.html.

Guarnizo, L. E., and M. P. Smith. 1999. "The Locations of Transnationalism." In *Transnationalism from Below*, edited by M. P. Smith and L. Guarnizo. New Brunswick, NJ: Transaction: 3–34.

Gupta, A., and J. Ferguson. 1999. "Beyond 'Culture': Space, Identity, and the Politics of Difference." In *Culture, Power, Place Explorations in Critical Anthropology*, edited by A. Gupta and J. Ferguson, 33–51. Durham, NC: Duke University Press.

Habu, T. 2000. "The Irony of Globalization: The Experience of Japanese Women in British Higher Education." *Higher Education* 39 (1): 43–66.

Hall, K., M. Ono, and A. Kohno. 2021. "British and Japanese International Retirement Migration and Creative Responses to Health and Care Challenges: A Bricolage Perspective." *Comparative Migration Studies* 9 (7): 1–18.

Hanami, M. 1995. "International Student Exchange Program at Hitotsubashi University: Policy and Perspective." *Hitotsubashi Journal of Social Studies* 72 (2): 113–125.

Hannerz, U. 1996. *Transnational Connections: Culture, People, Places*. New York: Routledge.

Hara, K. 1995. "Challenges to Education for Girls and Women in Modern Japan: Past and Present." In *Japanese Women: New Feminist Perspectives on the Past, Present and*

Future, edited by K. Fujimura-Fanselow and A. Kameda, 93–106. New York: Feminist Press.

Harmetz, A. 1982. "Center Rises on Coast for Japanese-Americans." *New York Times*, July 1, 1982.

Harvey, D. 2008. "The Right to the City." *New Left Review* 53 (September/October): 23–40.

Hasegawa, E. 2007. "Reconfiguring Boundaries: Expatriate Japanese Women in Shanghai." *Intersections: Gender, History and Culture in the Asian Context* 15 (May 2007). Accessed June 14, 2009. Available at http://intersections.anu.edu.au/issue15/hasegawa.htm.

Hasegawa, M. 2005. "Economic Globalization and Homelessness in Japan." *American Behavioral Scientist* 48 (8): 989–1012.

Hayano, D. M. 1981. "Ethnic Identification and Disidentification: Japanese American Views of Chinese Americans." *Ethnic Groups* 3 (2): 157–171.

Hayashi, K. K. 1985. "Kimura Sentenced to Probation, Released." *Pacific Citizen* (Los Angeles), December 6, 1985, 101.

Hayashi, M. 2014. "Urban Poverty and Regulation, New Spaces and Old: Japan and the US in Comparison." *Environment and Planning A* 46:1203–1225.

Hedegard, D. 2013. "Finding 'Strong' and 'Soft' Racial Meanings in Cultural Taste Patterns in Brazil." *Ethnic and Racial Studies* 36 (5): 774–794.

Hendry, J. 1993. "The Role of the Professional Housewife." In *Japanese Women Working*, edited by J. Hunter, 224–241. New York: Routledge.

Heung, V. C. S., H. Qu, and R. Chu. 2001. "The Relationship between Vacation Factors and Socio-demographic and Travelling Characteristics: The Case of Japanese Leisure Travellers." *Tourism Management* 22 (259–269).

Higashi, S. 2016. "Japanese Christians in the Sawtelle District of Los Angeles." JANM (Japanese American National Museum). Available at http://www.discovernikkei.org/en/journal/2016/10/21/sawtelle-christians/.

Higuchi, H., and A. Phillips. 2017. *South Bay Japanese American Community Needs Assessment Study*. Los Angeles: Little Tokyo Service Center.

Hirabayashi, J. A., and L. R. Hirabayashi. 2013. *A Principled Stand: The Story of Hirabayashi v. United States*. Seattle: University of Washington Press.

Hirabayashi, L. R. 1993. "Community Lost? The Significance of a Contemporary Japanese American Community in Southern California." In *Asians in America: A Reader*, edited by M. Collier, 169–181. Dubuque, IA: Kendall-Hunt.

———. 1995. "Back to the Future: Re-framing Community-Based Research." *Amerasia Journal* 2 (1–2): 103–118.

———. 2015. "Thinking about and Experiencing Mutuality: Notes on a Son's Formation." In *Mutuality: Anthropology's Changing Terms of Engagement*, edited by R. Sanjek, 118–129. Philadelphia: University of Pennsylvania Press.

———. 2016. "Introduction to Conjuring Communities." *Pan-Japan* 12 (1–2): i–xx.

Hirabayashi, L. R., and A. Kikumura-Yano. 2006. "Japanese Latin Americans during World War II." In *Japanese Diasporas: Unsung Past, Conflicting Presents, and Uncertain Futures*, edited by N. Adachi, 159–171. New York: Routledge.

Hirabayashi, L. R., and G. Tanaka. 1988. "The Issei Community in Moneta and the Gardena Valley, 1900–1920." *Southern California Quarterly* 70 (2): 127–158.

Hirakawa, H. 2000. "The Politics of Gender and Mass Media in Post-1975 Japan: Its Implications for 'Us.'" *U.S.-Japan Women's Journal* (19):49–82.

Honda, Y. 2005. "'Freeters': Young Atypical Workers in Japan." *Japan Labor Review* 2 (3): 5–25.

Hontz, J. 2007. "Visit Japan in California: Discover the Eateries, Tea Shops, Boutiques, and Galleries of West Los Angeles' Little Osaka." *Sunset Magazine*, November 7, 2007.

Horie, M. 2002. "The Internationalization of Higher Education in Japan in the 1990s: A Reconsideration." *Higher Education* 43 (1): 65–84.

Horiuchi, K., E. Hirai, and S. Matsuura. 2023. "Japanese Living as Permanent Residents Abroad Hits Record High." *Asahi Shimbun*, January 27, 2023. Accessed March 25, 2023. Available at https://www.asahi.com/ajw/articles/14825248.

Hosler, A. S. 1998. *Japanese Immigrant Entrepreneurs in New York City: A New Wave of Ethnic Business*. New York: Garland.

House Subcommittee on Immigration, Border Security, and Claims Hearing. 2006. "Dual Citizenship, Birthright Citizenship, and the Meaning of Sovereignty." Washington, DC. Accessed January 12, 2020. Available at http://judiciary.house.gov.

Hune, S. 1991. "Migrant Women in the Context of the International Convention on the Protection of the Rights of All Migrant Workers and Members of Their Families." *International Migration Review* 25 (4): 800–817.

Huong, T. B., and H. Wilkins. 2016. "The Mobility of Young Japanese: The Travel–Migration Nexus." *Journal of Travel and Tourism Marketing* 33 (5): 581–596.

Hyodo, H. 2013. "The Era of Dual Life: The Shin-Issei, the Japanese Contemporary Migrants to the U.S." *Electronic Journal of Contemporary Japanese Studies* 13 (1): article 7. Available at http://www.japanesestudies.org.uk/ejcjs/vol13/iss1/hyodo.html.

Iida, T., and J. Morris. 2008. "Farewell to the Salaryman? The Changing Roles and Work of Middle Managers in Japan." *International Journal of Human Resource Management* 19 (6): 1072–1087.

IIE (International Institute of Education). 2012. "International Students in the United States." Project Atlas. Accessed December 19, 2015. Available at http://www.iie.org/Services/Project-Atlas/United-States/International-Students-In-US.

Ikeda, Jordan. 2016. "LTSC Opens South Bay Office." *Rafu Shimpo*, February 22, 2016, 1.

Imamura, A. 1987. *Urban Japanese Housewives: At Home and in the Community*. Honolulu: University of Hawai'i Press.

Imamura, P. 1982. "Immigration Raids Alarm Little Tokyo." *Pacific Citizen* (Los Angeles), February 12, 1982, 1.

IMDb Reviews. 2005. "*Shogun*: User Reviews." IMDb. Accessed June 14, 2019. Available at https://www.imdb.com/title/tt0080274/reviews.

Ingersoll, L. A. 1908. *Ingersoll's Century History: Santa Monica Bay Cities*. Los Angeles: Ingersoll, LA.

International Monetary Fund. 1980. *Annual Report*. Washington, DC: International Monetary Fund.

Inutake, C. 2003. "Contemporary Japanese Migration to the United States: Nonimmigrant-Dominated and Female-Dominated Flows." Master's thesis, University of California Los Angeles.

Ishikawa, E. A. 2009. "The Return of Japanese-Brazilian Next Generations: Their Post-1980s Experiences in Japan." In *Return Migration of the Next Generations: 21st Cen-*

tury Transnational Mobility, edited by D. Conway and R. Potter, 59–78. Burlington, VT: Ashgate.

Isogai, M. 2010. "The Japanese Quit Hold of Their Passports: Four Million Japanese People Have Not Applied for Renewal of Passport for Five Years." April 1, 2010. Japan Travel Bureau. Accessed April 22, 2021. Available at https://www.tourism.jp/en/tourism-database/insights/2010/04/hold-passport/#:~:text=The%20number%20of%20valid%20passports%20has%20declined%20by,million%20to%2031%2C935%2C917%20at%20the%20end%20of%202008.

Itoh, R. 2006. "Overseas Experience among Wives of Japanese Businessmen in the United States." *Pan Japan: The International Journal of the Japanese Diaspora* 4 (1–2): 1–35.

Itzigsohn, J., and S. Giorguli-Saucedo. 2005. "Incorporation, Transnationalism, and Gender: Immigrant Incorporation and Transnational Participation as Gendered Processes." *International Migration Review* 39 (4): 895–920.

Iwao, S. 1993. *The Japanese Woman: Traditional Image and Changing Reality*. New York: Free Press.

Izuhara, M., and H. Shibata. 2001. "Migration and Old Age: Japanese Women Growing Older in British Society." *Journal of Comparative Family Studies* 32 (4): 571–586.

JANM (Japanese American National Museum). n.d. "What Is Nikkei?" Discover Nikkei. Accessed June 28, 2013. Available at http://www.discovernikkei.org/en/about/what-is-nikkei.

Japan Ministry of Foreign Affairs [Gaimusho Ryoji Iju Bu Seisaku Kai]. 1987. *Diplomatic Bluebook 1987*. Tokyo: Japan Ministry of Foreign Affairs.

Japan Travel Bureau. 2009. "A Survey of Women's Leisure Travel Preferences." News release, April 7, 2009. Available at https://www.jtbcorp.jp/en/press_release/pdf/release20090407.pdf.

Japan Up! 2018. "Trends in Job Openings: Let's Work at Japanese Companies!" *Japan Up!* 125:26–32.

———. 2019. "Discover South Bay." *Japan Up!* 146:22–25.

Jenks, H. 2008. "Urban Space, Ethnic Community, and National Belonging: The Political Landscape of Memory in Little Tokyo." *GeoJournal* 73 (3): 231–244.

———. 2011. "Bronzeville, Little Tokyo, and the Unstable Geography of Race in Post–World War II Los Angeles." *Southern California Quarterly* 93 (2): 201–235.

———. 2014. "Seasoned Long Enough in Concentration: Suburbanization and Transnational Citizenship in Southern California's South Bay." *Journal of Urban History* 40 (1): 6–30.

Jiobu, R. 1988. "Ethnic Hegemony and the Japanese of California." *American Sociological Review* 53 (3): 353–367.

Johnson, A. 2016. "Who Gets to Be 'Hapa'?" NPR, August 8, 2016. Available at https://www.npr.org/sections/codeswitch/2016/08/08/487821049/who-gets-to-be-hapa.

Johnson, C. 1983. "The Internationalization of the Japanese Economy." In *The Challenge of Japan's Internationalization: Organization and Culture*, edited by H. Mannari and H. Befu, 31–58. Tokyo: Kodansha International.

Justice (U.S. Department of Justice). 1991. *Statistical Yearbook of the Immigration and Naturalization Service, 1990*. Washington, DC: Immigration and Naturalization Service.

———. 1996. *1996 Statistical Yearbook of the Immigration and Naturalization Service*. Washington, DC: Department of Justice.

———. 2017. "Owner of Schools That Illegally Allowed Foreign Nationals to Remain in U.S. as Foreign 'Students' Pleads Guilty to Federal Fraud Charges." Central District of California. Accessed June 19, 2018. Available at https://www.justice.gov/usao-cdca/pr/owner-schools-illegally-allowed-foreign-nationals-remain-us-foreign-students-pleads.

Kambayashi, R., and T. Kato. 2011. "The Japanese Employment System after the Bubble Burst: New Evidence." In *Japan's Bubble, Deflation, and Long Term Stagnation*, edited by K. Hamada, A. K. Kashyap, and D. E. Weinstein, 217–262. Cambridge, MA: MIT Press.

Kameyama, E. 2012. "Nikkei Chronicles #1: Itadakimasu! A Taste of Nikkei Culture Temaki Zushi; A Welcome-Home Party." Japanese American National Museum. Accessed July 10, 2014. Available at http://www.discovernikkei.org/en/.

Kanaiaupuni, S. M. 2000. "Reframing the Migration Question: An Analysis of Men, Women, and Gender in Mexico." *Social Forces* 78 (4): 1311–1347.

Kao, M. A. 2016. "Through the Fire: Keiro—Too Little Too Late? Sez Who?!!!" *Rafu Shimpo* (Los Angeles), February 18, 2016.1.

Kasamatsu, E. 2005. *Historia de la Asociación Panamerica: Nikkei Presencia e imigración japonesas en las Américas*. Asociación Panamericananikkei. Asuncion: Servilibro.

Kashu Mainichi. 1961. "It's Not Just Cheap Labor Which Makes Japan Competitive." *Kashu Mainichi* (Los Angeles), April 29, 1961, 1.

Kasza, G. J., and T. Horie. 2011. "Welfare Policy." In *Japanese Politics Today: From Karaoke to Kabuki Democracy*, edited by T. Inoguchi and P. Jaim, 143–162. New York: Palgrave Macmillan.

Kawano, S., G. S. Roberts, and S. O. Long. 2014. *Capturing Contemporary Japan: Differentiation and Uncertainty*. Honolulu: University of Hawai'i Press.

Kawashima, Y. 1995. "Female Workers: An Overview of Past and Current Trends." In *Japanese Women: New Feminist Perspectives on the Past, Present, and Future*, edited by K. Fujimura-Fanselow and A. Kameda, 271–293. New York: Feminist Press.

Keiro. 2021. "60 Years of Family History: George Aratani's Legacy through the Eyes of Sakaye and Linda Aratani." Keiro.org. Accessed March 12, 2022. Available at https://www.keiro.org/features/george-aratanis-legacy.

Keizer, A. B. 2008. "Non-regular Employment in Japan: Continued and Renewed Dualities." *Work, Employment and Society* 22 (3): 407–425.

Kelly, P., and T. Lusis. 2006. "Migration and the Transnational Habitus: Evidence from Canada and the Philippines." *Environment and Planning A* 38:831–847.

Kelly, W. W. 1986. "Rationalization and Nostalgia: Cultural Dynamics of New Middle-Class Japan." *American Ethnologist* 13 (4): 603–618.

Kelsky, K. 1994. "Postcards from the Edge: The 'Office Ladies' of Tokyo." English supplement, *U.S.-Japan Women's Journal*, no. 6, 3–26.

Kempner, K., and M. Makino. 1996. "The Modernistic Traditions of Japanese Higher Education." In *The Social Role of Higher Education: Comparative Perspectives*, edited by K. Kempner and W. G. Tierney, 27–54. New York: Garland.

Kenmochi, K. 1987. "The Hollowing: A New Threat to Japan's Super-Economy." *AMPO* 19 (1): 30–33.

Kensho, T. 1998. "American Educational Influences on Japanese Music Education from the End of World War II (1945) to the First Tentative Course of Study (1947)." *Bulletin of Historical Research in Music Education* 19 (2): 115–137.

Kikuchi, C. 1973. *The Kikuchi Diary: Chronicles from an American Concentration Camp.* Urbana: University of Illinois Press.

Kim, B.-L. 1977. "Asian Wives of U.S. Servicemen: Women in Shadows." *Amerasia Journal* 4 (1): 91–115.

Kim, Y. 2011. "Diasporic Nationalism and the Media: Asian Women on the Move." *International Journal Of Cultural Studies* 14 (2): 133–151.

Kitano, H. L. 1969. *Japanese Americans: The Evolution of a Subculture.* New Jersey: Prentice-Hall.

Kitano, H. L., W.-T. Yeung, L. Chai, and H. Hatanaka. 1984. "Asian-American Interracial Marriage." *Journal of Marriage and Family* 46 (1): 179–190.

Kitazawa, Y. 1987. "Setting Up Shop Shutting Up Shop." *AMPO* 19 (1): 10–29.

Kivisto, P. 2003. "Social Spaces, Transnational Immigrant Communities, and the Politics of Incorporation." *Ethnicities* 3 (1): 5–28.

Kobayashi, A. 2013. "Critical 'Race' Approaches." In *The Wiley-Blackwell Companion to Cultural Geography*, edited by N. C. Johnson, R. H. Schein, and J. Winder, 57–92. Sussex, UK: John Wiley and Sons.

Kobayashi, T. 1986. "The Internationalisation of Japanese Education." *Comparative Education* 22 (1): 65–71.

Kolpashnikova, K., and M.-Y. Kan. 2021. "Eldercare in Japan: Cluster Analysis of Daily Time-Use Patterns of Elder Caregivers." *Journal of Population Ageing* 14:441–463.

Komamura, K. 2008. "The Working Poor, the Borderline Poor and Developments in Public Assistance Reform." *Japan Labor Review* 5 (4): 67–94.

Konno, Y. 2012. "Localism and Japanese Emigration at the Turn of the Twentieth Century." *Amerasia Journal* 38 (3): 98–123.

Kosaku, Y. 1992. *Cultural Nationalism in Contemporary Japan: A Sociological Inquiry.* London: Routledge.

Kubo, K. 2008. "Japan: The Resilience of Employment Relationships and the Changing Conditions of Work." In *Globalization, Flexibilization, and Working Conditions in Asia and the Pacific*, edited by S. Lee and F. Eyraud, 153–185. Oxford: Chandos.

Kumazawa, M. 1996. *Portraits of the Japanese Workplace: Labor Movements, Workers and Managers.* New York: Westview.

Kurashige, L. 2002. *Japanese American Celebration and Conflict: A History of Ethnic Identity and Festival, 1934–1990.* Berkeley: University of California Press.

Kurashige, S. 2008. *The Shifting Grounds of Race: Black and Japanese Americans in the Making of Multiethnic Los Angeles.* Princeton, NJ: Princeton University Press.

Kurotani, S. 2005. *Home Away From Home: Japanese Corporate Wives in the United States.* Durham, NC: Duke University Press.

Lai, C. 2013. "Saving Japantown, Serving the People: The Scalar Politics of the Asian American Movement." *Environment and Planning D: Society and Space* 31:467–484.

Laratta, R. 2010. "From Welfare State to Welfare Society: Toward a Viable System of Welfare in Japan and England." *International Journal of Social Welfare* 19:131–141.

Le Blanc, R. M. 2016. "What High-Rise Living Means for Tokyo Civic Life: Changing Residential Architecture and the Specter of Rising Privacy." *Journal of Japanese Studies* 42 (2): 315–341.

Lee, C. 1992. "International Trade." *Los Angeles Times*, June 26, 1992. Accessed August 30, 2017. Available at http://articles.latimes.com/1992-06-26/business/fi-1140_1_hate-crime.

Lee, S., and M. Boyd. 2008. "Marrying Out: Comparing the Marital and Social Integration of Asians in the US and Canada." *Social Science Research* 37:311–329.

Lee, S. M. 1996. "Issues in Research on Women, International Migration and Labor." *Asian and Pacific Migration Journal* 5 (1): 5–26.

Lee, S. M., and B. Edmonston. 2005. "New Marriages, New Families: U.S. Racial and Hispanic Intermarriage." *Population Bulletin* 60 (2): 3–36.

Lee, S. M., and M. Fernandez. 1998. "Trends in Asian American Racial/Ethnic Intermarriage: A Comparison of 1980 and 1990 Census Data." *Sociological Perspectives* 41 (2): 323–342.

Lee, S. M., and K. Yamanaka. 1990. "Patterns of Asian American Intermarriage and Marital Assimilation." *Journal of Comparative Family Studies* 21 (2): 287–305.

Lee, Y., and K. Park. 2008. "Negotiating Hybridity: Transnational Reconstruction of Migrant Subjectivity in Koreatown, Los Angeles." *Journal of Cultural Geography* 25 (3): 245–262.

Lefebvre, H. 1991. *The Production of Space*. Oxford: Basil Blackwell.

Leistyna, P. 2001. "Racenicity: Understanding Racialized Ethnic Identities." In *Multi/Intercultural Conversations: A Reader*, edited by S. R. Steinberg, 423–462. New York: Peter Lang.

Lesser, J. 2007. *A Discontented Diaspora: Japanese Brazilians and the Meanings of Ethnic Militancy, 1960–1980*. Durham, NC: Duke University Press.

Levitt, P., and N. Glick Schiller. 2007. "Conceptualizing Simultaneity: A Transnational Social Field Perspective on Society." In *Sociology of Diaspora: A Reader*, edited by A. Sahoo and B. Maharaj, 1:156–193. Jaipur: Rawat.

Lie, J. 2001. *Multi-ethnic Japan*. Cambridge, MA: Harvard University Press.

Lim, L. L., and N. Oishi. 1996. "International Labor Migration of Asian Women: Distinctive Characteristics and Policy Concerns." *Asian and Pacific Migration Journal* 5 (1): 85–116.

Little Tokyo Service Center. 2018. "Ties That Bind: Looking Back and Looking Ahead for the Nikkei Community." LTSC conference program presented at Ties that Bind, Little Tokyo, Los Angeles, October 20, 2018.

———. n.d. "About Us." Accessed August 12, 2018. Available at https://www.ltsc.org/about-2/.

Liu, J., P. Ong, and C. Rosenstein. 1991. "Dual Chain Migration: Post-1965 Filipino Immigration to the United States." *International Migration Review* 25 (3): 487–513.

Liu, L. Y. 2000. "The Place of Immigration in Studies of Geography and Race." *Social and Cultural Geography* 1 (2): 169–182.

Liu-Farrar, G. 2020. *Immigrant Japan*. Ithaca, NY: Cornell University Press.

Los Angeles Conservancy. n.d. "History of Beverly Hills." Accessed July 15, 2015. Available at https://www.laconservancy.org/history-beverly-hills.

Los Angeles Times. 1943. "Here Are Results of Jap Questionnaire." December 6, 1943, A4.

———. 2016. "Hot Property: Westside, Central, South Bay." Advertisement, June 4, 2016.

———. 2017. "Rightly or Wrongly, Parker Center's Dark History Appears to Have Paved the Way for Its Demise." February 17, 2017. Available at http://www.latimes.com/opinion/editorials/la-ed-parker-center-little-tokyo-20170217-story.html.

Louie, S., and G. Omatsu, eds. 2001. *Asian Americans: The Movement and the Moment*. Los Angeles: UCLA Asian American Studies Center.

Low, S. 1994. "Cultural Conservation of Place." In *Conserving Culture: A New Discourse on Heritage*, edited by M. Hufford, 66–77. Urbana: University of Illinois Press.

———. 2000. *On the Plaza: The Politics of Public Space and Culture*. Austin: University of Texas Press.

Machimura, T. 2003. "Living in a Transnational Community within a Multi-ethnic City: Making a Localised 'Japan' in Los Angeles." In *Global Japan: The Experience of Japan's New Immigrant and Overseas Communities*, edited by R. Goodman, C. Peach, A. Takenaka, and P. White, 147–156. New York: RoutledgeCurzon.

Madrigal, A. 2014. "The Racist Housing Policy That Made Your Neighborhood." *The Atlantic*, May 22, 2014.

Mahler, S. 1999. "Theoretical and Empirical Contributions toward a Research Agenda for Transnationalism." In *Transnationalism from Below*, M. Smith and L. Guarnizo, 6:64–100. New Brunswick, NJ: Transaction.

Mahler, S. J. 1995. *American Dreaming: Immigrant Life on the Margins*. Princeton, NJ: Princeton University Press.

Mahler, S. J., and P. R. Pessar. 2001. "Gendered Geographies of Power: Analyzing Gender across Transnational Spaces." *Identities: Global Studies in Culture and Power* 7 (4): 441–459.

———. 2006. "Gender Matters: Ethnographers Bring Gender from the Periphery toward the Core of Migration Studies." *International Migration Review* 40 (1): 27–63.

Maki, M., H. Kitano, and S. M. Berthold. 1999. *Achieving the Impossible Dream: How Japanese American Obtained Redress*. Urbana, IL: University of Illinois Press.

Mallan, K., B. Ashford, and P. Singh. 2010. "Navigating iScapes: Australian Youth Constructing Identities and Social Relations in a Network Society." *Anthropology and Education Quarterly* 41 (3): 264–279.

Mannari, H., and H. Befu. 1983. "The Challenge of Japan's Internationalization: Organization and Culture." Preface to *The Challenge of Japan's Internationalization: Organization and Culture*, edited by H. Mannari and H. Befu. Tokyo: Kodansha International.

Marcu, S. 2014. "Geography of Belonging: Nostalgic Attachment, Transnational Home and Global Mobility among Romanian Immigrants in Spain." *Journal of Cultural Geography* 31 (3): 326–345.

Martin, P. 2007. "Managing Labor Migration in the 21st Century." *City and Society* 19 (1): 5–18.

Martin, S. F. 2004. "Women and Migration." United Nations Division for the Advancement of Women, consultative meeting, "Migration and Mobility and How This Movement Affects Women," 1–35. New York: United Nations.

Massey, D., J. Durand, and K. A. Pren. 2014. "Explaining Undocumented Migration to the U.S." *International Migration Review* 48 (4): 1028–1061.

———. 2015. "Border Enforcement and Return Migration by Documented and Undocumented Mexicans." *Journal of Ethnic and Migration Studies* 41 (7): 1015–1040.

Massey, D., and N. Malone. 2002. "Pathways to Legal Immigration." *Population Research and Policy Review* 21 (6): 473–504.

Masterson, D. 2004. "From Plantation Workers to the Presidency: The Immigrant Journeys of Peru's Japanese, 1899 to the Present Day." *Pan-Japan* 3 (1): 13–37.

Masuda, M., G. H. Matsumoto, and G. M. Meredith. 1970. "Ethnic Identity in Three Generations of Japanese Americans." *Journal of Social Psychology* 81 (2): 199–207.

Mathews, J. 1982. "Economic Invasion by Japan Revives Worry about Racism." *Washington Post*, A26, May 14, 1982.

Matsuda, G. 1990. "'Only the Beginning': Continuing Our Battle for Empowerment." *Amerasia Journal* 16 (1): 159–169.

Matsuda, T. 2007. *Soft Power and Its Perils: U.S. Cultural Policy in Early Postwar Japan and Permanent Dependency*. Stanford, CA: Stanford University Press.

Matsumoto, K., and D. Britain. 2022. "Diaspora Japanese: Transnational Mobility and Language Contact." *International Journal of the Sociology of Language* 273 (1): 1–29.

Matsumoto, V. 2014a. *City Girls: The Nisei Social World in Los Angeles, 1920–1950*. Oxford: Oxford University Press.

———. 2014b. "Omoide No Shotokyo: Remembering Old Little Tokyo." In *New Small Museums in North America: Multicultural Sites of Minority Memory*, edited by K. Tanaka and I. Yanagisawa, 3:311–320. Tokyo.

Matsunaga, L. 2000. *The Changing Face of Japanese Retail: Working in a Chain Store*. New York: Routledge.

McAndrew, M. 2014. "Beauty, Soft Power, and the Politics of Womanhood during the U.S. Occupation of Japan, 1945–1952." *Journal of Women's History* 26 (4): 83–107.

McGarvey, S., and A. Seiden. 2010. "Health, Well-Being, and Social Context of Samoan Migrant Populations." *NAPA Bulletin (National Association for the Practice of Anthropology)* 34:213–228.

McKinnon, R. I. 2007. "Japan's Deflationary Hangover: Wage Stagnation and the Syndrome of the Ever-Weaker Yen." Asian Development Bank Institute. Discussion Paper, August, 2007. Accessed November 28, 2012. Available at https://www.adbi.org/discussionpaper/2007/08/20/2345.exchange.rate.stabilization.yen/.

Miller, L. 1995. "Introduction: Looking beyond the *Sarariiman* Folk Model." *American Asian Review* 13 (2): 19–27.

———. 2006. *Beauty Up: Exploring Contemporary Japanese Body Aesthetics*. Berkeley: University of California Press.

Ministry of Foreign Affairs of Japan. 2010. "Annual Report of Statistics on Japanese Nationals Overseas." Tokyo: Consular and Migration Affairs Department. http://www.mofa.go.jp/mofaj/toko/tokei/hojin/index.html.

Minoura, Y. 1980. *Life In-Between: The Acquisition of Cultural Identity among Japanese Children Living in the United States*. Los Angeles: University of California Los Angeles.

Miyake, L. 2008. "Forsaken and Forgotten: The U.S. Internment of Japanese Peruvians During World War II." *Asian American Law Journal* 9 (5): 163–193.

Miyawaki, C., T. Shibusawa, R. Hamaguchi, and K. Ikeda. 2020. *Needs Assessment for Japanese American Senior Facilities*. Los Angeles.

Modell, J. 1977. *The Economics and Politics of Racial Accommodation: The Japanese of Los Angeles*. Urbana: University of Illinois.

Morimoto, T. 1997. *Japanese Americans and Cultural Continuity: Maintaining Language and Heritage*. New York: Garland.

Morito, T. 1955. "Educational Reform and Its Problems in Post-war Japan." *International Review of Education / Internationale Zeitschrift für Erziehungswissenschaft / Revue Internationale de l'Education* 1 (3): 338–351.

Moriyama, A. 1985. *Imingaisha: Japanese Immigration Companies and Hawaii, 1894–1908*. Honolulu: University of Hawai'i Press.

Morley, P. 1999. *The Mountain Is Moving: Japanese Women's Lives.* Vancouver: University of British Columbia Press.

Morrison, A. R., M. Schiff, and M. Sjoblom, eds. 2008. "The International Migration of Women." Washington, DC: World Bank and Palgrave Macmillan.

Mouer, R. E., and Y. Sugimoto. 1983. "Internationalization as an Ideology in Japanese Society." In *The Challenge of Japan's Internationalization: Organization and Culture*, edited by H. Mannari and H. Befu, 267–297. Tokyo: Kodansha International.

Murakami, S., and C. Baird. 2018. "Dual Citizenship in Japan: A 'Don't Ask, Don't Tell' Policy Leaves Many in the Dark." *Japan Times* (Tokyo), April 19, 2018.

Murakami, Y. 1982. "The Age of New Middle Mass Politics: The Case of Japan." *Journal of Japanese Studies* 8 (1): 29–72.

Muranaka, G. 2015a. "J-Town Beat: Fathers, Sons and a Community in Discord." *Rafu Shimpo* (Los Angeles), October 22, 2015.

———. 2015b. "A Sign for Sawtelle Japantown: Historic Westside Japanese American Neighborhood Recognized at Official Unveiling." *Rafu Shimpo* (Los Angeles), 1.

Murasaki, S. 1960. *The Tale of Genji.* New York: Modern Library.

Murase, I. M. 1983. *Little Tokyo: 100 Years in Pictures.* Los Angeles: Visual Communications/Asian American Studies Central.

Murase, M. 2006. *Cooperation over Conflict: The Women's Movement and the State in Postwar Japan.* New York: Routledge.

Nagase, N. 1997. "Wage Differentials and Labor Supply of Married Women in Japan: Part Time and Informal Sector Work Opportunities." *Japanese Economic Review* 48 (1): 29–42.

Nagata, D., J. H. J. Kim, and K. Wu. 2019. "The Japanese American Wartime Incarceration: Examining the Scope of Racial Trauma." *American Psychologist* 74 (1): 36–48.

Nagatomo, J. 2011. "De-territorialized Ethnic Community: The Residential Choices and Networks among Japanese Lifestyle Migrants in South-East Queensland." *Japanese Studies* 31 (3): 423–440.

———. 2017. "Changes of Social Cohesion within Ethnic Communities: A Case Study of the Japanese Community in Sydney, Australia." *International Journal of Arts and Sciences* 9 (4): 45–60.

Nakajima, M. 1997. "Has the Equal Opportunity Law Brought Equality?" *AMPO* 27 (3): 8–10.

Nakaji Monnier, M. 2016. "Year of Keiro: A Community at a Crossroads." *Rafu Shimpo* (Los Angeles), January 1, 2016.

Nakaji Monnier, M., and N. Nakanishi. 2015. "Keiro Addresses Community at Open Meeting: Questions and Anger Remain after Discussion." *Rafu Shimpo* (Los Angeles), October 17, 2015.

Nakamatsu, T. 2005. "Faces of Asian Brides: Gender, Race, and Class in the Representations of Immigrant Women in Japan." *Women's Studies International Forum* 28: 405–417.

Nakamura, E. 2015. "The Last Day for Satsuma Imports on Sawtelle." *Giant Robot.* October 30, 2015. Accessed September 5, 2019. Available at https://www.giantrobot.com/blogs/giant-robot-store-and-gr2-news/74432067-the-last-day-for-satsuma-imports-on-sawtelle.

Nakamura, T. 1994. *Lectures on Modern Japanese Economic History: 1926–1994.* Tokyo: LTCB International Library Foundation.

Nakane, C. 1974. "Cultural Anthropology in Japan." *Annual Review of Anthropology* 3:57–72.

Nakano, D. 2019. "To Be Yonsei in Southern California." In *Japanese American Millennials: Rethinking Generation, Community, and Diversity*, edited by M. Omi, D. Nakano, and J. Yamashita, 62–81. Philadelphia: Temple University Press.

Nakano, L. Y. 2014. "Single Women in Marriage and Employment Markets in Japan." In *Capturing Contemporary Japan: Differentiation and Uncertainty*, edited by S. Kawano, G. S. Roberts, and S. O. Long, 163–182. Honolulu: University of Hawai'i Press.

Nakano Glenn, E. 1986. *Issei, Nisei, War Bride: Three Generations of Japanese American Women in Domestic Service*. Philadelphia: Temple University Press.

Nakao, K. 2007. "Shared Abodes, Disparate Visions: Japanese Anthropology during the Allied Occupation." *Social Science Japan Journal* 10 (2): 175–196.

Nakaoka, S. 2012. "Cultivating a Cultural Home Space: The Case of Little Tokyo's Budokan of Los Angeles Project." *AAPI Nexus* 10 (2): 23–36.

Nakatomi, J. 1991. "A Study of Shin-Issei through the Case of Fumiko Kimura." Master's thesis. University of Hawai'i Manoa.

Nakayama, T. 2015. "Sawtelle Recognized by Los Angeles as Japantown." *Nichi Bei Weekly* (San Francisco). Accessed October 12, 2018. Available at https://www.nichibei.org/2015/06/sawtelle-recognized-by-los-angeles-as-japantown/.

———. 2016. "Escrow Closes but Criticism of Keiro Sale Continues." *Nichi Bei Weekly* (San Francisco), June 23, 1016. Accessed July 24, 2020. Available at https://www.nichibei.org/2016/06/escrow-closes-but-criticism-of-keiro-sale-continues/.

Naples, N. 2003. *Feminism and Method: Ethnography, Discourse Analysis, and Activist Research*. New York: Routledge.

Navarro, M. 2004. "Young Japanese-Americans Honor Ethnic Roots." *New York Times*, August 2, 2004.

Neilson, B., and N. Rossiter. 2008. "Precarity as a Political Concept, or Fordism as Exception." *Theory, Culture and Society* 25 (7–8): 51–72.

Nemoto, K. 2006. "Intimacy, Desire, and the Construction of Self in Relationships between Asian American Women and White American Men." *Journal of Asian American Studies* 9 (1): 27–54.

———. 2008. "Postponed Marriage: Exploring Women's Views of Matrimony and Work in Japan." *Gender and Society* 22 (2): 219–237.

———. 2009. *Racing Romance: Love, Power, and Desire among Asian American/White Couples*. New Brunswick, NJ: Rutgers University Press.

Neuliep, J., M. Chaudoir, and J. C. McCroskey. 2001. "A Cross-Cultural Comparison of Ethnocentrism among Japanese and United States College Students." *Communication Research Reports* 18 (2): 137–146.

Niiya, B. "Return to West Coast." n.d. Densho Encyclopedia. Accessed August 22, 2019. Available at https://encyclopedia.densho.org/Return_to_West_Coast/.

Nikkei for Civil Rights and Redress. 2018. *NCRR: The Grassroots Struggle for Japanese American Redress and Reparations*. Los Angeles: University of California Asian American Studies Center.

Nishi, M., and Y. I. Kim. 1964. "Recent Japanese Settlement Changes in the Los Angeles Area." *Yearbook of the Association of Pacific Coast Geographers* 26:23–36.

Nixon, R. 2016. "U.S. Uncertain of How Many Overstay Visas." *New York Times*, January 2, 2016.

Nobuhito, K. 1995. "Japan's Invisible Unemployment Problem." *Japan Echo* 22 (3): 38–43.

Norman, E. H. 1940. *Japan's Emergence as a Modern State: Political and Economic Problems of the Meiji Period.* New York: Comet.

Nozawa, H. 1992. "A Marketing Analysis of Japanese Outbound Travel." *Tourism Management* 13 (2): 226–234.

Nurchayati. 2011. "Bringing Agency Back In: Indonesian Migrant Domestic Workers in Saudi Arabia." *Asian and Pacific Migration Journal* 20 (3–4): 479–502.

Ochiai, E. 1994. *The Japanese Family System in Transition: A Sociological Analysis of Family Change in Postwar Japan.* Tokyo: LTCB International Library Foundation.

———. 1997. "Decent Housewives and Sensual White Women—Representations of Women in Postwar Japanese Magazines." *Japan Review* 9:151–169.

Oda, M. 2014. "Rebuilding Japantown: Japanese Americans in Transpacific San Francisco during the Cold War." *Pacific Historical Review* 83 (1): 57–91.

OECD (Organisation for Economic Cooperation and Development). 2007. "Highlights Japan: Babies and Bosses—Policies towards Reconciling Work and Family Life." *OECD Japan Policy Brief,* November 29, 2007. Accessed November 5, 2017. Available at https://www.oecd.org/els/social/family.

———. 2017. "The Pursuit of Gender Equality: An Uphill Battle; How Does Japan Compare?" Paris: OECD.

Office of Policy and Planning. 2001. "Estimates of the Unauthorized Immigrant Population Residing in the United States: 1990 to 2000 Introduction." Washington, DC: U.S. Immigration and Naturalization Service.

Ogawa, Dennis. 1978. *Kodomo No Tamei Ni: For the Sake of the Children, the Japanese American Experience in Hawaii.* Honolulu: University Press of Hawaii.

Ohnuki-Tierney, E. 1997. "McDonald's in Japan: Changing Manners and Etiquette." In *Golden Arches East: McDonald's in East Asia,* edited by J. L. Watson, 161–182. Palo Alto: Stanford University Press.

Oishi, N. 2007. "Pacific: Japan, Australia, New Zealand." In *The New Americans: A Guide to Immigration since 1965,* edited by M. Waters and R. Ueda, 543–556. Boston: Harvard University Press.

Okamoto, Y., K. Hayakawa, S. Noguch, and M. Shinya. 2004. *Homelessness and Housing in Japan.* Toronto: University of Toronto Centre for Urban and Community Studies.

Okamura, R. 1985. "Undesirable Culture." *Pacific Citizen* (Los Angeles), December 6, 1985, 101.

Okano, K. 1993. *School to Work Transition in Japan.* Avon, U.K.: Multilingual Matters.

Okazaki, M. 2017. "Sawtelle Japantown: A Return to One's Roots? A Los Angeles Neighborhood Is Struggling to Preserve Its Unique Cultural Identity." *Japan Times* (Tokyo), November 4, 2017.

Okihiro, G. 1973. "Japanese Resistance in America's Concentration Camps: A Re-evaluation." *Amerasia Journal* 2 (1): 20–34.

Omatsu, G. 1990. "Movement and Process: Building Campaigns for Mass Empowerment." *Amerasia Journal* 16 (1): 63–80.

Omi, M., D. Nakano, and J. Yamashita. 2019. Introduction to *Japanese American Millennials: Rethinking Generation, Community, and Diversity,* edited by M. Omi, D. Nakano, and J. Yamashita. Philadelphia: Temple University Press.

Omi, M., and H. Winant. 1994. *Racial Formation in the United States: From the 1960s to the 1990s.* New York: Routledge.

Ong, A. 1991. "The Gender and Labor Politics of Postmodernity." *Annual Review of Anthropology* 20:279–309.

———. 1996. "Cultural Citizenship as Subject-Making: Immigrants Negotiate Racial and Cultural Boundaries in the United States." *Current Anthropology* 37 (5): 737–762.

Ono, H., and N. Piper. 2004. "Japanese Women Studying Abroad, the Case of the United States." *Women's Studies International Forum* 27:101–118.

Ono, M. 2009. "Japanese Lifestyle Migration/Tourism in Southeast Asia." *Japanese Review of Cultural Anthropology* 10:43–52.

Ortner, S. 1996. *Making Gender: The Politics and Erotics of Culture*. Boston: Beacon.

Outlook (Santa Monica Daily Outlook). 1925. "Help Wanted," July 15, 1925.

Paret, M. 2016. "Towards a Precarity Agenda." *Global Labor Journal* 7 (2): 111–122.

Patessio, M. 2011. *Women and Public Life in Early Meiji Japan: The Development of the Feminist Movement*. Ann Arbor: University of Michigan.

Pearce, S. C. 2011. *Immigration and Women: Understanding the American Experience/ Susan C. Pearce, Elizabeth J. Clifford, and Reena Tandon*. New York: New York University Press.

Peng, I. 2002. "Social Care in Crisis: Gender, Demography and Welfare State Structuring in Japan." *Social Politics* 9 (3): 412–443.

Percival, J. 2013. "Charting the Waters: Return Migration in Later Life." In *Return Migration in Later Life: International Perspectives*, edited by J. Percival, 1–16. Bristol: Policy.

Pharr, S. J. 1981. *Political Women in Japan: The Search for a Place in Political Life*. Berkeley: University of California Press.

———. 2003. "Targeting by an Activist State: Japan as a Civil Society Model." In *The State of Civil Society in Japan*, edited by F. J. Schwartz and S. J. Pharr, 316–336. New York: Cambridge University Press.

Pigliasco, G. C. 2005. "Lost in Translation from Omiyage to Souvenir: Beyond Aesthetics of the Japanese Office Ladies' Gaze in Hawaii." *Journal of Material Culture* 10 (2): 177–196.

Polunin, I. 1989. "Japanese Travel Boom." *Tourism Management* 10 (3): 4–8.

Portes, A. 1997. "Immigration Theory for a New Century: Some Problems and Opportunities." *International Migration Review* 31 (4): 799–825.

Pratsinakis, M. 2018. "Established and Outsider Nationals: Immigrant–Native Relations and the Everyday Politics of National Belonging." *Ethnicities* 18 (1): 3–22.

Prewitt, K. 2002. "Demography, Diversity, and Democracy: The 2000 Census Story." *Brookings Review* 20 (1): 6–9.

Psychology Today. 2015. "Clinical Social Work/Therapist." Accessed June 10, 2020. Available at https://www.psychologytoday.com/us/therapists/sayaka-kawase-torrance-ca/179006.

Puig, C. 1986. "'School of the Rising Sun': Surroundings Are American but Classes, Traditions Are Strictly Japanese." *Los Angeles Times*, November 13, 1986. Accessed August 4, 2018. Available at http://articles.latimes.com/1986-11-13/news/we-25047_1_american-school.

Qian, Z., S. L. Blair, and S. Ruf. 2001. "Asian American Interracial and Interethnic Marriages: Differences by Education and Nativity." *International Migration Review* 35 (2): 557–586.

Quayson, A. 2010. "Signs of the Times: Discourse Ecologies and Street Life on Oxford St., Accra." *City and Society* 22 (1): 72–96.
Rafu Shimpo. 1938. "Nisei Club Directory 1938," *Rafu Shimpo*, December 24, 1937.
———. 2013. "LTSC Staff Honored During National Social Workers Month." *Rafu Shimpo*, April 1, 2013.
———. 2018. "Ties That Bind—Looking Back and Looking Ahead for the Nikkei Community." *Rafu Shimpo*, October 5, 2018.
Rafu Staff. 2015. "Sawtelle Gets Official 'Japantown' Designation." *Rafu Shimpo*. February 27, 2015. Accessed March 3, 2015. Available at https://rafu.com/2015/02/sawtelle-gets-official-japantown-designation/.
Ramakrishnan, S. K. 2001. "Immigrant Incorporation and Political Participation in the United States." *International Migration Review* 35 (3): 870–909.
Rannveig Agunias, D., and K. Newland. 2007. *Circular Migration and Development: Trends, Policy Routes, and Ways Forward.* Washington, DC: Migration Policy Institute.
Rebick, M. 2011. "Gender Inequality in the Workplace in Japan." In *Japan's New Inequality*, edited by Y. Sato and J. Imai, 71–95. Melbourne: Trans Pacific.
Reid, T. 2014. "Toyota Withdrawal a Bombshell, Economic Blow to California City." *Reuters*, April 28, 2014. Accessed June 21, 2016. Available at https://www.reuters.com/article/idUSBREA3R1EW20140428.
Ribeiros, G. 2006. "Cosmopolitics for a New Global Scenario in Anthropology." *Critique of Anthropology* 26 (4): 363–386.
Rindfuss, R., M. K. Choe, L. L. Bumpass, and N. Tsuya. 2004. "Social Networks and Change in Japan." *American Sociological Review* 69 (6): 838–861.
Roberston, J. 2002. "Blood Talks: Eugenic Modernity and the Creation of New Japanese." *History and Anthropology* 13 (3): 191–216.
Rocha, R. R., D. P. Hawes, A. H. Fryar, and R. D. Wrinkle. 2014. "Policy Climates, Enforcement Rates, and Migrant Behavior: Is Self-Deportation a Viable Immigration Policy?" *Policy Studies Journal* 42 (1): 79–100.
Rosaldo, R. 1994. "Cultural Citizenship in San Jose, California." *Political and Legal Anthropology Review* 17 (2): 57–64.
Rosenberger, N. 2001. *Gambling with Virtue: Japanese Women and the Search for Self in a Changing Nation.* Honolulu: University of Hawai'i Press.
———. 2013. *Dilemmas of Adulthood: Japanese Women and the Nuances of Long-Term Resistance.* Hawai'i: University of Hawai'i Press.
Rosenblum, M., and A. G. R. Soto. 2015. "An Analysis of Unauthorized Immigrants in the United States by Country and Region of Birth." August 2015. Washington, DC: Migration Policy Institute.
Ruppenstein, A. 1993. *Legal Foreign Immigration to California: Size and Characteristics of the Flow according to the INS Statistics for 1993.* Sacramento: State of California, Department of Finance.
Ruyssen, I., and S. Salomone. 2018. *Gender and Migration.* Brussels: Leuven University Press.
Saito, L. 1998. *Race and Politics: Asian Americans, Latinos, and Whites in a Los Angeles Suburb.* Urbana: University of Illinois Press.
Sakai, J. 2011. Review of *Cultural Migrants from Japan: Youth, Media, and Migration in New York and London* by Yuiko Fujita. *Journal of Japanese Studies* 37 (2): 476–479.

Sakurai, T. 2004. "The Generation Gap in Japanese Society since the 1960s." In *Japan's Changing Generations: Are Young People Creating a New Society?* edited by G. Mathews and B. White, 12–30. New York: RoutledgeCurzon.

Sanchez, M., and J. Batalova. 2021. "Naturalized Citizens in the United States." Migration Policy Institute. Available at https://www.migrationpolicy.org/article/naturalization-trends-united-states#Birth.

Sanger, D. 1993. "Off to U.S., Japanese Pack Words, Like 'Police!'" *New York Times*, January 10, 1993, 1, late final edition.

Sanjek, R. 2002. "Worth Holding Onto: The Participatory Discrepancies of Political Activism." *City and Society* 14 (1): 103–117.

Sasagawa, A. 2004. "Centered Selves and Life Choices: Changing Attitudes of Young Educated Mothers." In *Japan's Changing Generations: Are Young People Creating a New Society?*, edited by G. Mathews and B. White. New York: RoutledgeCurzon.

Sasaki-Uemura, W. M. 2001. *Organizing the Spontaneous: Citizen Protest in Postwar Japan*. Honolulu: University of Hawai'i Press.

Sassen, S. 1994. "Economic Internationalization: The New Migration in Japan and the United States." *Social Justice* 21 (2): 62–82.

Sato, B. 2003. *The New Japanese Woman: Modernity, Media, and Women in Interwar Japan*. Durham, NC: Duke University Press.

Sato, M. 1993. *Farewell to Nippon: Japanese Lifestyle Migrants in Australia*. Melbourne: Trans Pacific.

Saulny, S. 2011. "Census Data Present Rise in Multiracial Population of Youths." *New York Times*, March 25, 2011. Accessed July 28, 2020. Available at https://www.nytimes.com/2011/03/25/us/25race.html.

Sawada, M. 1996. *Tokyo Life, New York Dreams: Urban Japanese Visions of America, 1890–1924*. Berkeley: University of California Press.

Scholars (Woodrow Wilson International Center for Scholars). 2002. *Women Immigrants in the United States*. Washington, DC: Woodrow Wilson International Center for Scholars.

Security (Department of Homeland Security). 1996. *Yearbook of Immigration Statistics*. Washington, DC: Department of Homeland Security.

———. 2000. *Yearbook of the Immigration Statistics*. Washington, DC: Department of Homeland Security. Accessed September 12, 2016. Available at https://www.dhs.gov/xlibrary/assets/statistics/yearbook/2000/.

———. 2015. *Yearbook of Immigration Statistics*. Washington, DC: Department of Homeland Security. Accessed June 24, 2017. Available at https://www.dhs.gov/sites/default/files/publications/Yearbook_Immigration_Statistics_2015.pdf.

———. 2017. *Yearbook of Immigration Statistics*. Washington, DC: Department of Homeland Security. Accessed July 25, 2020. Available at https://www.dhs.gov/sites/default/files/publications/yearbook_immigration_statistics_2017_0.pdf.

———. 2018a. *Fiscal Year 2018 Entry/Exit Overstay Report*. Washington, DC: Department of Homeland Security. Accessed July 26, 2020. Available at https://www.dhs.gov/sites/default/files/.

———. 2018b. *Yearbook of Immigration Statistics 2018*. Washington, DC: Department of Homeland Security. Accessed July 25, 2020. Available at https://www.dhs.gov/immigration-statistics/yearbook/2018.

———. n.d. Green Card Eligibility Categories. Washington, DC: Department of Homeland Security. Available at https://www.uscis.gov/green-card/green-card-eligibility-categories.

———. n.d. Green Card through the Diversity Immigrant Visa Program. Washington, DC: Department of Homeland Security. Available at https://www.uscis.gov/green-card/green-card-eligibility/green-card-through-the-diversity-immigrant-visa-program.

Sekine, Y. 2008. "The Rise of Poverty in Japan: The Emergence of the Working Poor." *Japan Labor Review* 5 (4): 49–66.

Seltzer, W., and M. Anderson. 2001. "The Dark Side of Numbers: The Role of Population Data Systems in Human Rights Abuses." *Social Research* 68 (2): 481–513.

Service (Immigration and Naturalization Service). 1999. *1999 Statistical Yearbook*. Washington, DC: U.S. Department of Justice. Accessed July 25, 2013. Available at https://www.dhs.gov/sites/default/files/publications/Yearbook_Immigration_Statistics_1999.pdf.

Services (U.S. Citizenship and Immigration Services). n.d. "Naturalization Oath of Allegiance to the United States of America." Accessed December 11, 2019. Available at https://www.uscis.gov/us-citizenship/naturalization-test/naturalization-oath-allegiance-united-states-america.

Shibuhara, T. 2014. *Japanese Women and the Transnational Feminist Movement before World War II*. Philadelphia: Temple University Press.

Shichinohe-Suga, M. 2004. "Little Tokyo Reconsidered: Transformation of Japanese American Community through the Early Redevelopment Projects." *Japanese Journal of American Studies*, no. 15, 237–255.

———. 2006. "Diversity within 'Nikkei': The Demographic Background and Multiple Identities of the Japanese Population in the United States." In *The World of Transnational Asian Americans*, edited by D. Yui, 181–192. Tokyo: Center for Pacific and American Studies, Tokyo University.

Shirahase, S. 1995. "Diversity in Female Work: Female Part-Time Workers in Contemporary Japan." *American Asian Review* 13 (2): 257–282.

———. 2001. "Women and Class Structure in Contemporary Japan." *British Journal of Sociology* 52 (3): 391–408.

Shiraki, J. 2008. "Remembering Sawtelle." *Nichi Bei Times*. Accessed October 5, 2018. Available at https://www.californiajapantowns.org/newsevents.html.

Shire, K. A. 2000. "Gendered Organization and Workplace Culture in Japanese Customer Services." *Social Science Japan Journal* 3 (1): 37–57.

Silverberg, M. 1992. "Constructing the Japanese Ethnography of Modernity." *Journal of Asian Studies* 51 (1): 30–54.

Silvey, R. 2013. "Political Moves: Cultural Geographies of Migration and Difference." In *The Wiley-Blackwell Companion to Cultural Geography*, edited by N. C. Johnson, R. H. Schein, and J. Winders, 409–422. West Sussex, U.K.: John Wiley and Sons.

Simonen, M., and N. Ndiaye. 2006. *Female Migrants: Bridging the Gaps through the Life Cycle*. New York: United Nations Population Fund.

Simonsen, K., and L. Koefoed. 2020. *Geographies of Embodiment: Critical Phenomenology and the World of Strangers*. Thousand Oaks, CA: Sage.

Simpson, K. 2012. "Three Waves of Little Tokyo Redevelopment." KCET, July 31, 2012. Accessed August 1, 2018. Available at https://www.kcet.org/shows/departures/three-waves-of-little-tokyo-redevelopment.

Smart, A. 1999. "Participating in the Global: Transnational Social Networks and Urban Anthropology." *City and Society* 11 (1–2): 59–77.
Smith, J. M. 2006. "Spatial and Identity Transformations in the Japanese American Ethnic Economy in Globalizing Los Angeles." In *Landscapes of the Ethnic Economy*, edited by D. H. Kaplan and W. Li, 177–192. Lanham, MD: Rowman and Littlefield.
Smith, M., and L. Guarnizo, eds. 1999. *Transnationalism from Below*. Comparative Urban and Community Research. New Brunswick, NJ: Transaction.
Smith, M. P. 2005. "Power in Place/Places of Power: Contextualizing Transnational Research." *City and Society* 17 (1): 5–34.
Soja, E. W. 1996. "Los Angeles, 1965–1992: From Crisis-Generated Restructuring to Restructuring-Generated Crisis." In *The City: Los Angeles and Urban Theory at the End of the Twentieth Century*, edited by J. Scott Alan and E. W. Soja, 426–462. Berkeley: University of California Press.
———. 2011. "Spatializing Justice—Part II." *City* 15 (1): 96–102.
———. 2014. *My Los Angeles: From Urban Restructuring to Regional Urbanization*. Berkeley: University of California Press.
Song, M. 2009. "Is Intermarriage a Good Indicator of Integration?" *Journal of Ethnic and Migration Studies* 35 (2): 331–348.
Sonksen, M. 2012. "West L.A.'s Little Osaka, Rollin' with Dre and Margaret Hermes." KCET Departures, November 16, 2012. Accessed August 30, 2015. Available at http://www.kcet.org/socal/departures.
———. 2015. "Battle for Boyle Heights' Last Japanese Retirement Home." KCET, December 14, 2015. Accessed March 12, 2022. Available at https://www.kcet.org/history-society/battle-for-boyle-heights-last-japanese-retirement-home.
Sooudi, O. K. 2014. *Japanese New York: Migrant Artists and Self-Reinvention on the World Stage*. Honolulu: University of Hawai'i Press.
Sorensen, A. 2009. "Neighborhood Streets as Meaningful Spaces: Claiming Rights to Shared Spaces in Tokyo." *City and Society* 21 (2): 207–229.
Spickard, P. 2009. *Japanese Americans: The Formation and Transformation of an Ethnic Group*. New Brunswick, NJ: Rutgers University Press.
Stambler, L. 1985. "Outgrowing the Past: Distinctive Sawtelle Neighborhood Gives Way to Development." *Los Angeles Times*, May 30, 1985. Accessed August 27, 2019. Available at https://www.latimes.com/archives/la-xpm-1985-05-30-we-4978-story.html.
State (U.S. Department of State). n.d. "Safety and Security of U.S. Borders: Biometrics." Accessed May 7, 2022. Available at https://travel.state.gov/content/travel/en/us-visas/visa-information-resources/border-biometrics.html?msclkid=5623e358ce6111eca2f62b611e803a64.
Steinberg, R. J. 1990. "Social Construction of Skill: Gender, Power, and Comparable Worth." *Work and Occupations* 17 (4): 449–482.
Sterngold, J. 1989. "Spurt in Travel Abroad Cuts Japan's Large Trade Surplus." *New York Times*, December 22, 1989. Accessed March 3, 2018. Available at https://search.proquest.com/docview/427466392?accountid=14512.
Stewart, R. 1985. "Probation Given to Mother in Drowning of Her Two Children." *Los Angeles Times*, November 22, 1985. Available at https://www.latimes.com/archives/la-xpm-1985-11-22-me-1070-story.html.
Stockman, N., N. Bonney, and S. Xuuewen. 1995. *Women's Work in East and West: The Dual Burden of Employment and Family Life*. London: Cambridge University Press.

Suehiro, A. 1998. "An Introduction to This Issue's Special Topic: Japanese Society and 'Community.'" *Social Science Japan Journal* 1 (2): 163–164.

Sukbin, C., K. W. Mccleary, and M. Uysal. 1995. "Travel Motivations of Japanese Overseas Travelers: A Factor-Cluster Segmentation Approach." *Journal of Travel Research* 34 (1): 33–39.

Sullivan, J. J. 1992. *Invasion of the Salarymen: The Japanese Business Presence in America*. Westport, CT: Praeger.

Susser, I. 2021. "Urban Precarity: The Destructiveness of Neoliberalism and Possibilities for Transformation." *City and Society* 33 (2): 403–412.

Suzuki, N. 2008. "Filipino Migration to Japan: From Surrogate Americans to Feminized Workers." In *Transnational Migration in East Asia: Japan in Comparative Focus*, edited by S. Yamashita, M. Minami, D. Haines, and J. Eades, 67–77. Osaka: National Museum of Ethnology.

Tachibanaki, T. 1987. "Labour Market Flexibility in Japan in Comparison with Europe and the U.S." *European Economic Review* 3 (1): 647–684.

Tachibanaki, T., and K. Sakurai. 1991. "Labour Supply and Unemployment in Japan." *European Economic Review* 35:1575–1587.

Tachiki, A., E. Wong, and F. Odo, eds. 1971. *Roots: An Asian American Reader*. Los Angeles: UCLA Asia American Studies Center.

Tajima, J. 2000. "A Study of Asian Immigrants in Global City Tokyo." *Asian and Pacific Migration Journal* 9 (3): 349–364.

Tajima, R. E. 1989. "Lotus Blossoms Don't Bleed: Images of Asian Women." *Making Waves: An Anthology of Writings by and about Asian American Women*, edited by Asian Women United of California, 308–317. Boston: Beacon.

Takagi, S. 1986. "Women on the Labor Front." *AMPO Japan-Asia Quarterly Review* 18 (2–3): 48–54.

Takahashi, J. 1997. *Nisei/Sansei: Shifting Japanese American Identities and Politics*. Philadelphia: Temple University Press.

Takaki, R. 1989. *Strangers from a Different Shore*. Boston: Little, Brown.

Takamori, Ayako. 2010. "Rethinking Japanese American 'Heritage' in the Homeland." *Critical Asian Studies* 42 (2): 217–238.

Takeda, A. 2013. "Weblog Narratives of Japanese Migrant Women in Australia: Consequences of International Mobility." *International Journal of Intercultural Relations* 37 (4): 415–421.

Takekawa, S. 2007. "Forging Nationalism from Pacifism and Internationalism: A Study of Asahi and Yomiuri's New Year's Day Editorials, 1953–2005." *Social Science Japan Journal* 10 (1): 59–80.

Takenaka, A. 2003. "Paradoxes of Ethnicity-Based Immigration: Peruvian and Japanese-Peruvian Migrants in Japan." In *Global Japan: The Experience of Japan's New Immigrant and Overseas Communities*, edited by R. Goodman, C. Peach, A. Takenaka, and P. White, 222–236. New York: RoutledgeCurzon.

Takeuchi, M. 2017. "At the Crossroads of Equality versus Protection: American Occupationnaire Women and Socialist Feminism in US Occupied Japan, 1945–1952." *Frontiers: A Journal of Women Studies* 38 (2): 114–147.

Tamanoi, M. A. 1990. "Women's Voices: Their Critique of the Anthropology of Japan." *Annual Review of Anthropology* 19:17–37.

Tanemori, R. 2017. "Memorandum: Planning and Community Development Department City of Santa Monica Planning Division." Santa Monica: City of Santa Monica.

Thang, L. L., and M. Toyota. 2015. "Making 'Traditional' Families in Transnational Settings: Japanese Women in Balinese-Japanese Marriages." In *Configurations of Family in Contemporary Japan*, edited by T. Aoyama, L. Dales, and R. Dasgupta, 107–119. London: Routledge.

Thomas, K., and R. B. Galemba. 2013. "Illegal Anthropology: An Introduction." *Polar Political and Legal Anthropology Review* 36 (2): 211–214.

Thompson, J. 2021. "What It Means to Be a 'True American': Ethnonationalism and Voting in the 2016 U.S. Presidential Election." *Nations and Nationalism* 27 (1): 279–297.

Tipton, E. K. 2000. "Being Women in Japan, 1970–2000." In *Women in Asia: Traditional, Modernity, and Globalisation*, edited by L. Edwards and M. Roces, 208–228. Ann Arbor: University of Michigan Press.

Toba, K. 1979. "Working Worldwide: Japanese Overseas." *Japan Echo* 6 (2): 85–91.

Toivonen, T., and Y. Imoto. 2012. "Making Sense of Youth Problems." *A Sociology of Japanese Youth: From Returnees to NEETs*, edited by R. Goodman, Y. Imoto, and T. Toivonen, 1–29. New York: Routledge.

Toji, D., and K. Umemoto. 2003. "The Paradox of Dispersal: Ethnic Continuity and Community Development among Japanese Americans in Little Tokyo." *AAPI Nexus* 1 (1): 21–45.

Tomlinson, J. 1991. *Cultural Imperialism*. Baltimore: Johns Hopkins University Press.

Torrance (City of Torrance). 2012. "City of Torrance: A Community Profile." Community Development Department, October, 2012. Accessed June 10, 2020. Available at https://www.torranceca.gov.

Toyama, C. 1926. *The Japanese Community in Los Angeles*. New York: Columbia University.

Toyokawa, T., and N. Toyokawa. 2002. "Extracurricular Activities and the Adjustment of Asian International Students: A Study of Japanese Students." *International Journal of Intercultural Relations* 26 (4): 363–379.

Toyota, T. 2010. *Envisioning America: New Chinese Americans and the Politics of Belonging*. Palo Alto, CA: Stanford University Press.

———. 2012. "The New Nikkei: Transpacific Shin Issei and Shifting Borders of Community in Southern California." *Amerasia Journal* 38 (3): 2–27.

Travel.state.gov. n.d. Employment. Available at https://travel.state.gov/content/travel/en/us-visas/employment.html.

———. n.d. Study and Exchange. Available at https://travel.state.gov/content/travel/en/us-visas/study.html.

Trinh Võ, L., and R. D. Torres. 2004. "Guest Editorial: Mapping Comparative Studies of Racialization in the US." *Ethnicities* 4 (3): 307–314.

Trouillot, M.-R. 1995. *Silencing the Past: Power and the Production of History*. Boston: Beacon.

Tsu, C. M. 2009. "Sex, Lies, and Agriculture: Reconstructing Japanese Immigrant Gender Relations in Rural California, 1900–1913." *Pacific Historical Review* 78 (2): 171–209.

Tsuda, T. 1999. "Transnational Migration and the Nationalization of Ethnic Identity among Japanese Brazilian Return Migrants." *Ethos* 27 (2): 145–179.

———. 2015. "Recovering Heritage and Homeland: Ethnic Revival among Fourth-Generation Japanese Americans." *Sociological Inquiry* 85 (4): 600–627.

———. 2016. *Japanese American Ethnicity: In Search of Heritage and Homeland across Generations*. New York: New York University Press.

Tsukashima, R. T. 1995/1996. "Continuity of Ethnic Participation in the Economy: Immigrants in Contract Gardening." *Amerasia Journal* 21 (3): 53–76.

Tsukuda, Y. 2004. "Where Is 'Home' for the Shin-Issei?" *Nikkei Heritage: Journal of the National Japanese American Historical Society* 16 (Spring): 6–7.

Tsurumi, E. 1990. *Factory Girls: Women in the Thread Mills of Meiji Japan*. Princeton, NJ: Princeton University Press.

Tuan, M. 2001. *Forever Foreigners or Honorary Whites? The Asian Ethnic Experience Today*. New Brunswick, NJ: Rutgers University Press.

Ueunten, W. 2002. "Japanese Latin American Internment from an Okinawan Perspective." In *Okinawan Diaspora*, edited by R. Y. Nakasone, 90–111. Honolulu: University of Hawai'i Press.

Umakoshi, T. 1997. "Internationalization of Japanese Higher Education in the 1980's and Early 1990's." *Higher Education* 34 (2): 259–273.

Uno, K. S. 1991. "Women and Changes in the Household Division of Labor." In *Recreating Japanese Women, 1600–1945*, edited by G. L. Bernstein, 18–42. Berkeley: University of California Press.

U.S. Census Bureau. 1990. *We Asked . . . You Told Us: Place of Birth, Citizenship, and Year of Entry*. Washington, DC: U.S. Census Bureau. Available at https://www2.census.gov/library/publications/decennial/1990/cqc/cqc-12.pdf.

———. 2000. *Census Briefs: The Asian Population*. Washington, DC: U.S. Census Bureau. Available at http://www.census.gov/population/www/documentation.

———. 2009. *American Community Survey: Year of Entry by Citizenship Status in the United States*. Washington, DC: U.S. Census Bureau. Accessed November 23, 2019. Available at https://factfinder2.census.gov/naturalization.

———. 2010a. *Asian Alone or in Combination with One or More Other Races, and with One or More Asian Categories for Selected Groups*. Washington, DC: U.S. Census Bureau. Available at https://factfinder.census.gov/faces/tableservices/jsf/pages/productview.xhtml?pid=DEC_00_SF1_PCT007&prodType=table.

———. 2010b. *Community Facts Zip Code 90025*. Washington, DC: U.S. Census Bureau. Available at https://factfinder.census.gov/faces/nav/jsf/pages/community_facts.xhtml.

———. 2010c. *Selected Population Profile in the United States: 2010 American Community Survey 1-Year Estimates*. Washington, DC: U.S. Census Bureau. Available at https://factfinder.census.gov/faces/tableservices/jsf/pages/productview.xhtml?src=bkmk.

———. 2012. *The Asian Population: 2010*. Washington, DC: U.S. Department of Commerce, Economics and Statistics Administration. Available at https://factfinder.census.gov/faces/tableservices/jsf/pages/productview.xhtml?pid=DEC_10_SF1_QTP8&prodType=table.

———. 2018. *American Community Survey*. Washington, DC: U.S. Census Bureau. Available at https://data.census.gov/cedsci/table?q=japanese&table=DP05&lastDisplayedRow=29&layer=state&cid=DP05_0001E&t=Populations%20and%20People&tid=ACSSPP1Y2018.S0201&hidePreview=true.

———. 2020. *How Many People Live in Census Tract 2677, Los Angeles County, California*. Washington, DC: U.S. Census Bureau. Available at https://data.sj-r.com/census/total-population/total-population-change/census-tract-2677-los-angeles-county-california/140-06037267700/.

Van Hear, N. 1998. *New Diasporas: The Mass Exodus, Dispersal and Regrouping of Migrant Communities*. Seattle: University of Washington Press.

Verge, A. C. 1994. "The Impact of the Second World War on Los Angeles." *Pacific Historical Review* 63, no. 3 (August): 289–314.

Villa, S. n.d. "Gabrielino-Tongva Tribe: A California Indian Tribe Historically Known as San Gabriel Band of Mission Indians." Accessed July 30, 2019. Available at http://www.gabrielinotribe.org/historical-sites-1/.

Võ, L. T. 2008. "Constructing a Vietnamese American Community: Economic and Political Transformation in Little Saigon, Orange County." *Amerasia Journal* 34 (3): 85–109.

Vogel, E. F. 1967. *Japan's New Middle Class: The Salary Man and His Family in a Tokyo Suburb*. Berkeley: University of California Press.

Vosko, L. F., M. MacDonald, and I. Cambell. 2009. "Gender and the Concept of Precarious Employment." In *Gender and the Contours of Precarious Employment*, edited by L. F. Vosko, M. MacDonald, and I. Campbell, 1–25. London: Routledge.

Wade, P. 2002. *Race, Nature and Culture: An Anthropological Perspective*. London: Pluto.

Wagatsuma, H. 1967. "The Social Perception of Skin Color in Japan." *Daedalus* 96 (2): 407–443.

Wang, H. L. 2019. "What You Need to Know about the 2020 Census." NPR, March 31, 2019. Available at https://www.npr.org/2019/03/31/707899218/what-you-need-to-know-about-the-2020-census.

War Agency Liquidation Unit (WALU). 1975. "People in Motion: The Postwar Adjustment of the Evacuated Japanese Americans." Washington, DC: Department of the Interior.

Warren, W. H. 1986–1987. "Maps: A Spatial Approach to Japanese American Communities in Los Angeles." *Amerasia Journal* 13 (2): 137–151.

Wasem, R. E. 2014. *Nonimmigrant Overstays: Brief Synthesis of the Issue*. Washington, DC: U.S. Congress, Congressional Research Service.

Watts, D. 1985. "The Rising Sun Outshines the U.S." *London Times*, December 16, 1985.

Weathers, C. 2001. "Changing White-Collar Workplaces and Female Temporary Workers in Japan." *Social Science Japan Journal* 4 (2): 201–218.

Weiner, M. 1997. *Japan's Minorities: The Illusion of Homogeneity*. London: Routledge.

Weisman, S. 1991. "Japanese Coin Word for Their Unease about U.S." *New York Times*. October 16, 1991.

West Los Angeles Neighborhood Council. 2014. "2014 Neighborhood Council Elections West Los Angeles Canvass of Votes." Accessed September 2019. Available at https://empowerla.org/wp-content/uploads/2014/02/West-LA-NC-Final-Canvass-of-Votes-2014.pdf.

Wilkins, M. 1990. "Japanese Multinationals in the United States: Continuity and Change, 1879–1990." *Business History Review* 64 (4): 585–629.

Wilkins, S., and J. Huisman. 2012. "The International Branch Campus as Transnational Strategy in Higher Education." *Higher Education* 64 (5): 627–645.

Wilkinson, C. 2013. "The Soldiers' City: Sawtelle, California, 1897–1922." *Southern California Quarterly* 95 (2): 188–226.
Williams, T. K. 1991. Marriage between Japanese Women and U.S. Servicemen Since World War II. *Amerasia Journal* 17 (1): 135–154.
Winant, H. 2015. "Race, Ethnicity and Social Science." *Ethnic and Racial Studies* 38 (13): 2176–2185.
Witz, A. 1992. *Professions and Patriarchy*. New York: Routledge.
Wong, K. 2015. "2015 Travel Trends and Statistics: Outbound Japanese Tourism." *Freshtrax*, February 10, 2015. Accessed March 3, 2018. Available at http://blog.btrax.com/en/2015/02/10/2015-travel-trends-statistics-japanese-tourists/.
Woo, R. 2015. "Naming Los Angeles." In *LAtitudes: An Angeleno's Atlas*, edited by P. Wakida, 1–9. Berkeley, CA: Heyday.
Woodyard, C. 1995. "Welcome Back: Southern California Lures Big-Spending Japanese Tourists Back by Making Them Feel at Home." *Los Angeles Times*, September 3, 1995, 1.
Workpermit.com. 2007. "Female Migration Increasing around the World." November 27, 2007. Accessed June 29, 2013. Available at http://www.workpermit.com/news/2007-11-27/global/world-bank-report-woman-immigrants-increasing.htm.
WRA (War Relocation Authority). 1945. *Returns to West Coast—City Cumulative Reports 1–12*. Washington, DC: WRA Statistics Section.
Wright, E. O. 2016. "Is the Precariat a Class?" *Global Labour Journal* 7 (2): 123–135.
Wuthnow, R. 1998. *Loose Connections: Joining Together in America's Fragmented Communities*. Cambridge, MA: Harvard University Press.
Wyzant. 2015. "Find Japanese Tutors in Torrance, California." Accessed June 10, 2020. Available at http://www.wyzant.com/Torrance_CA_japanese_tutors.aspx.
Yamada, K. 2009. "Past and Present Constraints on Labor Movements for Gender Equality in Japan." *Social Science Japan Journal* 12 (2): 195–209.
Yamamoto, D., and A. Gill. 1999. "Emerging Trends in Japanese Package Tourism." *Journal of Travel Research* 38 (2): 134–143.
Yamamoto, E. 2000. "Cheers for Japanese Athletes: The 1932 Los Angeles Olympics and the Japanese American Community." *Pacific Historical Review* 69 (3): 399–430.
Yamamoto, J. 2011. "Study Shows Changing Demographics in JA Community." *Rafu Shimpo* (Los Angeles), July 19, 2001. 1.
Yamamoto, L. E. 2010. "Gender Roles and Ethnic Identities in a Globalizing World: The Case of Japanese Brazilian Migrant Women." In *Japanese Nikkei at Home and Abroad: Negotiating Identities in a Global World*, edited by N. Adachi, 187–209. Amherst, NY: Cambria.
Yamanaka, K. 2003. "Feminization of Japanese Brazilian Labor Migration to Japan." In *Searching for Home Abroad: Japanese and Brazilian Transnationalism*, edited by J. Lesser, 163–200. Durham, NC: Duke University Press.
Yamashiro, J. 2017. *Redefining Japaneseness: Japanese Americans in the Ancestral Homeland*. New Brunswick, NJ: Rutgers University Press.
Yamashita, S. 2008. "Transnational Migration of Women: Changing Boundaries of Contemporary Japan." In *Multiculturalism in the New Japan: Crossing the Boundaries Within*, edited by N. H. Graburn, J. Ertl, and R. K. Tierney, 101–116. New York: Berghahn Books.

Yanagisako, S. 2002. "Asian Exclusion Acts." In *Learning Places: The Afterlives of Area Studies*, edited by M. Miyoshi and H. D. Harootunian, 175–189. Durham, NC: Duke University Press.

Yang, D. C. 2005. "Globalization and the Transnational Asian 'Knowledge Class.'" *Asian Law Journal* 12 (1) 137–160.

Yang, P. Q. 2002. "Citizenship Acquisition of Post-1965 Asian Immigrants." *Population and Environment* 23 (4): 377–404.

———. 2011. *Asian Immigration to the United States*. Cambridge: Polity.

Yasuike, A. 2005. "Maternalism—Japanese Patriarchal Bargaining in the Era of Globalization: Corporate Transnational Wives and Shin Issei Women in Southern California." PhD dissertation. University of Southern California.

Yasutake, R. 2004. *Transnational Women's Activism: The United States, Japan, and Japanese Immigrant Communities in California, 1859–1920*. New York: New York University Press.

Yializis, C. n.d. "Getting a U.S. Visa for a Short, Recreational or Part-Time Study Course." Available at https://www.nolo.com/legal-encyclopedia/getting-us-visa-short-recreational-part-time-study-course.html.

Yoda, T., and H. Harootunian. 2006. *Japan after Japan: Social and Cultural Life from the Recessionary 1990s to the Present*. Durham, NC: Duke University Press.

Yokota, R. M. 2008. "Japanese and Okinawan Cubans." In *Changing Cuba/Changing World*, 429–447. New York: Bildner Center for Western Hemisphere Studies, City University of New York.

Yoo, D. 2000. *Growing Up Nisei: Race, Generation, and Culture among Japanese Americans of California, 1924–49*. Urbana: University of Illinois.

Yoshikawa, H., and F. Ohtake. 1989. "An Analysis of Female Labor Supply, Housing Demand and the Savings Rate in Japan." *European Economic Review* 33 (5): 997–1030.

Yoshimi, S. 2003. "'America' as Desire and Violence: Americanization in Postwar Japan and Asia during the Cold War." *Inter-Asia Cultural Studies* 4 (3): 430–453.

Young, L. 1998. "Reinventing Agrarianism: Rural Crisis and the Wedding of Agriculture to Empire." In *Japan's Total Empire: Manchuria and the Culture of Wartime Imperialism*, edited by L. Young, 307–351. Berkeley: University of California Press.

Zlotnik, H. 1990. "International Migration Policies and the Status of Female Migrants." *International Migration Review* 24 (2): 372–381.

Index

Ad Hoc Committee to Save Keiro, 154–155
Aki-chan's House, 104–109, 124, 126, 186. *See also* Tomoko
Akogare, 13
Aratani Theatre, 93
Asahi Gakuen, 113. *See also* Hoshuukoo, Japanese heritage school
Aya, 36; employment in Japan, 36–37; employment in U.S., 72; migration to Los Angeles, 61–62

Bonin, Mike, 138
Bradley, Tom, 92–93
Bronzeville, 91. *See also* Little Tokyo: history
Bubble economy Japan, 8, 45, 46, 96; stagnation, 54, 72, 176

Casualization of labor, 9, 33
Chain migration, 71
Chika, 80–81
Chisa, 55; education in Japan, 29; education in U.S., 61; employment in Japan, 61; employment in U.S., 72, 99; parental pressure, 35–36, 61
Christmas cakes, 39. *See also* Parasaito
Chuzai-in: residence in Southern California, 88, 91, 96; shin Issei differences, 94–95,
101–103, 112–113, 115, 169; temporary Japanese employees, 16, 23, 46–47, 52, 66, 177
Citizenship, 8, 23, 68, 71, 77, 114, 170, 187n1; Nikkei identity, 19, 79, 130, 131–132, 136, 141, 158, 169, 183; shin Issei identity, 65, 78, 80, 81–85, 142–143, 154, 179, 180. *See also* Dual citizenship; Immigration Reform and Control Act (IRCA); Jus sanguinis; Jus soli
Community activism: Nikkei, 19, 137, 148–150, 172; shin Issei, 24, 105, 146, 152–153, 160, 167–168, 173, 181
Community meanings: Nikkei, 151; shin Issei, 146, 147
Community transformation, 188n4; meanings of, 145–151, 156, 168, 172–173, 182, 184; in Nikkei space, 2–6, 8, 18–20, 46–47, 92–95, 114–115; in Sawtelle, 23, 110, 125, 133–134. *See also* Sawtelle
Contract gardening, 127. *See also* Sawtelle
Cultural migrants, 14

Dekasegi, 17
Department of Homeland Security (DHS), 178
Douglas Aircraft Company, 141
Dual citizenship, 81–82, 85. *See also* Citizenship

Economy: Japan restructuring, 2–3, 8, 9, 12, 13, 15, 17, 30–33, 34–35, 40–41, 45, 46, 72, 96, 176–177, 184, 187n2; migration motivations for shin Issei, 65, 68; postwar Japan, 21, 26–32; transpacific ties, 23, 26, 46–47, 51, 52–54, 56, 63, 70, 73, 91, 169, 181; U.S. restructuring, 15, 22, 46, 69, 71, 92–94, 113, 127. *See also* Bubble economy Japan

Education: chuzai-in, 47, 112–113; foreign students, 56, 59, 62, 63, 187n6, 187n7, 188n8; foreign travel and, 54–60; Japan postwar reforms, 28–29; limits of, 35, 38, 43, 65, 148, 187n3; marriage/partners, 77–78; naturalization, 80–84; Nikkei, 128, 186n8; shin Issei in Japan, 2, 6, 13, 22, 25; shin Nisei, 104, 110, 164, 183–184

Enryo, 125

Equal Employment Opportunity Law (EEOL) Japan, 42–43, 187n4

Ethnonationalism, 83, 88, 116

Ethnoracial, 162

Exogamy: Nikkei, 77; shin Issei women, 73, 77, 106

Family reunification, 15, 7
Feminization of migration, 11, 12, 68, 180
Fertility rates: Japan, 39, 86, 147

Gakuen, 112–113, 189n5
Gardena: demographics, 88, 168; history, 88, 169–170
Gardena Valley Japanese Cultural Institute (GVJCI), 168, 171
Gender: imbalance in migration, 12–13; Japanese housewife, 35, 37–38; Nikkei, 5, 11; shin Issei employment in United States, 23, 95–100, 113, 180; shin Issei in Japan, 3, 9–10, 13, 15–16, 27–28, 33–48, 73, 77, 167–168
Gosei, 5, 185n1, 186n8
Green card, 7, 186n7; lottery, 188n7; no desire for, 84, 96, 179; pursuit of, 64, 70–76, 78–79, 80–82, 98, 100, 103, 107, 142, 162, 170–172. *See also* Lawful permanent residency

Hafu, 189n3
Hana: employment in Japan, 60; employment in Los Angeles, 70, 72; migration to Los Angeles, 60, 69, 80, 188n5
Hapa, 106, 183. *See also* Hafu
Hollywood, 27, 98, 126
Hoshuukoo: differences with gakuen, 112. *See also* Japanese heritage school
Hostessing: employment in Japan, 97; shin Issei employment in U.S., 16, 23, 75, 96–99, 113, 115

Illegal Immigration Reform and Immigrant Responsibility Act of 1996 (IIRIRA), 68, 69
Immigration Act of 1924, 17
Immigration and Nationality Act of 1965, 15, 71, 72, 188n4. *See also* Family reunification
Immigration laws Japan, 16, 84, 171
Immigration Reform and Control Act (IRCA) of 1986, 72
Inaka, 120, 129
Incarceration WWII, 24; Nikkei experience, 117, 118, 129, 130, 148, 151, 160, 162; U.S. Census role, 68. *See also* Manzanar
Issei, 185n1, 186n4, 189n5; building Sawtelle, 125–129; nineteenth-century migration to U.S., 2, 8, 17; settlement in U.S., 91, 184; U.S. citizenship, 79

Japan bashing, 48
Japanese American, 3, 6; community, 125, 149, 156, 160, 170, 182; global connections, 93–94; identity as, 4, 18–19, 122, 140, 150, 174; ideological space, 23, 90–91, 114–115, 132, 136, 139, 141; prewar, 68; segregation, 128–129. *See also* Nikkei
Japanese heritage school (JHS), 110–112, 137, 157–166. *See also* Sawtelle
Jus sanguinis, 188n10
Jus soli, 188n10

Kaisha: definition, 16; incursions into Nikkei community, 90, 94–95, 97, 135, 153, 169, 177, 178, 187n2; transnationality, 17, 47, 63, 102, 112–115. *See also* Chuzai-in
Keiro Senior Healthcare, 153; sale of, 153–156
Kimura, Fumiko, 52; fair trial committee, 152, 189n4

Kyoko: employment in Tokyo, 39–41, 63; employment in U.S., 72; transnational influences, 51, 54; travel to the U.S., 49–50, 54, 56, 65, 99, 100, 189n1

Labor: 11, 17, 26, 71, 190n3; Japan gendered, 30, 31, 33–35, 38, 43, 167; Japan restructuring, 21, 34, 43, 68, 176; shin Issei, 12–14, 16, 47, 62, 65, 77, 90, 95, 96, 177, 180
Lawful permanent residency (LPR), 64, 179, 186n7, 187n1, 187n2, 188n3, 188n5. *See also* Green card
Little Osaka, 133, 139, 140
Little Tokyo, 6, 18, 24; history, 91–92, 129, 168–169; INS raids, 69, 75; Japanese investment and redevelopment, 92–94; postwar, 91–92; shin Issei destination and employment, 45, 55, 88, 96, 99, 100
Little Tokyo Service Center (LTSC), 152, 168, 181
Los Angeles: Nikkei history, 2, 18, 91, 125, 128; shin Issei destination, 1, 2, 45, 55, 57–58, 60, 61, 62, 66, 88–89, 135, 148; shin Issei employment, 1, 70, 72, 90, 99–100; urban transformation, 18, 23, 47, 92, 102, 127. *See also* West Los Angeles

M curve, 35
Manzanar: Nikkei experience, 160, 161, 162; shin Issei response, 148, 163, 190n2; shin Nisei response, 163, 164
Mariko, 39
Mar Vista, 99, 102, 135
Masami: children, 111–112; education, 74, 78; green card, 74; marriage, 74; migration to Los Angeles, 74
Meiji period, 13, 28, 48, 185n2, 186n6; Nikkei values, 117, 121–122, 132, 181, 189n2; shin Issei values, 118–119
Miki: dual citizenship, 82–83; education, 57–58, 59, migration to Los Angeles, 52
Multinational Japanese corporations (MNCs) 46, 48, 63, 115, 169
Multiracial Nikkei, 6, 106, 182–183

Nikkei: activism, 157–161, 168, 170–171, 183; collaboration with shin Issei, 145–147, 170–175; definition of, 4; generational belonging, 18, 19, 120, 161, 185n2; identity, 130–133, 181; importance of community, 135–138; intergroup differences with shin Issei, 19, 115, 122, 141; racialization, 18, 19, 21. *See also* Japanese American; Sawtelle
Naturalization: Nikkei, 131; shin Issei, 23, 65, 78, 79, 80, 81, 82, 188n9; shin Issei identity as Japanese, 85–86, 142, 179

OL: gendered employment Japan, 41, 53, 59, 102; office ladies, 25–26
Overstayers, 5, 67, 102, 177–178; definition of, 64. *See also* Undocumented Japanese migrants
Oyako-shinju, 109, 189n4. *See also* Kimura, Fumiko

Paato, 33–34. *See also* Part-time work
Parasaito, 39, 77
Part-time work, 3, 9, 84; gendered work in Japan, 9, 22, 33–34, 35, 40, 43, 176; shin Issei work in Japan, 25, 36–37, 39–40, 44, 49, 55, 61, 63, 67, 69, 102; shin Issei work in U.S., 7, 170, 183n2
Passports, 52, 53, 54, 82, 176
Postwar Japan, 26, 167; American occupation, 27–29, 48
Precarity, 8–9, 10, 21, 22, 23, 33, 36, 39, 41, 147; migration status, 63, 64–66, 72, 73, 75–76, 79, 86, 102; shin Issei in U.S., 69, 87, 96, 101, 113, 180

Racial geography, 24, 91, 93, 94, 126–129, 146, 168–169, 172
Racial identity: Japan, 83, 85, 97, 162
Racialization: intergroup differences, 115, 116–117, 122–123, 143–144, 174, 181; Japanese ideology, 48, 69; shin Issei in U.S., 100, 180
Rieko: 1; education in Japan, 58; education in U.S., 59; employment in Japan, 2, 8, 59; employment in Los Angeles, 101; marriage and children, 78, 101, 108; migration to Los Angeles, 59
Risa: activism, 162, 164–166, 168; employment in Los Angeles, 161; green card, 162; migration to Los Angeles, 161; parental influences, 166–167
Ryosei kenbo (good wife, wise mother), 30, 38, 77, 101, 166, 186n2

Sachiko: employment in U.S., 72; migration to Los Angeles, 55
Sansei, 5, 6, 84, 185n2, 186n8; activism, 93, 135, 137, 138, 150–151, 157, 181, 182; identity, 120–121, 126–127, 130–132; intergroup differences with shin Issei, 122, 140–141, 171
Sarariman, 30, 38, 96
Sawtelle, 2, 6, 19, 23, 24, 90, 190n5; gentrification, 133–136; Nikkei community, 110, 119, 123, 136–139, 141, 151, 158, 166, 169; racialized space, 125–130; shin Issei in, 139–140
Sawtelle Japantown Association (SJA), 136; activism, 138–139, shin Issei response, 139–140
Seina: activism, 148–149, 168, 169; education in Japan, 142; migration to Los Angeles, 142, 148; naturalization, 143
Shelley: activism, 157–158, 159; intergroup differences with shin Issei, 159
Shin Issei: children, 106–109; community activism, 105, 143, 157, 180; definition of, 3, 4, 5, 78; education in Japan, 58; fieldwork sources, 6–8; foreign students, 57, 61–63; intergroup differences with Nikkei, 18–19, 24, 116–125; marriage and divorce, 73–74, 75–78, 100–103; migration to U.S., 20, 22, 23, 45, 176; racialization, 10, 16, 23, 87, 105; reasons for migration, 8–16, 26–29, 35, 38–44; social differences with chuzai-in, 17, 47, 63, 95, 102, 103, 112, 115, 153; transnational linkages, 46–56, 96–97; undocumentation, 64–66, 68–69, 79, 177–178; visa overstay, 67, 70, 72, 178. *See also* Dual citizenship; Exogamy; Naturalization; Nikkei
Shin Nisei, 107; education, 110–112, 182–183; travel, 107
Social class: in Japan, 3, 11, 13, 33; women, 37, 45, 97; shin Issei in U.S., 23, 95, 100, 103, 114, 115–116, 119–120, 123, 128, 147
South Bay, 2, 6, 24, 88, 96, 115, 169, 170, 190n4

Takako: activism, 156–157, 180; identity, 154; naturalization, 154

Tanaka Farms, 164
Terri, 141; acceptance of shin Issei, 160
Teruko, 111
Tomoko: activism, 101, 103–105, 124, 143, 145, 183–184, 189n2; employment in Los Angeles, 76; marriage and children, 75, 100; migration to Los Angeles, 51; undocumented status, 76, 78
Torrance, 88, 95, 169–170, 190n4
Tourism and travel, 48, 51, 52, 53–54, 65, 67, 80, 177, 187n5, 188n1; shin Issei, 5, 22, 49–50, 54–55, 61, 65, 81, 83, 89, 90, 176, 178
Toyo Miyatake, 190n2
Transnational: migration, 4, 9, 14, 80, 85, 173; Japanese media, 95; U.S. communities, 46–47, 50–51, 88, 89, 91, 92–96, 169, 181. *See also* Chuzai-in; Kaisha; Shin Issei

Undocumented Japanese migrants, 7, 86, 99, 102, 103, 187n4. *See also* Overstayers
U.S. Census: characteristics of Japanese population, 179; fear of, 68; foreign born Japanese in U.S., 20; racial categories, 106, 182–183; Sawtelle demographics, 135, 190n5; unauthorized residents, 67–68
U.S. Occupation of Japan, 13, 26–29, 186n1

Visas: Japanese students in U.S., 1, 5, 22, 62, 63; kaisha use of, 22, 46, 66, 95, 187n1; restrictions, 69, 71, 74, 90, 177–178, 187n4, 187n6, 188n1, 188n2; shin Issei use of, 1, 2, 7, 16, 50, 55, 56–57, 58–59, 61, 64–65, 67, 70, 73, 74, 80, 88, 98–99, 102, 161
Visa Waiver Program, 52, 187n5

West Los Angeles: gentrification, 133, 135; Nikkei in, 110, 111, 118, 128, 130, 160; shin Issei presence, 60, 88, 90, 104, 109, 122, 139, 183
West Los Angeles Neighborhood Council (WLANC), 137

Yamato damashii, 118–119
Yonsei, 5, 84, 132, 151, 158, 162, 185n2, 186n8

Tritia Toyota is Associate Adjunct Professor in the Department of Anthropology and is a Research Scholar at the Asian American Studies Center at the University of California, Los Angeles. She is the author of *Envisioning America: New Chinese Americans and the Politics of Belonging*. She also wrote and produced the documentary *Asian America*.

Also in the series *Asian American History and Culture*:

Edward Tang, *From Confinement to Containment: Japanese/American Arts during the Early Cold War*
Patricia P. Chu, *Where I Have Never Been: Migration, Melancholia, and Memory in Asian American Narratives of Return*
Cynthia Wu, *Sticky Rice: A Politics of Intraracial Desire*
Marguerite Nguyen, *America's Vietnam: The Longue Durée of U.S. Literature and Empire*
Vanita Reddy, *Fashioning Diaspora: Beauty, Femininity, and South Asian American Culture*
Audrey Wu Clark, *The Asian American Avant-Garde: Universalist Aspirations in Modernist Literature and Art*
Eric Tang, *Unsettled: Cambodian Refugees in the New York City Hyperghetto*
Jeffrey Santa Ana, *Racial Feelings: Asian America in a Capitalist Culture of Emotion*
Jiemin Bao, *Creating a Buddhist Community: A Thai Temple in Silicon Valley*
Elda E. Tsou, *Unquiet Tropes: Form, Race, and Asian American Literature*
Tarry Hum, *Making a Global Immigrant Neighborhood: Brooklyn's Sunset Park*
Ruth Mayer, *Serial Fu Manchu: The Chinese Supervillain and the Spread of Yellow Peril Ideology*
Karen Kuo, *East Is West and West Is East: Gender, Culture, and Interwar Encounters between Asia and America*
Kieu-Linh Caroline Valverde, *Transnationalizing Viet Nam: Community, Culture, and Politics in the Diaspora*
Lan P. Duong, *Treacherous Subjects: Gender, Culture, and Trans-Vietnamese Feminism*
Kristi Brian, *Reframing Transracial Adoption: Adopted Koreans, White Parents, and the Politics of Kinship*
Belinda Kong, *Tiananmen Fictions outside the Square: The Chinese Literary Diaspora and the Politics of Global Culture*
Bindi V. Shah, *Laotian Daughters: Working toward Community, Belonging, and Environmental Justice*
Cherstin M. Lyon, *Prisons and Patriots: Japanese American Wartime Citizenship, Civil Disobedience, and Historical Memory*
Shelley Sang-Hee Lee, *Claiming the Oriental Gateway: Prewar Seattle and Japanese America*
Isabelle Thuy Pelaud, *This Is All I Choose to Tell: History and Hybridity in Vietnamese American Literature*
Christian Collet and Pei-te Lien, eds., *The Transnational Politics of Asian Americans*
Min Zhou, *Contemporary Chinese America: Immigration, Ethnicity, and Community Transformation*

Kathleen S. Yep, *Outside the Paint: When Basketball Ruled at the Chinese Playground*
Benito M. Vergara Jr., *Pinoy Capital: The Filipino Nation in Daly City*
Jonathan Y. Okamura, *Ethnicity and Inequality in Hawai'i*
Sucheng Chan and Madeline Y. Hsu, eds., *Chinese Americans and the Politics of Race and Culture*
K. Scott Wong, *Americans First: Chinese Americans and the Second World War*
Lisa Yun, *The Coolie Speaks: Chinese Indentured Laborers and African Slaves in Cuba*
Estella Habal, *San Francisco's International Hotel: Mobilizing the Filipino American Community in the Anti-eviction Movement*
Thomas P. Kim, *The Racial Logic of Politics: Asian Americans and Party Competition*
Sucheng Chan, ed., *The Vietnamese American 1.5 Generation: Stories of War, Revolution, Flight, and New Beginnings*
Antonio T. Tiongson Jr., Edgardo V. Gutierrez, and Ricardo V. Gutierrez, eds., *Positively No Filipinos Allowed: Building Communities and Discourse*
Sucheng Chan, ed., *Chinese American Transnationalism: The Flow of People, Resources, and Ideas between China and America during the Exclusion Era*
Rajini Srikanth, *The World Next Door: South Asian American Literature and the Idea of America*
Keith Lawrence and Floyd Cheung, eds., *Recovered Legacies: Authority and Identity in Early Asian American Literature*
Linda Trinh Võ, *Mobilizing an Asian American Community*
Franklin S. Odo, *No Sword to Bury: Japanese Americans in Hawai'i during World War II*
Josephine Lee, Imogene L. Lim, and Yuko Matsukawa, eds., *Re/collecting Early Asian America: Essays in Cultural History*
Linda Trinh Võ and Rick Bonus, eds., *Contemporary Asian American Communities: Intersections and Divergences*
Sunaina Marr Maira, *Desis in the House: Indian American Youth Culture in New York City*
Teresa Williams-León and Cynthia Nakashima, eds., *The Sum of Our Parts: Mixed-Heritage Asian Americans*
Tung Pok Chin with Winifred C. Chin, *Paper Son: One Man's Story*
Amy Ling, ed., *Yellow Light: The Flowering of Asian American Arts*
Rick Bonus, *Locating Filipino Americans: Ethnicity and the Cultural Politics of Space*
Darrell Y. Hamamoto and Sandra Liu, eds., *Countervisions: Asian American Film Criticism*
Martin F. Manalansan IV, ed., *Cultural Compass: Ethnographic Explorations of Asian America*
Ko-lin Chin, *Smuggled Chinese: Clandestine Immigration to the United States*
Evelyn Hu-DeHart, ed., *Across the Pacific: Asian Americans and Globalization*

Soo-Young Chin, *Doing What Had to Be Done: The Life Narrative of Dora Yum Kim*
Robert G. Lee, *Orientals: Asian Americans in Popular Culture*
David L. Eng and Alice Y. Hom, eds., *Q & A: Queer in Asian America*
K. Scott Wong and Sucheng Chan, eds., *Claiming America: Constructing Chinese American Identities during the Exclusion Era*
Lavina Dhingra Shankar and Rajini Srikanth, eds., *A Part, Yet Apart: South Asians in Asian America*
Jere Takahashi, *Nisei/Sansei: Shifting Japanese American Identities and Politics*
Velina Hasu Houston, ed., *But Still, Like Air, I'll Rise: New Asian American Plays*
Josephine Lee, *Performing Asian America: Race and Ethnicity on the Contemporary Stage*
Deepika Bahri and Mary Vasudeva, eds., *Between the Lines: South Asians and Postcoloniality*
E. San Juan Jr., *The Philippine Temptation: Dialectics of Philippines–U.S. Literary Relations*
Carlos Bulosan and E. San Juan Jr., eds., *The Cry and the Dedication*
Carlos Bulosan and E. San Juan Jr., eds., *On Becoming Filipino: Selected Writings of Carlos Bulosan*
Vicente L. Rafael, ed., *Discrepant Histories: Translocal Essays on Filipino Cultures*
Yen Le Espiritu, *Filipino American Lives*
Paul Ong, Edna Bonacich, and Lucie Cheng, eds., *The New Asian Immigration in Los Angeles and Global Restructuring*
Chris Friday, *Organizing Asian American Labor: The Pacific Coast Canned-Salmon Industry, 1870–1942*
Sucheng Chan, ed., *Hmong Means Free: Life in Laos and America*
Timothy P. Fong, *The First Suburban Chinatown: The Remaking of Monterey Park, California*
William Wei, *The Asian American Movement*
Yen Le Espiritu, *Asian American Panethnicity*
Velina Hasu Houston, ed., *The Politics of Life*
Renqiu Yu, *To Save China, To Save Ourselves: The Chinese Hand Laundry Alliance of New York*
Shirley Geok-lin Lim and Amy Ling, eds., *Reading the Literatures of Asian America*
Karen Isaksen Leonard, *Making Ethnic Choices: California's Punjabi Mexican Americans*
Gary Y. Okihiro, *Cane Fires: The Anti-Japanese Movement in Hawaii, 1865–1945*
Sucheng Chan, *Entry Denied: Exclusion and the Chinese Community in America, 1882–1943*